MACHINE POLITICS
CHICAGO MODEL

WHEN A LADY NEEDS A LOT OF FRIENDS

From the "Chicago Tribune," February 7, 1931

MACHINE POLITICS
Chicago Model

HAROLD F. GOSNELL

Foreword by
WILLIAM F. OGBURN

SECOND EDITION
With a Foreword by THEODORE J. LOWI *and a
Postscript by the Author*

THE UNIVERSITY OF CHICAGO PRESS
CHICAGO AND LONDON

Library of Congress Catalog Card Number: 68-16692

THE UNIVERSITY OF CHICAGO PRESS, CHICAGO 60637

The University of Chicago Press, Ltd., London W.C.1

Printed in the United States of America

FOREWORD TO THE SECOND EDITION

GOSNELL'S CHICAGO REVISITED VIA LINDSAY'S NEW YORK

Theodore J. Lowi

The political machine is an institution peculiar to American cities. Militant parties of various kinds abound in the histories of most modern democracies, but similarities between them and the machine are inevitably superficial. Both militant parties and American machines, as classic types, are centralized, integrated, and relatively ruthless. But there the similarity ends.

Machines are integrated from within, as fraternities; they do not arise out of the opposition of the state or a hostile class. The power of the machine rests upon integration within a dispersed, permissive, and unmobilized society. Most machines were created and maintained without legal reinforcement; only quite late in their histories did laws develop to protect them from opposition, and yet throughout their existence they tended to hold a monopoly on the political process. On the other hand, despite their mastery of government they did not attempt to become a party-state in the European sense. In fact, the machines seemed to thrive on petty resources. A machine might be removed from office, its leaders indicted, but more than likely the organization suffered very little. Morale often seemed higher in defeat than in victory.

The most militant parties of Europe have depended upon homogeneity—enforced if necessary. Machines have capitalized upon the very opposite; in fact, ingenious techniques for capitalizing upon ethnic and racial heterogeneity have been invented in city after city. Militant parties have typically been based on common ends at the center, holding the periphery together by fear. The machines were based upon a congeries of people with uncommon ends, held together at the center by logrolling and at the periphery by fraternité, égalité, and ignorance.

v

As to the significance of the machine for the development of the city, the returns are still not in. Typically, the European observers were the first to appreciate this unusual, American phenomenon. Ostrogorski, Bryce, Weber, Michels, Schumpeter, and Duverger each in his own way made outstanding efforts to evaluate urban democracy in America. Gosnell, in *Machine Politics*, is one of the first Americans to join that distinguished company with anything approaching a systematic treatment of the subject. (By this standard, the muckrakers do not count.)

Gosnell, however, in focusing directly on a real machine, failed to give a lasting and completely convincing evaluation. This he could not have done in the 1930's, first, because the job of political scientist as it was defined at that time did not provide for formulating generalizations and erecting general normative or explanatory theories. This was especially true of Gosnell's school of Chicago social scientists, all of whom placed high value upon careful research and description.[1] A second and more important reason is that there was at that time insufficient experience with alternative forms of big city politics. Too few big cities in the United States had been reformed significantly enough or long enough to warrant comparison.

By now, in the 1960's, sufficient time has passed. Political science has matured; a post-behavioral generation of political scientists embraces broad generalization as well as systematic evidence. And perspectives have been broadened by lengthy periods of Reform government, the almost complete demise of machines, and the trial and failure of various experiments with new democratic and totalitarian forms of politics at home and abroad.

Properly understood, *Machine Politics* could now become one of the best bases for a comparative study of city politics. At times Gosnell may seem to the contemporary reader somewhat quaint in his hope that civic virtue would reemerge with the withering away of the machine. But he was most realistic in

[1] Compare James Q. Wilson's Introduction to Harold F. Gosnell, *Negro Politicans: The Rise of Negro Politics in Chicago*, 2d ed. (Chicago: University of Chicago Press, 1967).

his recognition of the staying power of those elements whose withering away would be required. The book is realistic and yet systematic. It is a masterpiece in the imaginative use of aggregate data in the study of political phenomena. A direct predecessor to the work of V. O. Key, this study is unexcelled to this day as an effort to understand political behavior in its institutional setting. The opportunity afforded by *Machine Politics* must simply be prepared for by addition of the perspective it could not have had in the 1930's.

We can begin to introduce perspective by immediately setting aside Gosnell's opening claim, in the Preface, to the representativeness of the Chicago experience. It is the very uniqueness of Chicago's experience with the machine that gives the study value. New York is the representative big city, not Chicago. In 1967, political power in Chicago has an extremely strong machine base; political power in New York has an entirely new and different base. As New York was being revolutionized by the. New Deal and its successors, Chicago politics was being reaffirmed. When New York was losing its last machine and entering into the new era of permanent Reform, Chicago's machine politics was just beginning to consolidate. New York became a loose, multiparty system with wide-open processes of nomination, election, and participation; Chicago became a tight, one-party system. New York sought to strengthen a weak mayor already operating under a strong-mayor government; Chicago has had the opposite problem of an already strong mayor in a weak-mayor government.

To evaluate the machine we must ask whether, by surviving, machine politics, Chicago model, in any way distorted Chicago's growth and development. How much change would there have been in Chicago's history if the nationalization of politics had made possible in Chicago, as it did in virtually every other big American city, ways of "licking the ward boss" and altering precinct organization, means of loosening the hold of the county organization on city hall, power for freeing the personnel and policies of the professional agencies of government? We cannot answer these questions for Chicago because the basis of machine strength still exists, and the conditions for its continuity, as Gosnell so accurately captures them, may continue through the remainder of the century.[2] We might be able to answer them, however, at least better than before, by looking at Gosnell's Chicago through the contemporary experience of New York.

New York city government, like government in almost all large American cities except Chicago, is a product of Reform. It is difficult to understand these cities without understanding the two strains of ideology that guided local Reform movements throughout the past three-quarters of a century. *Populism* and *efficiency*, once the foundations of most local insurgency, are now, except in rare holdout cases like Chicago, triumphant. These two tenets are now the orthodoxy in local practice.

Populism was originally a statement of the evils of every form of bigness and scale in the city, including big business, big churches, and big labor as well as big political organizations. Decentralization was an ultimate goal. In modern form it has tended to come down to the charge to eliminate political parties, partisanship, and, if possible, politics itself.

Efficiency provided the positive program to replace what populist surgery excised. The doctrine calls essentially for a new form of centralization; that is, centralization and rationalization of government activities and services to accompany the decentralization of power. Some assumed that services do not constitute power. Others assumed the problem away altogether by defining a neutral civil servant who would not abuse centralized government but could use it professionally to reap the economies of scale and specialization. That was the secret of the business system; and, after all, the city is rather like a business. ("There is no Republican or Democratic way to clean a street.")

While there are many inconsistent assumptions and goals between these two doctrines, they lived well together. Their coexistence was supported by the fact that different wings of this large, progressive movement were responsible for each.

[2] See Gosnell's own summary, p. 193.

Populism was largely the province of the working-class, "progressive" wing. Doctrines of efficiency were very much the responsibility of the upper-class wing. Populism resided with the politician-activists. Efficiency was developed by the intellectuals, including several distinguished university presidents, such as Seth Low, Andrew Dickson White, Harold Dodd, and, preeminently, Woodrow Wilson, who wrote a classic essay while still a professor of political science proclaiming the virtues of applying Prussian principles of administration in the United States.

These two great ideas were, by a strange and wonderful chemistry, combined into a movement whose influence is a major chapter of American history. Charters and laws have consistently insulated government from politics (meaning party politics). It became increasingly necessary with each passing decade to grant each bureaucratic agency autonomy to do the job as its professional commissioner saw fit.

On into the 1960's the merit system extends itself "upward, outward and downward," to use the Reformers' own dialectic. Recruitment to the top posts comes more and more often from the ranks of lifetime careerists in the agencies, party backgrounds increasingly signifying automatic disqualification. Reform has succeeded in raising the level of public morality and in making politics a dirty word. "Good press" for mayors consists of a determination to avoid intervening in the affairs of one department after another. The typical modern mayor is probably eager to cooperate, because this is a release from responsibility. Absolution-before-the-fact has become part of the swearing-in ceremony.

Reform has triumphed, and the cities are better run than ever before. But that, unfortunately, is not the end of the story, nor would it have been even without a Negro revolution. The triumph of Reform really ends in paradox: Cities like New York are now *well run but ungoverned*.

Politics under Reform is not abolished. Only its form is altered. *The legacy of Reform is the bureaucratic state*. Destruction of the party foundation of the mayoralty cleaned up many cities but also destroyed the basis for sustained, central, popularly based action. This capacity, with all its faults, was replaced by professionalized agencies. But this has meant creation of new bases of power. Bureaucratic agencies are not neutral; they are only independent. The bureaucrat may be more efficient and rational and honest than the old amateur. But he is no less political. If anything, he is more political because of the enormously important decisions so willingly entrusted to his making.

Modernization in New York and other modern cities has meant replacement of Old Machines with New Machines. The bureaucracies—that is, the professionally organized, autonomous career agencies—are the New Machines.

Sociologically, the Old Machine was a combination of rational goals and fraternal loyalty. The cement of the organization was trust and discipline created out of long years of service, probation and testing, slow promotion through the ranks, and centralized control over the means of reward. Its power in the community was based upon services rendered.

Sociologically, the New Machine is almost exactly the same sort of organization. There are more New Machines in any given city. They are functional rather than geographic in their scope. They rely on formal authority rather than upon majority acquiescence. And they probably work with a minimum of graft and corruption. But these differences do not alter their definition; they only help to explain why the New Machine is such a successful form of organization.

The New Machines are machines because they are relatively irresponsible structures of power. That is, each agency shapes important public policies, yet the leadership of each is relatively self-perpetuating and not readily subject to the controls of any higher authority.

The New Machines are machines in that the power of each, while resting ultimately upon services rendered to the community, depends upon its cohesiveness as a small minority in the midst of the vast dispersion of the multitude.

The modern city is now well run but ungoverned because it

now comprises islands of functional power before which the modern mayor stands impoverished.[3] No mayor of a modern city has predictable means of determining whether the bosses of the New Machines—the bureau chiefs and the career commissioners—will be loyal to anything but their agency, its work, and related professional norms. Our modern mayor has been turned into the likeness of a French Fourth Republic premier facing an array of intransigent parties in the National Assembly. The plight of the mayor, however, is worse: at least the premier could resign. These modern machines, more monolithic by far than their ancient brethren, are entrenched by law and are supported by tradition, the slavish loyalty of the newspapers, the educated masses, the dedicated civic groups, and, most of all, by the organized clientele groups enjoying access under existing arrangements.

The Reform response to the possibility of an inconsistency between running a city and governing it would be based upon the assumption of the Neutral Specialist, the bureaucratic equivalent to law's Rational Man. The assumption is that if men know their own specialties well enough they are capable of reasoning out solutions to problems they share with men of equal but different technical competencies. That is a very shaky assumption indeed. Charles Frankel's analysis of such an assumption in Europe provides an appropriate setting for a closer look at it in modern New York: "[D]ifferent [technical] elites disagree with each other; the questions with which specialists deal spill over into areas where they are *not* specialists, and they must either hazard amateur opinions or ignore such larger issues, which is no better. . . . "[4]

During the 1950's government experts began to recognize that, despite vast increases in efficiency flowing from defeat of the machine, New York City government was somehow lacking. These concerns culminated in the 1961 Charter, in which the

[3] Compare Wallace Sayre and Herbert Kaufman, *Governing New York City* (New York: Russell Sage, 1960), pp. 710 ff.
[4] Charles Frankel, "Bureaucracy and Democracy in the New Europe," *Daedalus* (Winter, 1964), p. 487.

Office of Mayor was strengthened in many impressive ways. But it was quickly discovered that no amount of formal centralization could definitively overcome the real decentralization around the mayor. It was an organized decentralization, and it was making a mockery of the new Charter. The following examples, although drawn from New York, are virtually universal in their applicability:

(1) Welfare problems always involve several of any city's largest agencies, including Health, Welfare, Hospitals, etc. Yet, for more than forty years, successive mayors of New York failed to reorient the Department of Health away from a regulative toward more of a service concept of organization.[5] And many new aspects of welfare must be set up in new agencies if they are to be set up at all. The new poverty programs were very slowly organized in all the big cities—except Chicago.[6]

(2) Water pollution control has been "shared" by such city agencies as the Departments of Health, Parks, Public Works, Sanitation, Water Supply, and so on. No large city, least of all New York, has an effective program to combat even the local contributions to pollution. The same is true of air pollution control, although for some years New York has had a separate department for such purposes.

(3) Land-use patterns are influenced in one way or another by a large variety of highly professional agencies. It has proved virtually impossible in any city for any one of these agencies to impose its criteria on the others. In New York the opening of Staten Island by the Narrows Bridge, in what may be the last large urban frontier, found the city with no plan for the revolution of property values and land uses in that Borough.

(4) Transportation is also the province of agencies too numerous to list. Strong mayors throughout the country have been unable to prevent each agency from going its separate way. For just one example, New York pursued a vast off-street parking program, at a cost of nearly $4,000 per parking space, at

[5] Sayre and Kaufman, op. cit., p. 274.
[6] Compare Paul Peterson, unpublished doctoral dissertation, University of Chicago, 1967.

the very moment when local rail lines were going bankrupt.

(5) Enforcement of civil rights is imposed upon almost all city agencies by virtue of federal, state, and local legislation. Efforts to set up public, then City Council review of police processes in New York have been successfully opposed by professional police officials. Efforts to try pairing and busing of school children on a very marginal, experimental basis have failed. The police commissioner resigned at the very suggestion that values other than professional police values be imposed upon the Department, even when the imposition came via the respected tradition of "legislative oversight." The superintendent of education, an outsider, was forced out. He was replaced by a career administrator. One education journalist at that time said: "Often . . . a policy proclaimed by the Board [of Education], without the advice and consent of the professionals, is quickly turned into mere paper policy . . . . The veto power through passive resistance by professional administrators is virtually unbeatable . . . ."

The decentralization of city government toward its career bureaucracies has resulted in great efficiency for the activities around which each bureaucracy was organized. The city is indeed well run. But what of those activities around which bureaucracies are not organized, or those which fall between or among agencies' jurisdictions? For these, as suggested by the cases above, the cities are suffering either stalemate or elephantitis—an affliction whereby a particular activity, say urban renewal or parkways, gets pushed to its ultimate success totally without regard to its balance against the missions of other agencies. In these as well as in other senses, the cities are ungoverned.

Mayors have tried a variety of strategies to cope with these situations. But the 1961 mayoral election in New York is the ultimate dramatization of their plight. This election was confirmation of the New York system in the same way the 1936 election was confirmation of Gosnell's Chicago. The 1961 New York election will some day be seen as one of the most significant elections in American urban history. For New York it was the culmination of many long-run developments. For the country it may be the first of many to usher in the bureaucratic state.

The primary significance of the election can be found in the spectacle of a mayor attempting to establish a base of power for himself in the bureaucracies. The mayor's "organization" included the following persons: his running mate for president of the City Council had been commissioner of sanitation, a position which culminated virtually a lifetime career in the Department of Sanitation. He had an impressive following among the sanitation workers, who, it should be added, are organized along precinct lines. The mayor's running mate for comptroller had been for many years the city budget director. As a budget official he had survived several administrations and two vicious primaries pitting factions of the Democratic Party against one another. Before becoming director he had served a number of years as a professional employee in the Bureau. The leaders of the campaign organization included a former, very popular fire commissioner who retired from his commissionership to accept campaign leadership and later to serve as deputy mayor; it also included a former police commissioner who had enjoyed a strong following among professional cops as well as in the local Reform movement. Added to this was a new and vigorous party, the Brotherhood Party, which was composed in large part of unions with broad bases of membership among city employees. Before the end of the election most of the larger city bureaucracies had political representation in the inner core of the new Administration.

For the 1961 election Mayor Wagner had put his ticket and his organization together just as the bosses of old had put theirs together. In the old days the problem was to mobilize all the clubhouses, districts, and counties in the city by putting together a balanced ticket about which all adherents could be enthusiastic. The same seems true for 1961, except that by then the clubhouses and districts had been replaced almost altogether by new types of units.

The main point is that destruction of the machine did not,

in New York or elsewhere, elevate the city into some sort of political heaven. Reform did not eliminate the need for political power. It simply altered what one had to do to get it. In the aftermath of twenty or more years of modern government it is beginning to appear that the lack of power can corrupt city hall almost as much as the possession of power. Bureaucracy is, in the United States, a relatively new basis of collective action. As yet none of us knows quite what to do about it.

These observations and cases are not supposed to indict Reform cities and acquit Chicago. They are intended only to put Chicago in a proper light and to provide some experimental means of assessing the functions of the machine form of collective action. Review of Reform government shows simply and unfortunately that the problems of cities, and the irrational and ineffectual ways city fathers go about their business, seem to be universally distributed without regard to form of government or type of power base.

All cities have traffic congestion, crime, juvenile delinquency, galloping pollution, ghettoes, ugliness, deterioration, and degeneracy. All cities seem to be suffering about equally with the quite recent problems of the weakening legitimacy of public objects, resulting in collective violence and pressures for direct solution to problems. All cities seem equally hemmed in by their suburbs and equally prevented from getting at the roots of many of their most fundamental problems. Nonpartisan approaches, even approaches of New York's Republican mayor to Republican suburbs and a Republican governor, have failed to prevent rail bankruptcy in the vast Eastern megalopolis, to abate air or water pollution, to reduce automobile pressure, or to ease the pain of the middle-class Negro in search of escape.

The problems of the city seem to go beyond any of the known arrangements for self-government. However, low morality and lack of what Banfield and Wilson call "public-regardingness" may be a function simply of mass pressure, poor education, and ethnic maladjustment. The old machine and its abuses may have been just another reflection of the same phenomena. If that is so, then the passage of more time and the mounting of one sociocultural improvement after another might have reformed the machines into public-regarding organs, if they had not been first too much weakened to be repaired.

Are there any strong reasons to believe that real reform could have come without paying the price of eliminating the popular but unseemly base of political action? Intimations can be found in the last of the machine-recruited leaders of Tammany, Carmine DeSapio and Edward Costikyan. Each was progressively more public-regarding than any of his predecessors. Costikyan was a model of political responsibility for whom the new New York had no particular use. For this question, however, the best answers may lie in looking afresh at Gosnell's Chicago. With a scientific rigor superior to most political analysis of the 1960's, his book goes further than any other single work to capture what political behavior was like under machine conditions. The sum total of his findings, despite Gosnell's own feelings, does not constitute a very damning indictment of the Chicago machine—if contemporary experience is kept clearly in mind.

Even amidst the most urgent of depression conditions the machine in Chicago does not seem to have interfered with the modest degree of political rationality distributed throughout the United States. Gosnell's data strongly suggest that the New Deal did not win by purchasing masses of the electorate with favorable public policies. Nor did the hungry local Democratic candidates. Persons who benefited most by Roosevelt's relief policies were already Democrats before 1932, certainly before 1936 when the true character of the New Deal was beginning to be grasped by the masses. Party tradition was important in Chicago, as it is everywhere in the United States. Democrats gained an important margin in Chicago through the general disaffection voters were experiencing with parties in power during economic reverses; but again this is typical. Another marginal gain to the Democrats came from the prohibition issue, certainly a rational basis at that time for choosing between the two parties nationally and locally.

What of voting behavior on referendum proposals, the most

issue-laden situation an electorate ever faces? Gosnell's criticism of the referendum as subject to fraud and other types of
abuse constitutes damnation of the practice everywhere, even
though it must have been particularly true of Chicago referenda
during the 1920's and '30's. But even so, his figures show that
the electorate, despite the machine, did not behave indiscriminately. The theory that universal suffrage provides no check
against irresponsible acceptance of financing schemes that pass
the real burden on to future generations is simply not borne out
in Chicago. Conservative and propertied appeals were effective.
Over a twelve-year period, including six fat years and six lean
years, sixty-six local bond issues were approved and forty-eight
rejected. Those rejected included some major bond issues offered for agencies whose leaders had been discredited. Other
issues showed responsiveness to appeals other than those of
the local precinct or county organizations. As the anti-prohibi-
tion campaign began to grow, so did the vote on the prohibition
repealer. Clear irrationalities tended to be associated primarily
with highly technical proposals involving judicial procedure or
taxation; but even so, there were clear variations according to
education, class lines, and other factors that suggest sensitivity
to things other than the machine.

In a bold stroke, Gosnell also tried to assess the influence
of the newspapers, the best source for rational—at least non-
machine—voting decisions. For this particular purpose Gosnell's data were weak, but fortunately he was not deterred
from asking important questions merely for lack of specially
designed data. Factor analysis helped Gosnell tease out of
census tract data and newspaper subscription patterns a fairly
realistic and balanced sense of the role of the local newspapers.
Gosnell was led to conclude that the influence of news media
is limited but that this was a limitation imposed far less by the
machine than by the limitations on the distribution of readers.
Newspaper influence on issues was measurably apparent wherever daily readership was widely established—*the machine not-
withstanding.* Here again is the possibility that real machine
domination rested upon a level of education and civic training

that was at the very time of Gosnell's research undergoing a great deal of change.

Taking all the various findings together, and even allowing for abuses that were always more frequent in cities than in towns, and probably more frequent in Gosnell's Chicago than in other cities, we can come away from Gosnell's analysis with a picture not at all contrary to Key's notion of the "responsible electorate."[7] It was, in fact, sufficiently self-interested to subdivide into hostile constituencies, and for this phenomenon Gosnell offers his only positive statement about the machine: "On the credit side of the ledger should be placed the success of the bosses in softening class conflicts." This single proposition, anticipating by more than a decade Merton's famous essay on the "latent functions" of the machine,[8] tends to confirm, in a perverse way, the existence and the problems of rational voters. It also suggests that machine politics is a special phase in the development of all American cities, a solution to problems that tends to pass when the problems for which it is appropriate pass.

In the end Gosnell may have felt his book to be an indictment of machine politics. Perhaps it is only a sad commentary upon our loss of innocence that we can look at his data a generation later and come away morally uplifted.

[7] V. O. Key, *The Responsible Electorate* (Cambridge: Belknap-Harvard Press, 1966)

[8] Robert K. Merton, *Social Theory and Social Structure* (New York: Free Press, 1949), chap. 1.

PREFACE TO THE FIRST EDITION

The present study is closely related to a larger study of the theory of democracy which the author has projected and partially completed. It happens that most, but not all, of the materials which are used in this book are drawn from the experience of Chicago with democratic institutions; but this does not lessen their value as evidence which can be used to verify or disprove certain hypotheses regarding governmental practices. As far as the number of people studied is concerned, there are many more in the city than in all of ancient Greece, and about as many as in Switzerland today or as in the entire continental United States at the time the federal Constitution was being framed.

Thomas Jefferson was afraid of a democracy built upon an urban civilization. He said: "When they [the American people] get piled upon one another in large cities, as in Europe, they will become corrupt as in Europe." If Jefferson were alive today, he would see many things in the city that carry out his prophecy. Some discerning reader may discover in these pages a Jeffersonian skepticism of urban democracy. However, the writer has tried to be objective, relegating his functions as a citizen, a voter, and a taxpayer to the background, and emphasizing his role as an observer.

The present book is based on a careful perusal of the Chicago newspapers for ten years, upon interviews which have been spaced over this period of time, upon personal observation of political meetings and election-day activities, upon participation in court trials, and upon observations made as an active party worker. As a participant observer the writer has aided in the publicity work of several aldermanic campaigns, and in 1935 undertook to manage an aldermanic campaign for an independent candidate. His success as a campaign manager was not flattering, but he learned a great deal about Chicago politics.

If time and money had permitted, the present study would
have been entirely comparative. Wherever possible, an attempt
has been made to show how typical of other cities the patterns of
political behavior are in Chicago. Fortunately, in the past ten
years a number of studies of the party politics of other cities
has appeared; and, in so far as these studies yielded comparable data, they have been compared with the findings reached
in Chicago. Peel's study of New York City political clubs,
Salter's and Kurtzman's quite different analyses of Philadelphia
district leaders, and Mosher's research on upstate committeemen in New York State have all furnished the basis of significant
comparisons. However, none of these studies of other cities
purports to cover as broad a field as the present analysis. The
present study not only attempts to examine the party machine
and the characteristics of the party workers but also presents an
analysis of voting behavior in candidate and proposition elections. Among the influences studied are the circulations of the
important daily newspapers in Chicago. To the writer's knowledge, in no other city has so exhaustive a study been made of the
social and economic background of voting behavior.

The present analysis is a highly condensed presentation of the
main findings of a number of studies. Preliminary manuscripts
on the operation of the referendum in Chicago and on the 1928
committeemen are each longer than this book itself. The case
stories of ward and precinct committeemen could be amplified
and multiplied. Records were obtained regarding one hundred
and seventy-five ward leaders and nine hundred precinct captains. As far as possible, the materials presented are the most
representative. Those who are interested in a detailed study of
two typical ward leaders in Chicago and the groups they serve
should consult the author's *Negro Politicians: The Rise of Negro
Politics in Chicago.*

When it was not possible to obtain comparable material for
other cities, data concerning Chicago as of two different time
periods were used. One of the themes which runs through this
book is that the profound economic changes of the period 1928–
36 have left their lasting imprint upon urban politics in the

United States. Certainly Chicago politics was not as corrupt, as violent, as vulgar, and as subservient to vested business interests in 1936 as in 1928. However, there is still vast ground for improvement in the morality of Chicago politics, and one of the antitheses of the thesis presented above is that many outstanding characteristics of the politics of the city are just the same after seven hard years of economic depression as they were in the boom days of the carefree twenties. Economic insecurity and deprivation, while great, were not sufficient to alter fundamentally the pattern of the party organizations. If the whole seven years had been like the trying last two years of the Hoover administration, when the government was deadlocked and protest groups were rampant, perhaps the parties would have had to change their tactics. The city is now showing definite signs of economic recovery, and it appears that the old-line politicians will not be challenged in the immediate future.

As far as possible, the materials in the chapters that follow are presented in nontechnical language. Those who are interested in the questionnaire, tabular, correlational, and factorial procedures used as a basis for the theoretical interpretations can consult the appendixes. Portions of two chapters have appeared in slightly different form in various periodicals. I am indebted to the *American Political Science Review*, the *Journalism Quarterly*, the *Journal of the American Statistical Society*, the *Journal of Social Psychology*, and the *Annals of the American Academy* for permission to quote from my published articles.

It will soon be apparent to anyone who examines these pages that the writer did not do all the interviewing and tabulating by himself. The Social Science Research Committee of the University of Chicago very generously supplied him with research assistants and an allowance for overhead. The present book would not be possible without the efficient services of David Maynard, Sonya Forthal, Norman N. Gill, and Margaret J. Schmidt. In addition to these research assistants, the Board of Vocational Guidance and Placement of the University of Chicago has referred many other valuable student-assistants to the author.

The author is indebted to his colleagues Professors Charles E. Merriam, William F. Ogburn, James Weber Linn, Harold D. Lasswell, T. V. Smith, and to Professor S. McKee Rosen, Mr. Edward M. Martin, and Miss Schmidt for reading the manuscript and offering many valuable suggestions, some of which were not followed for practical reasons. As is customary, the author assumes full responsibility for all statements of fact or judgment. The writer also wishes to acknowledge here the obligation he owes to Professor Ogburn for the Foreword and for an inspiring example of pioneering statistical work in the field of American politics.

HAROLD F. GOSNELL

CHICAGO
March 1937

FOREWORD TO THE FIRST EDITION

This book, to which I have the honor of writing a foreword, is something new in the study of politics. It is new because it brings to political science the whole battery of scientific techniques of modern social science. The effect is most interesting, as may be indicated by an observation.

I once heard of a man who was wonderfully skilled as wool-tester. He could feel a piece of wool with his fingers and tell how durable it would be, how much warmth it would hold, how much shoddy was in it, and could describe many other qualities of the wool and of the sheep that produced it. He could not, though, transmit his art to others, for he scarcely knew how he did it, though his results were good. About the same time I read an account of a method, developed in a laboratory, of measuring the properties of wool with the aid of a microscope, by counting the fibers, by measuring thickness, and by dimensioning air pockets and enumerating them per unit of area. By this means the weight of blankets necessary on a night with a temperature of, say, 30 degrees to keep the air surrounding the body at 98.6 degrees could be determined by anyone who could count and measure.

In politics the politicians who are clever are like the wool-tester. They seem to know the job. But it is difficult for anyone to learn from them how they do it. But the scientific methods of Professor Gosnell are well organized and laid out, so that one may readily see just how his conclusions have been reached. Many of them, indeed, are better than those of the so-called "practical" politician, as might have been expected from his superior techniques. An illustration is his proof of the degree of effectiveness in the election of the Chicago newspapers, which were hostile to Roosevelt, despite the widely prevalent view that, because the President won overwhelmingly, the press was without influence. His method also permits deductions that the politicians would not be able to make, as, for instance, those regarding the influences of the business cycle in politics.

The essence of scientific method is to hold constant all factors except the one whose influence is to be measured. This is what the chemist does in his laboratory and what the psychologist does with his guinea pigs. The author does the same thing with partial correlation. Social science, unlike mathematics, is not an arm-chair science. That the author knows his data, as well as his method, is evident from his apparent wide acquaintance with Chicago political leaders, big and little, with ward boundaries, locales of operations, and services of precinct captains and ward bosses. This orientation with the realities of everyday politics makes his book more readable than others dealing with less concrete material.

The modern scientific methods of trend lines, variance, multiple correlation, and factorial analysis have in recent years made much of economics, sociology, and psychology exact science. But for some reason their advance in political science has been slow. Perhaps Dr. Gosnell's work is a signal for a general forward movement which is surely inevitable some time in the distinguished field of political science.

WILLIAM FIELDING OGBURN

TABLE OF CONTENTS

TABLE OF CONTENTS

LIST OF ILLUSTRATIONS

LIST OF MAPS AND CHARTS

LIST OF TABLES

CHAPTER I
CHANGING PARTY FORTUNES

The world-wide economic crisis which struck the United States with full vigor in the fall of 1929 undermined the popularity of existing political regimes in many democratic countries.

MAYOR EDWARD J. KELLY

In Canada, the Liberal government was swept from power in 1930; in Great Britain and Australia, Labour governments were overwhelmed in the elections of 1931; and in Germany, the postdepression elections brought about a Fascist revolution. On the other hand, the swing of the pendulum in France, Sweden, and Denmark was toward the left. From the standpoint of political theory it is a matter of prime importance to examine the conditions which are associated with changing political attitudes.

In the United States, the economic deprivations which accompanied the downward trend of the business cycle brought varying responses. The voters in the New England states and the rural sections of the northeastern part of the United States changed their political attitudes least. A comparison of the 1928 and 1936 presidential election returns for the state of Maine shows a shift of only 10 per cent away from the Republican party which dominated the political scene in the prosperous twenties. On the other hand, there has been a 34 per cent shift from Republican-party presidential candidates in the state of California. These states are typical, in this respect, of the regions in which they are found.

An examination of the changes in state and local politics in the United States during the past nine years shows a similar wide variation. In the state of Louisiana, a consummate dema-

1

gogue, the late Senator Huey Long, was able to emulate the
example of European dictators. By clever propaganda techniques, force, trickery, and bribery he was able to eliminate all
effective opposition to his control of his state; and he was on
his way to extend his domain when his life was cut short in 1935
by an assassin's bullet. In the state of California, a former
Socialist, Upton Sinclair, was able to win the Democratic nomination for governor in 1934 on the appealing platform, "Eliminate Poverty in California." While the state was Democratic
in national affairs, the forces of reaction were able to turn back
the Sinclair attack upon the *status quo*. On the other hand, the
voters of Wisconsin and Minnesota turned in increasing numbers to the leaders of new party movements which promised
far-reaching changes in the economic order.

In some of the great metropolitan centers of the United States
the depression brought at least a temporary defeat for the political organizations which had been long intrenched in power.
The Tammany machine in New York City and the Republican
machine in Philadelphia suffered severe reverses during the
period. Economic discontent, plus the damaging disclosures of
the Seabury Committee, brought the fiery Mayor La Guardia
to office in New York. Philadelphia, corrupt but no longer
contented, turned some of the Republican grafters out of power.

What was happening in Chicago during these times of far-
reaching political changes? Was there a turn to the right or a
turn to the left? Did the voters show a disposition to support
reform movements, as in New York City? Was there a drift
away from the spoils tradition? In large measure none of these
things happened in the second largest city in the United States.
It is true that there was a shuffling of the political cards. Democrats were substituted for Republicans in practically all of the
local offices. But these Democrats were not New Deal Democrats at heart. They were just like their Republican predecessors—spoils politicians. It is the purpose of this book to consider why there have been so few fundamental changes in the
outlook of Chicago politicians during this period of economic
crisis.

vealed that one of the Democratic city hall wheel horses
andled the "junk" of the utility interests for the modest
of over half a million dollars a year.[8]

reaction of the public to the Insull trial shows one of the
s why economic adversity has changed political practices
orals in Chicago so little. Insolent, defiant, the white-
fallen monarch of a far-flung utility empire told the
"I'd do it again."[9] The lawyers were sentimental; the
ragged on; the people forgot the millions that they had
Insull's holding companies; the jury brought in the ver-
Not guilty."

le the blot of Insull's connections marred the records of
he major parties, the Republicans were the worst suf-
A year and a half before the stock market crash the
lican party was torn asunder by a primary election battle
which various Insull "deals" were made principal issues
press. Such a destructive internal quarrel was not the
reparation for the lean years which were to follow. And
ars were lean not only because of the loss of the patron-
ices but also because of the absence of large contributions
he utility interests. A political party which finances itself
out of the public treasury and out of the pockets of the
-users is in a deplorable condition when both of these two
s of revenue dry up. The Democrats likewise lost the
t of the famous Insull chest, but they still retained the
share of the public jobs and the privileges which are
d thereto.

local governments in the Chicago region practically
own when the depression hit the trough. An antiquated
e system and a chaotic governmental setup were not
o the emergency. Without federal aid, misery and want
city would have reached alarming proportions. While

Democratic politician who handled the "junk" was Moe Rosenberg, who died
United States government was investigating his income-tax returns. Rosen-
e sensational charges about the sums of money he gave to politicians. See
s and *Chicago Evening American* for March 12, 13, 14, and 15, 1934.
hell Dawson, "Insull on Trial," *Nation* for November 28, 1934, CXXXIX,

How was Chicago affected by the depression in comparison
with other large cities of the United States? Of the ten largest
cities in the United States, one of the hardest hit by the depression was Chicago. Over half of the employees of the electrical industries, and a large proportion of those engaged in the
furniture, packing, clothing, printing, and transportation industries, were put out on the streets. Rents declined more

TABLE 1

DWELLING UNITS BY MONTHLY RENTALS FOR CHICAGO, 1930 AND 1934
NUMBER AND PERCENTAGE DISTRIBUTION

DWELLING UNITS BY RENTAL	1930*		1934†	
	Number of Families	Percentage Distribution	Number of Families	Percentage Distribution
Total.................	561,189‡	100.0	580,876§	100.0
Under $10.00.............	5,100	0.9	16,981	2.9
$10.00–$14.99.............	17,380	3.1	69,272	11.9
$15.00–$19.99.............	33,805	6.0	73,410	12.7
$20.00–$29.99.............	81,194	14.5	143,922	24.8
$30.00–$49.99.............	146,256	26.1	212,687	36.6
$50.00–$74.99.............	186,484	33.2	48,582	8.4
$75.00–$99.99.............	60,500	10.8	8,774	1.5
$100.00–$149.99.............	20,730	3.7	4,651	0.8
$150.00–$199.99.............	4,820	0.8	1,383	0.2
$200.00 and over..........	4,920	0.9	1,214	0.2

* *Census Data of the City of Chicago, 1930.*
† *Census Data of the City of Chicago, 1934.*
‡ Cases (10,980) with no information on rental excluded from percentage distribution.
§ Cases (7,632) with no information on rental excluded from percentage distribution.

drastically than in any other large city except Detroit.[1] In 1935,
rents were only one-half of what they had been in the period
1923–25. Table 1 shows how precipitous was the fall of higher
rentals in the city. Whereas nearly one-half of the dwelling
units rented for $50 a month or more in 1930, only 12 per cent
rented for this in 1934. New building was practically at a standstill. As a matter of fact, more buildings were wrecked each
year since 1931 than were erected.[2]

Certainly all of these economic hardships must have brought

[1] Chicago Tribune, *The 1936 Chart Book*, p. 115.   [2] *Ibid.*, p. 113.

their political repercussions. Unemployed persons have plenty of time to think about their woes. Were there no radical agitators in the region that produced the Haymarket riot and the Pullman strike?

The city of Chicago produced practically no nationally known agitators in the period from 1928 to 1936. While the national government embarked upon tremendous schemes of public spending and governmental regulation, the local officials in Chicago had no program but retrenchment. Expenditures and services were cut, not willingly, but out of necessity and under terrific pressure from the banking interests.

What was there about the social and economic structure of the city which made it so impervious to the tensions of the depression? In real estate, in banking, in trade, and in industry the leaders of Chicago during the boom period had been violent, offensive boosters. As one writer has put it, "A want of deference for ceremony and tradition corresponded to a sometimes brutal disregard for the values inherent in human life, a defiance of established moral codes."[3] The possessors of economic power were, for the most part, self-made men who had shown themselves more ruthless than their rivals. These men were not heir to any tradition which impressed upon them their responsibility to the general public. Instead, they were loud in their praise of business, vigorous in their opposition to any kind of governmental control over business, and scornful of the efficiency of governmental enterprises.

Perhaps no one illustrated the old Chicago spirit better than Samuel Insull, the former utilities magnate. There is no doubt that he was a man of vision and a great industrial leader. Concerning his decision to come to Chicago to head the old Chicago Edison Company, he said: "It seemed to me that this great community must inevitably become the center of manufacturing for this populous and rich central valley of the country."[4] As the head of the Chicago electrical power industries, which

[3] Louis Wirth, "Chicago: The Land and People," *Survey Graphic*, XXIII (October, 1934), 522.

[4] Lloyd Lewis and Henry Justin Smith, *Chicago: The History of Its Reputation* (New York, 1929), p. 412.

he soon became, Insull was greatly inter
larger and larger turbines. At a time when
their heads, he was bold enough to experi
ward the engineering techniques. Insull's
was to build a newer and bigger opera h
bludgeoning his business associates to mal
for governmental officials, party leaders,
and the editors of the lesser newspapers, h
ciple that each man had his price. Donald
nent in the gas case, said:

Insull was more responsible than any other one
for the degradation of municipal government to its
and incompetence. It was this misuse of political po
stroyed his economic power. Honest, watchful gove
Insull from himself.[5]

There is no question that the collapse
empire constructed by Samuel Insull was
which greatly aggravated the economic w
habiting the Middle West. Not until his
around him did he give up his optimism.
greater because he tried to hang on too
cians be held in any way responsible for
losses suffered by the public on account o
The American system of government was
to prevent business men from making mis
disaster to many innocent persons. In Chi
cratic and the Republican leaders aided
his savage struggle for economic power.
huge campaign-fund contributions from t
return for which they left him relatively
his economic ends.[6] The responsibility of t
cratic and Republican, was made doubly
depression by the sensational disclosures,
sull trial, of the lists of insiders in Insull

[5] Donald Richberg, "Gold-plated Anarchy: An Inte
Giants," *Nation* for April 5, 1933, CXXXVI, 368–69.

[6] C. H. Wooddy, *The Case of Frank L. Smith* (Chicag

[7] *Chicago Daily News*, September 30, 1932, gives the l

also re
had h
profit
The
reason
and n
haired
judge,
case d
lost in
dict, "
Whi
both
ferers.
Repub
during
in the
best p
the ye
age off
from t
largely
utility
source
suppor
lion's
attach
The
broke
revenu
equal
in the

[8] The
while the
berg ma
Daily Ne
[9] Mit
611–13.

the credit facilities of all American cities were damaged by the economic crisis, the city of Chicago was in a particularly vulnerable financial position because of drastic revision in its real estate assessment, which had just been started. This revision was necessary because of the favoritism and corruption discovered in the assessment office during the days of expanding real estate values and the political fix.[10] Out of the lessened and disappearing revenues, new and unexpected demands were made upon the local treasuries. For many years the city of Chicago had been noted for its "hobohemias," its havens for transient and homeless men. To these were now added a great army of unemployed. In October, 1933, there were 384,206 persons on the relief rolls, or 12 per cent of the total population of the city.

If the tax machinery had been administered honestly and fairly during the period of rising real estate values, the various local governments would have been in a better position to meet the greatly increased demands placed upon them. The tax "racket" had been run by a bipartisan combination which included the leaders of the Democratic and Republican parties. Conditions grew so bad that the State Tax Commission ordered a reassessment in 1928. This action delayed the levying of taxes for a whole year and added to the financial difficulties which confronted the city when the depression began to pile up tax delinquencies.

The governmental problems which confronted the Chicago region during the worst of the economic crisis were solved for the most part by the national government. The federal relief program, the public works program, the works progress program, the R.F.C. loans to Chicago banks, the loans to homeowners, and the loan to the board of education enabled the citizens to weather the severest of storms. One of the curious characteristics of the American form of government is that the local representatives of the party which put these national policies into effect operated in accordance with an entirely different political philosophy from that of the nation-wide leaders.

[10] Herbert D. Simpson, *Tax Racket and Tax Reform in Chicago* (Chicago, 1930).

These local leaders capitalized the popularity of their national leaders to their own political benefit. The national leaders, on the other hand, had very few means of disciplining the city bosses.

The net result of the economic crisis, as far as the politics of the city of Chicago is concerned, has been the establishment of a political machine of unprecedented power.

At the beginning of 1928 there was a fairly even balance between the two major parties in the city. This balance was a delicate one, which depended in part on the Republican factions knifing each other and dealing with the Democrats. Of course, all factions, Republican and Democratic alike, were the handmaidens of the business interests, i.e., they were not interested in disturbing existing economic relationships except for their own benefit or the benefit of the leaders of industry and finance.

In 1928 the Republicans controlled the city hall, the two United States senatorships, the state government, and many of the county offices. The Democrats of this era were pretty well united, ably led, and not without important key positions. They controlled the county board, a majority of the "non-partisan" aldermen, and a disproportionate share of the state and congressional representatives. A failure to reapportion the city, the state, and the congressional districts worked to the benefit of the Democratic party, which was strong in the poorer residential areas where the population of the city had been declining.

In 1936 the Democrats were in complete control of all the governmental agencies selected by, or represented in, the territorial limits of the city of Chicago. Only a few judges and five county commissioners from the country towns remained of the once haughty and confident band of Republican office-holders. Not since the formation of the Republican party in the city had the Democrats so completely dominated the political scene. As the depression deepened, the grip of the new Tammany grew tighter and tighter about the various corporate bodies located at the mouth of the Chicago River. That their success was hardly due to their own efforts bothered these new bosses not at all.

While the Democrats were in a position to take advantage of the general swing of public sentiment in their favor after 1929, it took several years for them to reap the full benefits of their new position, since the terms of some of the Republican office-holders did not expire immediately. The first notable Democratic victory was in 1930, when the Republicans lost control of the county treasurer's office, the sanitary district board, the county board, and the board of tax assessors. Each of these victories meant important additions to the patronage which the Democrats already enjoyed. In 1931 the Democrats captured practically all the city hall jobs when they won the position of mayor in a great civic uprising. After the general elections of 1932, Democrats replaced Republicans in the state's attorney's office and on the board of review (of tax assessments). The local Republicans likewise lost all state and federal patronage at the same election, since their candidates for governor, United States senator, and president went down to defeat. Two years later the Democrats again swept all of the county offices and made some gains in their representation in the state legislature. It took six years to put the finishing touch upon the job of eliminating the Republicans from governmental posts in Chicago, but the work was practically complete by 1933. In viewing the wreck of his party, one Republican ward committeeman said, "In my opinion, the Democrats now have greater power than any party has ever had in Chicago. Before they secured it, they promised open consultation and decision on all matters. Now it is practically impossible to see anyone in the city hall."[11] This Republican boss was not complaining about any changes in governmental policies brought about by the Democrats; he was whining about his loss of patronage.

The depression years saw the elimination, one after the other, of the old-time leaders of the Republican party in Chicago. In Wisconsin the La Follettes were nominally Republican at the beginning of the economic crisis. While they suffered some setbacks, in the main they have weathered most of the political

[11] Interview, 1936.

storms in the past nine years. The city of Chicago and the state of Illinois had no Republicans of this stripe.

One of the first of the elder Republican statesmen to taste defeat was Charles S. Deneen, who failed to secure a renomination as Republican candidate for United States senator in the primary of 1930. Since 1896, when he was first elected as state's attorney for Cook County, Deneen had been the leader of a powerful faction in local politics. While a master at compromise and combination, he was regarded as a cold figure personally; and his faction directed many of its appeals to the so-called respectable elements in the Republican party. As state's attorney, as governor, as United States senator, he followed in a cool and calculating fashion the general rule of Chicago politics that all racial, linguistic, religious, economic, and neighborhood groups should be recognized on a balanced ticket. A dignified speaker, he never stooped to the arts of demagoguery, and he fell short of ever becoming a popular idol. While he lost his direct control of the federal patronage when his term as senator expired in 1931, his faction held the state's attorney's office and a position on the board of review until 1933. The man who had remained a regular Republican when Theodore Roosevelt was battling for the Lord in 1912 was not the person to lead the bewildered citizens of Chicago out of the morass they found themselves in in the dismal thirties. Deneen was a Hoover Republican—honest, well meaning, sincere—and, like the great humanitarian, he lost in popularity when the storm broke. The depression had likewise made disastrous inroads upon the ranks of his banking and business associates.[12]

A second of the older leaders to be relegated to the background was William Hale Thompson, the picturesque and bizarre mayor, who had been a storm center for more than twenty years. Thompson had wealth and social position, and he might have taken a place among the élite of Chicago. However, he was not diligent at his studies, and he was not interested in society. As mayor of the city from 1915 to 1923 and from

[12] On the failure of the Bain banks, see *People* v. *John Bain et al.*, 358 Ill. 177, and W. H. Stuart, *The Twenty Incredible Years* (Chicago, 1935), p. 532.

1927 to 1931, he was hailed as "Big Bill, the Builder," Chicago's greatest booster, the defender of the weak, the champion of the people, while at the same time in certain newspapers the word "Thompsonism" came to be a symbol for spoils politics, police scandals, school-board scandals, padded pay rolls, gangster alliances, betrayal of the public trust, grotesque campaign methods, and buffoonery in public office. He was the clown who distracted the people's attention while his political associates ran the city's business. He was a good clown and a firm believer in the principle that bad publicity is better than none. He believed in the campaign rule, "If your opponent calls you a liar, call him a thief." His slight of General Joffre during the war, his expedition to photograph the tree-climbing fish, his rat show at which he tried to discredit two former associates, his slogan "Kick the snoot of King George out of Chicago," and his campaign properties, such as a halter, a burro, and a donkey, started reports that went around the world. The people laughed and said that "Big Bill" was a "good guy." As one political observer put it, "his genius for the spectacular made him an international figure. He might produce dismay and ridicule, but he was a force to be reckoned with."[13] As he grew older, Thompson grew cynical about the motives of some of his associates. As far as can be ascertained, he personally derived no pecuniary benefit from his activities in politics. He liked the game and the crowds. However, with a World's Fair in the city approaching, the voters grew tired of his antics. Samuel Insull, who had been the financial godfather of many of his campaigns, had troubles of his own. As Thompson had contributed to defeat Deneen and his cohorts, so the Deneen faction helped turn some of the voters away from Thompson. During the mayoralty campaign of 1931 the state's attorney's office indicted Thompson's city sealer on the ground that he had conspired with merchants to rob the people of $54,000,000 by

[13] Phillip Kinsley, in the obituary which was removed from the *Chicago Tribune* office and used in Thompson's campaign pamphlet for the 1931 mayoralty election. For further details on Thompson's methods of winning local groups, see H. F. Gosnell, *Negro Politicians*, chap. iii.

short weights.[14] At a time when incomes were rapidly dropping, these charges did not do Thompson any good.

But Thompson was not completely eliminated by his defeat in 1931. His friends and enemies were amazed at his vitality. If he had been younger and if he had not had to carry such a load of unfavorable publicity, he might have been one of the big figures of depression politics. His faction succeeded in nominating Len Small for governor in the Republican primary of 1932. Len Small's platform seemed to recognize the fact that there had been an economic crisis. However, in the fall election Small ran behind the head of the Republican ticket, and the Thompson machine was smashed beyond all recognition. In spite of this, Thompson refused to go into retirement. In the fall of 1936 he came out of seclusion to run for governor on the Lemke ticket in order to make doubly sure the defeat of Brooks, the Republican candidate who had the support of the *Chicago Tribune*. The effort was needless, and the former great campaigner could not muster 100,000 votes in the city that had been the scene of many triumphs. He cut a pitiful figure, indeed. Insull's money and the city hall patronage had made a tremendous difference.

On the ruins of the Republican organization in the city the Democrats have built the most powerful political machine that the city has ever seen. None of the leaders of the Democratic party has been a member of Chicago's Four Hundred in recent years, as far as could be ascertained. One of them, Patrick Nash, was listed among the highest income-receivers in 1925, but his name could not be found in the social register. The Democratic bosses have been recruited, for the most part, from the second-generation immigrant classes in Chicago. They are self-made men and can easily understand the point of view of Chicago self-made business men.

The leadership of the Chicago Tammany first fell to Anton J. Cermak, who became one of the important cogs in the Demo-

[14] Daniel Serritella, state senator and friend of Alphonse Capone, was city sealer under Mayor Thompson. For an account of his trial, see *Chicago Daily News*, April 1, 2, 1931; *Chicago Tribune*, April 2, 1931. On appeal the conviction secured in the lower court was reversed. See *People* v. *Serritella*, 272 Ill. Appellate Ct. (1933), 616.

cratic party when he was elected president of the county board in 1922. Cermak was born in Prague, Bohemia, and brought to the United States when he was very young. In deriding his humble origin, Mayor Thompson said, "Tony, where is your pushcart at? Can you imagine a World's Fair mayor with a name like that?"[15] But Cermak had demonstrated by years of hard work and clever maneuvering that he could hold his own with any of Chicago's professional politicians. As state representative, as alderman, as bailiff of the Municipal Court, as president of the county board, and as mayor, he was noted for his force, firmness, persistence, and shrewdness. He was charged with profiting from his position on a number of occasions, but he always managed to win over his accusers. In the 1931 campaign Thompson bellowed, "Saving Tony . . . . saved six million out of a $10,000 salary . . . . built the county jail without a boiler . . . . grafts on coal and paving."[16] However, the reports about his connection with real estate deals, bootlegging, and gambling were never made matters of court record. Before the days of prohibition he had been the archrepresentative of the liquor-dealers; during the prohibition era, when he was president of the county board, the country towns under his jurisdiction were said to be wetter than Chicago; and as mayor his personal bodyguard was accused of being involved in the shooting of a gangster who furnished no resistance.[17] Hard times and a lack of cash had not decreased the interest in gambling, the most profitable of all the political rackets. The fact remained that Cermak was more willing than Mayor Thompson to meet the demands of the bankers and business groups for reform of the tax machinery and drastic economy in local government.

As party boss, Cermak ruled with an iron hand, kept all the patronage under his thumb, and dealt ruthlessly with those who

[15] Stenographic record of Thompson s speech.

[16] *Ibid.*

[17] *Chicago Daily News*, September 26, 1933. For a discussion of this case, see M. Mayer, "Corrupt and Discontented?" *Survey Graphic*, XXIII (October, 1934), 480–81.

furnished any opposition. In the Democratic primary of 1932, things were not as harmonious as they had been under Brennan's leadership; and Cermak did not hesitate to ride his machine rough shod over the Irish contingent under the leadership of Michael Igoe, Democratic leader in the state legislature, who had been bold enough to challenge the machine. On the other hand, Cermak was a master at the art of conciliating business, labor, reform, nationalistic, and neighborhood associations. His 1932 primary slate included representatives of the Jews, the Poles, the Italians, the Czechs, organized labor, organized business, and many other groups.

Cermak was destined never to be a World's Fair mayor. While his local victory was complete in 1932, he had backed the wrong horse in the Democratic national convention. Using Senator J. Hamilton Lewis as a favorite-son candidate, he had joined the anti-Roosevelt forces that hoped to renominate Al Smith. Cermak had the social philosophy of a business man and an organization politician. Senator Lewis did not lend himself to this game and abruptly withdrew his name from consideration without consulting the mayor on his move. In order to prevent the federal patronage from being used against him by Senator Lewis, operating under the rule of senatorial courtesy, Cermak tried to make peace with James A. Farley, chairman of the Democratic national committee, and with President-elect Roosevelt. To this end he went to Miami, Florida, in February, 1933, where both Farley and Roosevelt were enjoying a rest.[18] There were a number of federal positions in which Cermak was particularly interested, such as the local postmastership, the district attorney's post, and the federal judgeships which might become vacant. At the climax of his career, at the age of fifty-nine, Cermak's life was cut short by an assassin's bullet which was aimed at Roosevelt.

The question as to who would succeed Cermak was not decided immediately. When Cermak became mayor in 1931, his lifelong friend, Patrick A. Nash, became the chairman of the Democratic county committee. From the standpoint of age,

[18] *Chicago Tribune*, February 9, 1933.

experience, and financial standing, Nash was logical successor to Cermak. Born in 1863, he inherited with his brothers a prosperous business as sewer contractor. He had been a neighbor and close friend of Roger Sullivan, Democratic state leader. It was said that the Nash Brothers firm did more sewer work than any other around Chicago. At any rate, when the federal government made public the income returns for 1925, Nash was among the ten highest income-receivers in the city of Chicago.[19] Although he served nine months by appointment on the board of assessors and in 1918 was elected to the board of review, he usually preferred to remain behind the scenes and manipulate the wires. However, he could not prevent some unfavorable publicity in connection with Insull's lists, his income tax, and the loss of certain federal contracts. His hobby was the breeding of thoroughbred horses for racing. Since he was known as the great harmonizer of the organization and since he had met many of the business men as tax-reviewer, he was asked to assume the position of leadership left vacant by Cermak.

For the asking, Nash could have been made mayor; but he felt that the work would be too onerous for a man of his age. Legislation was rushed through the general assembly at Springfield authorizing the city council to choose the new mayor. It was claimed that this would save half-a-million dollars, the cost of a special municipal election. After refusing to take the position himself, Nash suggested the name of Edward J. Kelly, president of the South Park Board and chief engineer of the sanitary district. The Democratic caucus agreed to this suggestion, and since thirty-eight out of the fifty aldermen were Democrats, the election followed as a matter of course.[20] As the sanitary district has control of sewage disposal in the Chicago area, it was natural that Nash and Kelly would be well known to each other. Governor Horner and Kelly had lived in the same ward in Chicago and were acquainted as neighbors and fellow-Democrats. In addition, Colonel Robert R. McCormick, the publisher of the independent Republican *Chicago Tribune*,

[19] *Ibid.*, September 1–30, 1925.
[20] *Ibid.*, April 14, 1933; *Chicago Daily News*, April 13, 1933.

was friendly toward Kelly since the days when McCormick was president of the sanitary district board. The business men who were backing the World's Fair had already made contacts with Kelly in connection with his position on the South Park Board. The press was kindly toward the new mayor at first and did not remind the public that he had been indicted in connection with the sanitary district scandals of the famous "whoopee era."[21] Nor did the papers bring out the fact that he was having trouble with his income tax. Here was another self-made man who was wholly in sympathy with the social philosophy of the business men.

At the age of fifty-seven, Edward J. Kelly, without turning a finger, became the mayor of Chicago. The son of a Chicago policeman who had immigrated from Ireland during the Civil War, Kelly had become in turn rodman, computer, subinstrument, subassistant engineer, assistant engineer, assistant chief engineer, and chief engineer of the sanitary district. His engineering training was entirely practical, since his education did not extend beyond high school. Politics became one of his early interests, since he was a member of the senatorial district convention which nominated Cermak for the state legislature in 1902. It was said that Kelly was very thrifty and had built up a comfortable income. As Horner put it, in the bitter primary campaign of 1936, in answer to Kelly's charge that he (Horner) was not a politician, "If to amass a huge fortune on a modest salary is to be a politician, I am not a politician."[22] Later Horner said, "And the national administration turned a deaf ear . . . . to 'Boss' Kelly when he was forced to pay from $105,000 to $110,000 to the federal government on his income of $450,000 during the years 1926, 1927, and 1928."[23] However, when Kelly was first made mayor, he had the good wishes of the press and the general public. Tall, athletic looking, modest in speech and manner, he made a fine-appearing mayor to wel-

[21] At the time of the indictment, the *Chicago Tribune* ran a story. See issue of May 30, 1930.

[22] *Chicago Evening American* and *Chicago Daily News*, March 3, 1936.

[23] *Ibid.*, March 16, 1936.

come the World's Fair guests. Furthermore, he was willing to listen to the suggestions of the bankers, editors, and business men.

While the new Kelly-Nash machine had its weak points, it would probably have gone ahead without mishaps had not certain mistakes been made. Shortly after coming into office, Kelly gained control of the school board, which up to that time had been run by Thompson holdovers. Although the school budget for the year had been passed, the new board, made up for the most part of practical business men, held a secret session and adopted a drastic program of economy which was condemned by educators everywhere.[24] The city junior college and the junior high schools were completely abolished; the work in music, manual training, household arts, and physical education was eliminated from the elementary schools; and the kindergartens were cut by 50 per cent. Teachers, pupils, parents, and civic leaders protested against the flouting of the superintendent and the interests of the school children, but the board was adamant. The callous attitude of the new board was the product of its ignorance, since it was persuaded, by experience, to reverse itself on many points, the demands of the bankers and business men for economy, and the indifference of the Catholic elements in the city, which had to support schools of their own which served half as many pupils as the public schools served. It is an axiom of wise boss rule in the United States that it is good politics to provide an efficient educational system. The well-intrenched boss of Kansas City, Missouri, Pendergast, has acted to his own advantage on this principle.

The Kelly-Nash machine was also brazen in its handling of the liquor question. President Roosevelt's election brought to an end the prohibition era in Chicago politics, with its gangster bootleggers and demoralization of the law-enforcing authorities. The repeal amendment which went into effect in November, 1933, was overwhelmingly indorsed by the voters in the city of Chicago. Here was a golden opportunity to contribute something to the solution of the difficult problem of liquor control.

[24] *Chicago Evening American*, July 13, 1933.

National Democratic leaders had promised in the 1932 platform
that there would be no return to the saloon and the evils of the
old liquor traffic. Public discussion of the question was widespread, and there were many research organizations which
publicized the experience of other countries. The Chicago
politicians were not interested in liquor control. Their main
concern was how much revenue would the city get from this
source and who would enjoy the political advantage of controlling the licensing of the traffic. This meant that they were
interested in promoting, not regulating, the liquor business. As
a local newspaper put it:

> It is true that the 8,000-odd saloons in Chicago now are called taverns, but
> that does not change the fact that they are saloons, with the appearance and
> the character of the old saloons that spread corruption and degradation be-
> fore prohibition.
>
> They are, in fact, somewhat worse than the old-time saloons because thou-
> sands of women frequent them now, many unescorted. That was not per-
> mitted in the "old days." . . . .
>
> The open saloon is HERE.
>
> Its "attendant evils" are here, too, all of them—drunkenness, brawling,
> moral deterioration, murder.[25]

The extent of the popular reaction to the highly political
solution of the liquor question is shown by the number of
precincts which voted "dry" in the 1936 general election. Although the law was cumbersome, a number of community
groups took advantage of it in order to get rid of the taverns in
their neighborhoods.

In spite of its mistakes and the lukewarm attitude of the
national administration, the Kelly-Nash machine functioned in
a very effective fashion in the congressional and county elections
of 1934 and the mayoralty election of 1935. After the sweeping
Democratic county victories of 1934 the Republican organization was completely bankrupt, financially and morally. Five
years earlier, a man with Kelly's record would have been regarded as an easy mark for the Republican organization. However, in 1935 there was no Republican faction which had the
ready cash for a real fight or which had a leader who was willing

[25] *Ibid.*, January 6, 1934.

to enter the lists with the odds appearing to be so strong against him. In previous Republican primaries, the *Chicago Tribune* was willing to give one of the Republican candidates considerable publicity, but in this campaign it kept entirely aloof. As a result the Republican nomination went by default to a man who was actually chosen by the Democrats on the basis of a bipartisan deal.[26] The Democratic organization wanted to pile up such a huge vote for Kelly that the national administration would be impressed and ready to recognize more of the claims of the local leaders. No hitch marred the working of this scheme, and Kelly received 800,000 votes to 167,000 for his Republican rival, who waged a listless "powder-puff" campaign. There were charges that 200,000 of these votes were stolen; but even granting some election irregularities, the vote was a striking indication of popular support. The result might be put in this fashion: About one-half of the registered voters supported Kelly. The other half stayed away from the polls, for the most part, since it did not see any real alternative to Kelly. Shortly after the election Kelly went to Washington in order to talk "turkey" with the federal officials about the Works Progress Administration money to be spent in Chicago. President Roosevelt went out of his way to congratulate the mayor on his splendid vote.[27]

Following the stunning victory of 1935, the machine met a few setbacks. The first was the famous Sweitzer case. On two occasions the genial "Bob" Sweitzer, popular after-dinner speaker and well-known race-track fan, had been the Democratic nominee for mayor. For twenty-four years he had held the office of county clerk, which meant that he had survived the severest Republican landslides. He had received the indorsement of independent Republican newspapers for the position as well as that of various business groups. In 1934 he was nominated and elected county treasurer. His successor in the

<hr/>

[26] This charge was made by the manager for the third-party candidate. See *Chicago Daily News* and *Chicago Tribune*, March 27, 1935. The author has substantiated it on the basis of private sources.

[27] *Chicago Tribune*, April 12, 1935.

county clerk's office refused to take over the books until there had been an audit. Early in May, 1935, there were rumors that this audit showed a shortage in the funds of around $400,000. The audit was finally made public; and on the basis of it the county board removed Sweitzer from the office of county treasurer, to which he had recently been elected. A most extraordinary series of events followed. By his own admission, it was obvious that he regarded the tax-redemption fund which had been in his charge, as county clerk, as "nobody's money," to be handled as he pleased—in his vest pocket or even in the stocks of questionable companies which were about to make fortunes manufacturing coal bricks, monkey wrenches, or what not, but never did. It was also obvious that this fund was a kind of "self-service" money reservoir for politicians, who were free to dip into it at any time with no thought of paying any of it back. Throughout the proceedings for his ouster from the county treasuryship, the *quo warranto* trial which he instituted to regain his office, and the criminal trial which was brought against him by the state's attorney, he maintained an air of injured innocence, always promising to produce the money but never doing so. The significance of this case is what it revealed about the operation of the machine. As one editorial writer put it:

It was all too evident that Sweitzer's party associates were not vigilant to protect the public from his weaknesses. They were not diligent to protect Sweitzer from himself. Ever since the famous incident in 1926, when Sweitzer made good a rubber check for $89,050 made out to the gambling king, Col. Edward R. Bradley, winner of the American Derby that year, Nash and his merry men have been on notice that their "good fellow" vote-getter was a playboy entrusted with millions of the people's money.

The story reeks of clandestine conspiracy to hoodwink the people and to cheat them of their rights. Sweitzer was only one poor pawn in this game. The whole Nash crowd became moral accessories after the fact. The outfit has shown that it regards public office as a private snap.[28]

Economic adversity had made the voters more tax conscious than they had been in the prosperous twenties, and Sweitzer's antics were not viewed with complacency. However, the genial

[28] *Chicago Daily News*, May 23, 1935.

Bob was a good witness for himself and a fine courtroom actor. The jury in the criminal trial brought in the cheering verdict, "Not guilty."

The first real test of the Kelly-Nash machine came in the Democratic primary of 1936 in connection with the gubernatorial nomination. Prior to his election as governor, Henry Horner had not had any experience in a large administrative office. During the first part of his governorship he felt it necessary to consult with his friends and party advisers very frequently. Although he was a great admirer of Mayor Cermak and was under obligations to him for his nomination and election, Horner did not follow Cermak's suggestions on all occasions. Horner had a streak of stubborn idealism in his make-up, which he displayed when he felt the issues were clear. Many of his friends felt that he did not show this side of his character soon enough. After Cermak was replaced by the Kelly-Nash combination, the governor became more and more independent. At the same time the Democratic organization became more shameless in its demands. In the summer of 1935, considerable friction developed between the governor and the Chicago Democratic leaders when the governor vetoed a bill to legalize race-track handbooks in the city. As has already been indicated, a number of prominent politicians were interested in race-track betting, and they were out to increase their business. The Citizens Association and a number of other civic groups prevailed upon the governor to veto the legislation.

Governor Horner and the Kelly-Nash machine broke openly when the mayor announced that he was going to support Herman N. Bundesen, city health commissioner, for the governorship. Horner had been asked to retire gracefully. He had even been offered a federal judgeship as an inducement to withdraw from the race,[29] but the blandishments of the machine could not remove the implication that he had not made good as governor. Rather than go on the bench, he preferred to take the risk of going down fighting. At any rate, he could turn to a lucrative private practice of the law with the feeling that he had done his

[29] *Chicago Herald and Examiner*, March 4, 1936.

best. It seemed at first as though he was going against hopeless odds.

As the primary campaign developed, the Horner forces gained considerable momentum. In addition to the handbook issue, which the organization had a hard time explaining, the governor took advantage of the rivalry between Chicago and downstate, the agitation for a sound system of registration of voters, a bitter newspaper war over the question of daylight saving, and the rising resentment of a large body of citizens at the high-handed methods of the Democratic organization leaders.

For many years the League of Women Voters and other civic organizations had carried on a campaign for legislation which would lessen fraudulent practices in connection with registration. At first the Republican machine in the state legislature had blocked this legislation; and then, when the Democrats came to power, the tables were reversed. Governor Horner kept the question alive by pressing it in a special message to the state legislature just before the primary. The bill passed the house, being supported by practically all of the Republicans and the downstate Democrats. In the senate the measure lost by a very narrow margin, owing to the absence of some of its potential supporters and the determined opposition of the Kelly-Nash bloc. This action on the part of the machine leaders put them in a position which was difficult to defend. The *Chicago Tribune* had supported Kelly on practically all of his policies, but it was against him in his opposition to a bill designed to secure honest and more economical administration of elections. When the mayor tried to defend himself, he appeared foolish. He failed to follow Frank Kent's rule of political behavior, "Never handle a hot poker on the front porch."[30] Election manipulation may be a common political technique in the largest American cities, but a wise boss does not try to apologize for it. The democratic symbols are sufficiently sacred to the rank and file that their cheapening and degrading is resented. Mayor Kelly's reference to the possible loss of 200,000 votes in the coming presidential

[30] *Political Behavior* (New York, 1928), chap. xvi.

election because of the disfranchisement of persons who could not sign their names was turned neatly against him. As Horner put it, "Do any of you think President Roosevelt would care to be elected in Illinois by crooked votes? . . . . They are still trying to vote butterflies, fence rails and ghosts, but it is not going to work this year. The people of Illinois are aroused against bossism and they are going to see that 'Boss' Kelly won't rule Illinois."[31]

Governor Horner's fight for votes in Chicago was greatly aided by the jealousy of the newspaper proprietors. It was obvious that the *Chicago Tribune* was the chief beneficiary of the city ordinance which provided for permanent daylight-saving time. This action cut the afternoon papers out of one of their early financial editions. The dailies affected did everything in their power to discredit this action and to undermine confidence in the city administration which was responsible for it. Governor Horner's campaign was a convenient channel into which they could direct their energies, and they gave full publicity to his crusading speeches. In the fall election the city hall machine and the *Tribune* were defeated on the issue of permanent daylight saving by the Horner forces, organized labor, and the afternoon papers. By a popular vote of two to one the electors supported propositions which called for a return to Central Standard Time during the winter months.

So rapidly did the sentiment in favor of Governor Horner grow that two of the local leaders of the Kelly-Nash organization deserted to the Horner camp within the last week of the campaign. Both of them were accused of following their own selfish interests, which bound them close to the state government; but, be this as it may, it did not lessen their shrewdness in picking a winner. If Horner had been defeated, they would have lost both their state and local contacts. In building up a rival organization Governor Horner did not hesitate to use state patronage freely. The Kelly-Nash group tried to discredit his campaign by sensational charges of pay-roll padding, and the

[31] *Chicago Evening American*, March 28, 1936; *Chicago Daily News*, March 30, 1936.

state treasurer went to the point of holding up some of the pay rolls. However, this line of attack fell flat, as it was a case of the kettle calling the pot "black."

The victory of Horner over Bundesen in the Democratic primary destroyed the myth of the invincibility which had grown up around the Kelly-Nash machine. To be sure, the governor lost the city of Chicago by 150,000 votes; but his margin of 300,000 votes downstate gave him a comfortable lead. The hardest blows to the prestige of the Democratic organization were the large size of the Horner vote in Chicago, the loss of eight wards by the organization candidate, and the loss of control over the governorship. Horner was more in sympathy with the policies of the New Deal than were the Chicago bosses. Three hundred thousand voters in Chicago sensed this.[32]

The momentum which Horner gained in the primary and the continued Democratic sweep in the nation were so strong that Horner was re-elected governor by a safe margin in the fall election, even though he ran behind the top of the ticket in Chicago instead of ahead of it, as he had in 1932. In spite of internal dissensions within its ranks, the Democratic party appears to be securely in the saddle in Illinois.

Harmony and rigid discipline used to be the order of the day for the minority party of the prosperity days. However, so intense did the struggle for power within this party become when it became a majority group that open factional warfare could not be avoided. The mad scramble for control over the liquor traffic, gambling, contracts, jobs, special favors, and public expenditures split the new machine, as it had broken party machines which held sway before it. Mistakes in judgment, lack of adroitness in campaigning techniques, and the rivalry between Chicago and the rest of the state accentuated the centrifugal forces which had been brought into play.

Seven years of depression in the city of Chicago have made practically no changes in the fundamental character of party

---

[32] The final returns for the city of Chicago were: Bundesen, 481,966; Horner, 319,927; Robertson, 12,508. Horner needed a big vote in Chicago to make his lead downstate effective. The vote downstate was: Bundesen, 133,105; Horner, 450,210.

organization, methods, and leadership. It is true that the fortunes of individual politicians and parties have been greatly altered, but the party system has remained about the same. The party which controlled only a minority of the local offices when the financial crash came was greatly benefited by its connection with the new national administration, but it did not change its outlook. Jobs and spoils were the currency of Chicago politics in 1936 as well as in 1928, and not issues which concerned the functions of municipal government in times of great economic stresses and strains.

The political bosses who found themselves in power in the great metropolis of the Middle West in the thirties were, for the most part, self-made men. Chicago, in contrast to New York, has been a center abounding in self-made men—industrialists, grain merchants, large department-store owners, and real estate speculators. Chicago business men and politicians were accustomed to dealing with men and materials directly in their everyday work. In New York City the bankers are more prominent than the industrialists. Investment bankers work largely by means of secondary contacts, established by reports, charts, and graphs. During the economic crisis many of the industrial leaders of the city of Chicago met financial reverses, but there were others who stepped into their places. The economic setup of the city was altered in details but not in its general pattern. The self-made politicians understood the self-made business men, as they talked the same language. While the sources of revenue available for local governmental purposes were greatly reduced, the politicians were able to use what there was to consolidate their positions. They said, in effect, to the business men: "You leave us alone and we will leave you alone." The economic crisis in Chicago was met not by the local governments but by the national government.

And what were the other groups doing during this period? What were the demands of organized labor and the organized consumers? The answer to the latter point is simple. There were practically no well-organized groups of consumers who could make articulate demands upon the local party leaders.

But surely Chicago has always been a well-organized labor town? During the depression the leaders of the trade-unions in Chicago were unusually silent. Some of them had been the heroes of the post–World War era of labor insurgence, when they had tried political methods, had failed to leave any lasting impression, and had been rebuked by their national leaders. Disillusionment, advancing age, and troubles with racketeering minorities stilled their voices during a time when many of their rank-and-file members had plenty of grievances.

Economic hardships undoubtedly created feelings of discontent which might have been used to bring about political changes, but the city lacked the kind of leadership which was necessary to guide the inarticulate demands of the masses. The new Tammany which was created on the ruins of its opponents' machines was led by men who were thoroughly in sympathy with the philosophy of big business. The conservative political outlook of the political, industrial, and financial leaders and a lack of local constitutional powers prevented the city government from becoming a major instrumentality of the citizens in meeting their problems during the crisis.

CHAPTER II

YOU CAN'T LICK A WARD BOSS

Of the economic and political changes which took place in Chicago during the period 1928–36, some were revolutionary in character. A complete new set of political leaders was brought in by the depression. What happened to the lesser political lights and the ward bosses?

COMMITTEEMAN PAT NASH

A comparison of the lists of ward committeemen for 1928 and 1936 shows some marked similarities. Twenty-one of the Democratic ward committeemen were the same in both lists, and eleven in the Republican lists. However, these figures do not reveal the real stability of the city committees. Thirteen Republicans and eight Democrats died in office. The proof of the hypothesis that a ward committeeman can't be "licked" is shown by the fact that only nine Republicans and five Democrats were "whipped" in straight contests for re-election. In other words, considering the fact that there were fifty Republican and fifty Democratic ward committeemen to be elected five times during the period under discussion, this turnover is amazingly small. Out of a total of five hundred ward contests, only thirteen city committeemen were "licked." Their superiors might change, but the ward bosses clung to their posts in spite of economic and political storms.

What is the secret of this longevity of ward bosshood? While economic changes bring about changes of party leaders and bring in entirely new leaders in the national and state fields, they have relatively little effect upon the ward bosses because these key men in the party hierarchy have their roots deeply planted in the spoils system which is characteristic of metropolitan regions in the United States.

In order to become a ward committeeman in Chicago, the aspirant must begin political work at an early age. Long years of apprenticeship seem to be one of the qualifications. Once elected, a ward boss who shows the ordinary amount of adroitness and party regularity is likely to be continued in office. He has the advantage of experience, patronage power, the prestige which is attached to the office itself, and the inertia of the rank-and-file party membership. The outstanding example of such a history in the city of Chicago is the famed Michael ("Hinky Dink") Kenna, who has been the ward boss of the First Ward, containing the central business section of the city, since 1897.

The invincibility of ward bosses in metropolitan sections like Chicago is in part due to their legal position. Every important political faction in both the Democratic and Republican parties tries to select the best possible representative for each of the fifty wards. While the legal position of these party officials has been confused during the past twenty years, their *de facto* functions have remained the same.[2] The official duties of the ward

---

[1] For an early description of Kenna, see H. G. Wells, *The Future in America* (New York, 1906).

"Now Alderman Kenna is a straight man, the sort of man one likes and trusts at sight, and he did not invent his profession. He follows his own ideas of right and wrong, and compared with my ideas of right and wrong, they seem tough, compact, decided things. He is very kind to all his crowd. He helps them when they are in trouble, even if it is trouble with the police; he helps them find employment when they are down on their luck; he stands between them and the impacts of an unsympathetic and altogether too-careless social structure in a sturdy and almost parental way. I can quite believe what I was told, that in the lives of many of these rough undesirables he's almost the only decent influence. He gets wives well treated, and he has an open heart for children. And he tells them how to vote, a duty of citizenship they might otherwise neglect, and sees that they do it properly. And whenever you want to do things in Chicago you must reckon carefully with him . . . ." (*ibid.*, p. 131).

[2] The Primary Law of 1910 failed to specify the term of the ward committeemen and the time of their election. Elections were held in 1914 and 1916 but not in 1918. The Primary Law of 1919 provided for the election of ward committeemen in 1920 for a four-year term. This law was declared unconstitutional in the case of *People* v. *Fox*, 294 Ill. 263, and both the 1916 and 1920 committees claimed to be the lawful committees. In 1921 the number of wards was changed from thirty-five to fifty. The Primary Law of 1927 was upheld by the courts (*People* v. *Kramer*, 328 Ill. 512). It provided for a two-year term, but a 1935 amendment extended the term to four years.

committeeman elected by the voters in his party primary include membership in the judicial circuit convention, which
nominates candidates for the Superior and Circuit Court bench;
membership in the county central committee, which sends delegates to the state convention, which in turn nominates candidates for the Illinois Supreme Court, trustees of the University of Illinois, and delegates at large to the national nominating
conventions; and membership in the congressional district and
city committees, which fill vacancies and manage the local
campaigns. Even though the Republican party in the city of
Chicago has received some very severe reverses during the past
seven years, it has still maintained a foothold on the bench. The
Democratic bosses have not been so brazen as to try to sweep
the bench clean of the sitting Republican judges. In Chicago
there is a tradition of long standing that a judge who serves
well on the bench should be allowed to remain there regardless
of the fortunes of his party. In the past, when political bosses
have defied this sentiment by a wholesale attack upon the sitting judges, the bosses have come to grief.[3] Besides, judicial
patronage has not been large enough to tempt the bosses to
make a strenuous fight for it. They have preferred to avoid the
trouble of a real contest by bipartisan arrangements. Consequently, a ward committeeman of a minority party is in a position to exercise some influence upon the nomination of judges.

In each of the party governing bodies the vote of a ward committeeman is in proportion to the total primary vote cast in
his ward by the members of his party. Thus, if in one ward
20,000 voters call for Democratic ballots, and in another ward
only 10,000, the successful candidate for ward committeeman
in the former ward would have twice the voting strength of the
one in the latter on the various Democratic committees. The
same rule holds for the Republican committee. Persons interested in the job of ward committeeman, then, try to get the
maximum primary vote for their party in their ward. The relative number of persons taking part in the Republican primaries

[3] E. M. Martin, *The Influence of the Bar upon the Selection of the Bench* (Chicago,
1936).

in Chicago has declined enormously during the past eight years, but it still behooves each Republican candidate for ward committeeman to seek to maximize his influence with reference to the other Republican ward committeemen.

The geographical boundaries of the wards are drawn largely to suit the wishes of the aldermen and the ward committeemen. According to law, the redistricting of the city into fifty wards after each decennial census is the function of the city council only, but in practice the ward committeemen have a great deal to say about how the ward lines will be drawn. In 1936 it happened that fourteen of the ward committeemen were also aldermen. This contingent in the city council would have been sufficient in itself to control apportionment, since a minority can hold up the entire redistricting ordinance. However, most of the other aldermen were under obligations to the ward committeemen of their particular party. In theory the aldermen were elected on a nonpartisan basis, but all of the members of the city council selected in 1935 had the backing of the Democratic or the Republican organization. The Democratic sweep of that year left only five nominally Republican aldermen out of a council of fifty. All the others were elected by means of Democratic backing.

In making a reapportionment, the city council keeps a number of things in mind. According to the city charter, the wards should be as nearly equal in population as possible. However, some wards are declining in population and others are growing very rapidly. A redistricting which was absolutely fair immediately after the census was taken would soon be grossly unjust to the outlying sections of the city, which are expanding by leaps and bounds. The 1921 and the 1931 ward lines, which are given in the accompanying chart (Fig. 1), discriminated in favor of the depreciated or blighted areas found near the business center of the city. The most glaring example of a rotten borough is the First Ward, where in 1936 "Hinky Dink" had only 14,119 registered voters, as compared with 52,675 registered voters for the Fifth Ward.

In drawing ward lines all the tricks of gerrymandering are

MAP OF CHICAGO
SHOWING
1921 AND 1931 WARD LINES

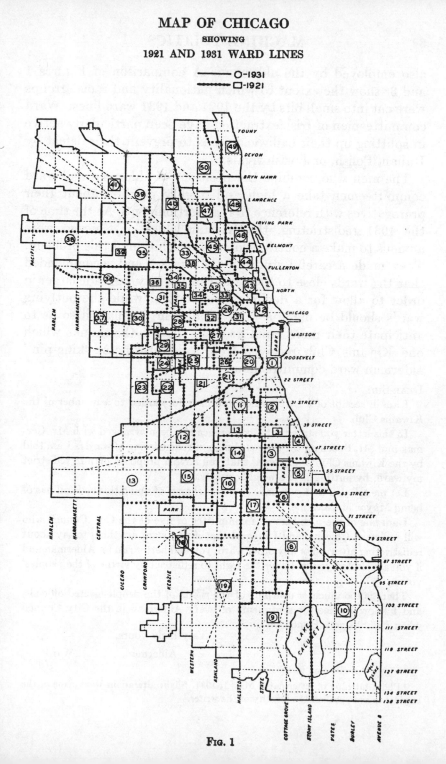

FIG. 1

also employed by the alderman. A comparison of Figures 1 and 3[4] show the extent to which nationality and racial groups were cut into small bits by the 1921 and 1931 ward lines. Ward committeemen of Irish extraction have been particularly active in splitting up their bailiwicks so as to prevent their defeat by Italian, Polish, or Jewish rivals.

The men who combine the positions of aldermen and ward committeemen take a high and mighty position about their prerogatives with reference to reapportionment. At the time of the 1931 redistricting, the Kiwanis clubs of Chicago were anxious to make a contribution to the solution of this problem. They made a careful study of the subject and recommended that the wards close to the center of the city be made larger in order to allow for a declining population, while the outlying wards should be made a little smaller in population so as to anticipate their more rapid growth. This is the thanks which one Kiwanis Club received from a dictator-boss, "king-pin" alderman ward committeeman:

DEAR SIR:

I am in receipt of a letter which you have forwarded to a member of the Kiwanis Club.

In this letter you state that a conference has been arranged with Mr. Cermak and Mr. Busch on the proposed plan of redistricting of wards. I am told by the Kiwanis Club of my ward that you have a proposed plan to redistrict my ward, by putting it in a neighboring ward

Let me tell you that you have as much chance of doing this as Ford has of being Mayor of Palestine.

I am one of the members of a committee of five of the City Council who will redistrict Chicago, and I suggest that if you want anything to say about redistricting my ward or any other ward, you had better run for Alderman and if you are elected you will have the right to redistrict by virtue of the peoples' votes.

There is too much of usurping of the rights of the people-elected officials, and I know I voice the sentiments of every Alderman in the City Council when I say to you, Hands Off.

Very truly yours,

Alderman,................Ward[5]

[4] Figure 3 is given on p. 103.

[5] Photostat copy of letter dated May 1, 1931. Slight alterations were made of the original so as to conceal the identity of the writer.

Although the Democratic party was a minority party in Chicago before 1930, nevertheless it dominated the redistricting because of its strength in the so-called "River wards," where population was declining.[6] This control of ward lines by a single party during the entire period was one of the elements which checked change.

Ward committeemen are difficult to defeat because practically all the elective office-holders are under obligations to them. In Illinois most of the candidates for elective positions are nominated by party voters in direct primary elections, but the ward committeemen are very influential in making up the pre-primary unofficial slates.[7] No person has much of any chance of winning a nomination in a direct party-primary election unless he has the backing of influential ward leaders. In general the more duly elected ward committeemen a candidate has in back of him, the greater are the chances of success in the primary. The complicated mechanism of the government of the Chicago region requires the voters within the city limits to exercise over one hundred and fifty primary- and election-day choices during a six-year period.[8] The drafting and circulation of petitions for the candidates for these one hundred and fifty different positions is largely in the hands of the ward committeeman. Even in an opposition party without patronage, like the Republican party in 1936, the nominations are controlled by the ward bosses.

Ward leaders perpetuate themselves because of the considerable control they have over the election machinery. A given political party is entitled to three of the five members of the precinct boards of election in every other precinct, according to the Illinois election law.[9] Even when a party is out of power in the county and city, it still retains the privilege of naming

[6] Wards, 1, 11, 20, 21, 28, 33, 42, and 43.

[7] C. H. Wooddy, *The Chicago Primary of 1926* (Chicago, 1926). At the time this book was written, the legal position of ward committeemen was confused, but the factional representatives in the various wards performed the functions of the office.

[8] C. E. Merriam, S. D. Parratt, and A. Lepawsky, *The Government of the Metropolitan Region of Chicago* (Chicago, 1933), pp. 81–82.

[9] Board of Election Commissioners of the City of Chicago, *General Election Laws* (Chicago, 1935), citing city Election Act, sec. 11.

one-half of the precinct judges and clerks of election for the entire city. The ward committeeman sends to the board of election commissioners what are called "submittal lists," and these lists are used in making appointments of precinct election officials.[10] This customary privilege exercised by the ward committeemen is of great importance not only because of the patronage involved but also because of the power over the election process itself. According to the parlance of the politicians, there are some wards which are "dependable," meaning that the wards can be depended upon to deliver the number of notes which are needed to win regardless of how the duly qualified voters may mark their ballots. Election frauds are possible only when the precinct election officials themselves are corrupt or so inefficient that they would not be likely to detect corruption.

In spite of the importance of the position of ward committeeman, only a portion of the voters take the trouble to indicate their preferences for this position. This situation is not peculiar to Chicago, as Mosher found a great deal of indifference among the voters of cities in upstate New York toward the selection of committeemen.[11]

During the eight-year period beginning with 1928 there were five occasions on which ward committeemen were elected by the members of the Democratic and Republican parties. According to Table 2, at no primary have as many as two-thirds of the registered voters marked their ballots for ward committeemen; and at two of the primaries (1930 and 1934) only slightly more than one-half of the voters performed this function. Most of the registered voters who do not concern themselves with voting for ward committeemen fail to come to the polls on primary days. Under the Illinois laws the primary voter has to ask for a Republican or Democratic ballot. He may not change his party affiliation in less than a two-year

[10] *In re Maguire* (hearing before the County Court, 1930).

[11] William E. Mosher, "Party and Government Control at the Grass Roots," *National Municipal Review*, XXIV (January, 1935), 16. He found that only 36 per cent of major party enrolment voted for committeemen in primary elections of 1932.

period. Many persons do not wish to reveal their party affiliations for fear that they will be charged with partisan activities, teachers wish to appear impartial before their students, many persons may be awaiting the lapse of the two-year period in order to change their party affiliation, certain business men who may have convictions which draw them to a party which is out of power may not be willing to expose themselves to persecution by the powers that be, and persons who are dissatisfied with both the major parties may wish to be available as signers of

TABLE 2

INTEREST IN VOTING FOR WARD COMMITTEEMEN: CHICAGO, 1928–36

YEAR	PERCENT- AGE OF REGIS- TERED VOTE CAST AT APRIL PRI- MARIES	PERCENTAGE OF TOTAL PRIMARY VOTE		PERCENTAGE OF REGISTERED VOTE CAST		AGGREGATE VOTE FOR REPUBLICAN AND DEMOCRATIC CANDIDATES FOR WARD COMMITTEEMEN	
		Republi- can	Demo- cratic	Republi- can Pri- mary	Demo- cratic Pri- mary	Percent- age of Total Vote at Primary	Percent- age of Total Regis- tered Vote
1928............	71.0	81.6	18.4	57.9	13.0	91.1	64.7
1930............	59.5	73.2	26.8	43.6	15.9	90.7	54.0
1932............	68.4	52.1	47.9	35.7	32.8	88.9	60.9
1934............	58.5	39.1	60.9	22.9	35.7	89.7	52.5
1936............	72.8	28.7	71.3	20.9	51.9	87.7	63.9

a third-party petition. These and many other reasons may be offered for not coming to the polls on primary day.

Table 2 shows that from 10 to 12 per cent of those who come to the polls on primary election days do not take the trouble to indicate their choice for ward committeeman. One obvious reason for this is that there is no contest for the position in many instances. Thus, for the entire period studied there were no contests in twenty-four Republican and none in ninety-one Democratic ward committeemen elections. Only in the Republican committeemen elections of 1932 were there contests in every one of the fifty wards. During the past eight years the

Democratic ward committeemen have been more successful in discouraging opposition to their re-election.

Certainly, it is strange that such a valuable post is not more vigorously sought after by aspiring party leaders! A closer examination of the situation reveals the fact that many of the contestants are eliminated by the board of election commissioners on the ground of technical deficiencies in their petitions. The names of these hopeful politicians do not appear upon the party ballots in the primary. Some have attempted to run anyway, by waging a "write-in" campaign; but such campaigns are extraordinarily difficult to conduct and require great zeal, money, intelligence, and organizing ability. Each individual voter must be instructed as to the proper spelling of the name to be written in on the ballot, as to the necessity of placing a square in front of the name, and finally as to the usual cross mark. There is no known instance of a candidate for ward committeeman who waged a successful "write-in" campaign against an opponent who had regular party organization support.[12] In other words, the device of raising technical objections to a petition is one which serves the purposes of the incumbent ward committeemen.

Many troublesome rivals have been eliminated by the sitting ward committeeman by means of legal technicalities raised in the hearings on the petitions. The objections raised include such trivialities as mistakes in the numbering of the pages of the petition, the failure to bind the petition in acceptable form, the omission of the word "street," the printing of the word "Chicago" where the law requires it to be written by the voters, and the use of ditto marks. These are requirements which can be observed by any candidate who makes an effort to find out the law and practice on such matters. On the other hand, a petition may be thrown out because of the detection of a similarity of handwriting. Prior to the fall of 1936 the City Election Act did not require the voter to sign his name when he registered, and the board of election commissioners had no real proof

[12] In the 1936 Republican primary in the Nineteenth Ward there were 2,284 "write-ins" for Northrup. Rohn won, with 6,761 votes.

as to the validity of such an objection and the most perfect petition ever presented could have been thrown out in an arbitrary fashion. This meant that the inside ring of a political organization had a strangle hold upon the office of ward committeeman. In the primary of 1936, only one sitting Democratic ward committeeman was defeated for re-election, and his opponent was in the good graces of the city hall machine.[13] Since the new permanent registration act went into effect with the signature requirement, it should be possible to check upon the validity of signatures on petitions.

But there are many contests for the position of ward committeeman. A rival candidate may be so strong that the ward committeeman who is coming up for re-election may think that it is better to win in a straight fight. Otherwise, the feeling against him might hurt his chances of securing a big primary vote in his ward and a large vote for his party in the final election. The figures show that, even where there is a contest, from 8 to 10 per cent of the voters fail to mark their ballots for ward committeeman. The names of the contestants for this position appear in the lower right-hand corner of the ballot, which requires some forty or more choices to be made. The voters who are not conscious of political affairs are likely to miss completely the significance of the position. They read in the daily paper about the city-wide candidates, but they know nothing about ward politics. In the primary of 1936 many persons asked for Democratic ballots, and then merely voted for Horner for governor and for Courtney for state's attorney.

Not only are ward committeemen elected by a minority of the registered voters, but it appears that those who exercise a choice for the position very frequently defeat their own ends by supporting a candidate who belongs to a city-wide faction which they oppose.

Thus in the famous Republican "pineapple" primary of 1928, the candidates of Mayor Thompson's faction for county

---

[13] After the hearings on petitions were over, regular Democratic ward committeemen deserted the city hall machine for the Horner forces. It was too late for the city hall machine to use its full weight against these recalcitrants.

and state positions were defeated in the city but the mayor
and his friends retained a two-thirds majority of the ward
committeemen posts. History repeated itself in the Democratic primary of 1936. Governor Horner was able to carry
wards in the city of Chicago which re-elected the ward committeemen who represented the city hall machine.[14] Many
party voters do not know that the man who is running for ward
committeeman belongs to a faction which they dislike. The
incumbent ward committeeman has many advantages over his
opponents. If his party controls certain patronage offices, he
has his job-holders and their friends who will work for him. In
addition the committeeman is likely to have superior financial
resources. If his party is in power, there will always be a large
fund available to pay canvassers, watchers, and other precinct
workers. The committeeman always makes sure that the
marked ballots and other literature emphasize the importance
of his election. I have attended many political meetings where
the ward committeeman told his workers to have the voters
vote for him first. In some wards the committeeman may bar-
gain with other factions for personal support. He is willing to
desert some of the candidates on his faction's slate in return
for votes for himself.

Reference has already been made to the fact that during the
past eight years there have been many more bitter contests
for Republican ward committeemen posts than there have been
for Democratic. Successful Republican candidates for ward
committeeman have never received much more than half of
the Republican primary votes in any year, and in 1932 they
received less than half. The disharmony in the ranks of the
Republican party has been partly caused by the varied composition of the party. Well-to-do white Protestants, Negroes
in less fortunate economic circumstances, and, from time to

---

[14] The results in the Democratic primary of April 14, 1936, in the Fifth Ward illus-
trate this clearly:

For Governor		For Ward Committeeman	
Henry Horner	11,083	H. G. Lindheimer (Kelly-Nash)	13,404
Herman N. Bundesen	10,411	Donahue (Horner)	5,429
		Sullivan	571
		Nelson	590

time, considerable numbers of Jews and Catholics of foreign origin, living in low rental areas, have voted in the Republican primaries. The leaders of these different elements have made appeals which fitted their own constituencies and have, as a result, found it difficult to work together. Discord has further been sponsored by bitter newspaper rivalry. Even prolonged adversity has not brought the Republican factions together.

In the Democratic party, on the other hand, harmony has usually been the rule until recently. In 1932 and in 1936 there were contests for ward posts which were encouraged by candidates who wished to break the organizational slate for state offices. When the Democratic party fought the Republicans more or less upon even terms, they presented a united front; but since they have controlled all important local offices for several years, they have quarreled among themselves regarding the division of the spoils. During the term that Mayor Cermak controlled the organization, the Irish were jealous of the power exercised by the Slavic elements in the party. Since the coming to power of the Kelly-Nash machine, the German Jews and the native American elements have been struggling for power within the organization.

Since the ward committeemen constitute the core of the party machine, a closer examination of their characteristics will throw light upon urban politics in a large American metropolitan community. Patronage is the cement which unites the party organization. What have the ward committeemen done for themselves?

The drastic changes in the fortunes of the Republican and Democratic parties that took place in Chicago during the years 1928–36 are reflected in the figures given in Table 3. At the beginning of the period, three-fourths of the Republican ward committeemen held elective or appointive positions in the government service; and at the end of the period, only one-sixth were directly connected with the public pay roll. Two-thirds of the 1936 Republican ward committeemen were former office-holders, and their continued interest in politics was an indication that they had hopes of future rewards. On the other hand, the Democratic ward committeemen strengthened a grip on the public pay roll which was already powerful in 1928. Patronage positions were fairly evenly divided between the two major parties in 1928, but eight years later the Democratic ward committeemen had almost a monopoly of the key posts. Of the seven Democratic ward committeemen who were not employed by some governmental agency in 1928, three were in occupations which enabled them to have many dealings with public authorities. One was in the sewer contracting business; the second was in a law firm which had many political ramifications; and the third was in the insurance business.

There is an amazing similarity between the distribution of public jobs held by the Chicago Republican committeemen of 1928, the Philadelphia committeemen of 1934, and the Chicago Democratic committeemen of 1936. In Chicago the depression has merely replaced a predominantly Republican with an overwhelmingly Democratic machine control. The main features of the spoils octopus, with its tentacles squeezing the life out of civic enterprises, is about the same. Labels have been changed.

The complete control which the Democrats gained over the governmental offices meant that all persons seeking governmental privileges or protection had to come to them. Now, some businesses are much more vulnerable to political pressures than others. Economic enterprises which were national in scope or which did not depend upon public franchises were, to some extent, immune from badgering by local politicians. However, the public utilities, the larger real estate interests, the local bankers, the contracting firms, the hotel and rooming-house proprietors, the small retailers, the liquor dealers, and other similar businesses were susceptible to political pressures. A street-car franchise, a rate structure, road improvements, deposit of public funds, the soundness of local governmental securities, the awarding of public contracts, the enforcement of the building code and fire regulations, the use of the sidewalks by shops, and the granting or withholding of licenses to do certain types of business were favors which the local machine had to hand out; and the political bosses usually stipulated conditions which helped to consolidate their power. If a business man failed to live up to these conditions, if he failed to make a con-

TABLE 3

WARD COMMITTEEMEN BY PARTY, AND GOVERNMENTAL POSITION
HELD: CHICAGO AND PHILADELPHIA

| GOVERNMENTAL BODY | CHICAGO | | | | PHILADELPHIA: REPUBLICAN CITY COMMITTEEMAN* 1934 |
| | Republican | | Democratic | | |
	1928	1936	1928	1936	
City:					
Elective.............	5	1	9	13	18
Appointive..........	7	....	2	7	1
County:					
Elective.............	8	....	2	8	4
Appointive..........	4	3	8	5	15
Sanitary district:					
Elective.............	4	....	3	2	....
Appointive..........	1	....	3	....	....
State:					
Elective.............	1†	4	6	4	4
Appointive..........	5	....	....	3	2
Federal:					
Elective.............	....	....	1	1	2
Appointive..........	2	....	....	....	....
Former office-holder:					
Elective.............	4	14	9	3	....
Appointive..........	6	19	2	1	....
Never held office........	3	9	3	1	4
No information........	....	....	2	2	....
Total..............	50	50	50	50	50

* D. H. Kurtzman, *Methods of Controlling Votes in Philadelphia* (Philadelphia, 1935), App. A.
† Held city appointed office as well.

tribution to the campaign fund, if he openly opposed the political machine, he would find the favor withheld, and in some circumstances he would find himself a butt for persecution. His taxes would be raised, the building inspectors would find many things wrong with his buildings, his desire to be permitted to extend his holdings or his operations would be blocked, and in some cases he would be openly intimidated. Mayor Kelly has been appealed to from time to time by bigger business men to hold off his political wolves. The mayor has complied. But the lesser fry cannot always get access to the big boss. There are many known cases where they knuckle under or go out of business.

If legitimate businesses of many sorts may be brought into line by a political machine, how much easier it is for the local bosses to bring the illegitimate enterprises under their influence. In a great metropolitan community like Chicago, the gambling privileges are perhaps the most important of all privileges at the command of the political machine. In the great cities of the United States, where there are many persons with liberal views on gambling, prostitution, drinking, and other human diversions, the existence of a powerful underworld, with its alliances with business men and machine politicians, may be taken for granted. Gambling kings, bookmakers, panders, thieves, bootleggers, racketeers, and other hoodlums enjoy extraordinary immunity from interference on the part of the law-enforcing agencies. These outlaws realize that this freedom from restraint depends upon how useful they can make themselves to the politicians. When asked to make campaign contributions or to produce results upon election day, the leaders of the underworld cannot very well refuse. If they do, their places will be promptly raided by the law-enforcing authorities.

Not only are the contributions from the underworld interests an important item in the campaign funds of the dominant party, but the services of the underworld personnel are also significant. When word is passed down from the gangster chiefs, all proprietors of gambling houses and speak-easies, all burglars, pickpockets, pimps, prostitutes, fences, and their like, are whipped into line. In themselves they constitute a large block of votes, and they frequently augment their value to the machine by corrupt election practices. Chain voters, colonized voters, and crooked election boards are recruited from the ranks of organized crime.[15] In connection with a proved case of ballot alteration, it was discovered that the election judge responsible for handling the ballots was a card shark in the local gambling dens.[16] Because the laws against gambling are very difficult to enforce, owing to the ease of concealing violations and the spasmodic interest of the public in such matters, the politicians and gambling kings unite their interests in the perpetuation of the political machine. In Chicago a number of the ward committeemen have been proprietors of gambling houses. During the time that the Republicans were in power a few of the Republican ward committeemen met violent ends in gang warfare.

The Republican ward committeemen who managed to survive the disasters that wrecked their party and to cling on to some public position in spite of the depression fall into two categories: those who were elected from districts which contained a concentration of Republican voters, and those who were appointed to administrative posts by one of the Republican judges. Two of these committeemen were state senators from districts which contained a large proportion of Negro voters, and two were state representatives from districts where at least one-third of the voters were Republicans. The cumulative system of voting used in Illinois for the election of state representatives insured minority representation in any district in which the minority party had at least one-third of the votes and the senatorial committee nominated only one candidate. Such action on the part of the Republican senatorial committee resulted in the "plumping" or accumulation of three votes for the Republican representative for every straight Republican vote cast. The other Republican committeemen who were known to have governmental jobs in 1936 were the appointees of Republican judges who remained on the bench because of bipartisan or nonpartisan backing. Thus, two of the committeemen were court bailiffs, and a third was a master in chancery.

[15] John Landesco, "Organized Crime in Chicago," Part III of *Illinois Crime Survey* (Chicago, 1929).

[16] H. F. Gosnell, "Fighting Corruption in Chicago," *Polity*, July–August, 1935, p. 138.

The remaining Republican office-holder was an alderman elected from a ward which had strong Republican leanings.

There is no question that other Republican committeemen received favors from Democratic officials. With the investigating facilities and time available, it was not possible to track down all of these relationships. About a half-dozen of the Republican committeemen were engaged in the wholesale or retail liquor business. Since the licensing of the sale of alcoholic beverages was completely in the control of the Democrats, these committeemen were in a vulnerable position. In addition, it appeared that a few of the committeemen had some connection with gambling in one form or another. With the Democrats controlling all the law-enforcing machinery, these Republican committeemen were under obligations to the Democratic party, which made it difficult for them to perform all of their duties as Republicans. They were paid in jobs or favors not to get out the Republican vote. These bipartisan dealers, although traitors to their party, were hard to dislodge upon primary days, since they could command the services of job-holders who were loyal to them personally on such occasions. These job-holders, of course, could not be used to help the Republican party on election days. Some Democratic committeemen found it easier to buy off the Republican committeemen in this fashion than to engage in genuine party warfare. When the Democrats were a minority group in the city, some of their committeemen were bribed in this fashion. Hard times reversed the roles of the Republican and Democratic committeemen in these bipartisan deals, but they did not lessen the effectiveness of these practices as means of self-perpetuation.

Ward committeemen held tenaciously to their positions during the period under discussion because, in the main, they were representatives of different racial, linguistic, and social groups found in the city. In the areas where there is a concentration of Negro population, both the Republican and Democratic parties had Negro committeemen.[17] In the areas where persons of Polish descent are found, the parties kept a Zintak, a Kon-

[17] See Gosnell, *Negro Politicians*, pp. 139, 153 ff.

kowski, a Rosenkowski, a Kucharski, a Golusinski, and a Peska
as committeemen; and in areas where many persons of Italian
extraction are located, the committeemen bore such names as
Serritella, Pacelli, Vignola, and Porcaro. Some of these committeemen were members of the famous Unione Sicilione, which
obtained much unfavorable publicity during the Al Capone-
prohibition era of Chicago politics. The same principle that the
dominant group should be represented by a member was followed in the sections populated largely by Jews. However,
persons of Irish Catholic extraction were far in the lead in both
committees. In the Democratic committee the lead was overwhelming, as over one-half of the committeemen were descend-
ants of Irish parents, three having been born in Ireland themselves. As far as the Republican party city committee was
concerned, there was a close race between the Irish and the
native Protestants of older American stocks, each constituting
about one-fourth of all of the committeemen, with the Irish
slightly in the lead. The Republicans likewise had a greater
contingent of persons of Swedish, German, and Italian extraction; but the Democrats led in their representation of the Polish
elements. In 1936, one-fifth of the Democratic committeemen
and only one-sixteenth of the Republican committeemen were
born abroad. The second generation of the foreign born were
the ones that made the greatest headway in Chicago politics.

While representative of the different nationalistic groups, the
ward committeemen were at the same time thoroughly acclimated to the city. As compared with the general population
of the city, a larger proportion of the committeemen were born
in Chicago. In 1928, over two-thirds of the Democratic committeemen were born in Chicago, as compared with slightly over
one-half of the Republican committeemen. Eight years later
the ratio of native Chicagoans among the committeemen was
about the same, both being in excess of 65 per cent. It appears
that those who grow up in the atmosphere of Chicago politics
are more likely to become attracted to party organization work
than those who are brought up elsewhere.

Although the personnel of the ward committees changes

slowly, there are some replacements. In addition to the re-
movals by death and by that rare event, defeat at the polls,
there were thirty-three voluntary retirements during the period
under discussion. What effect has the depression had upon
the type of new committeemen recruited?

Economic deprivations have increased the competition for
party posts, and this has resulted in the attraction of persons
of superior economic status. An analysis of the schooling of
the committeemen at the beginning and the end of the period
studied, shows an increase in the level of formal education
achieved. In 1928, about one-half of the Republicans and one-
fifth of the Democrats had gone beyond high school. Eight
years later the proportion of Republican committeemen with
more than secondary education had increased slightly and the
proportion of Democratic committeemen had jumped to over
one-third.

Has the competition for ward posts during the lean years of
the early thirties brought to the city committees men of higher
occupational status? It is very difficult to answer this question
because of the variety and changing character of the occupations pursued by ward committeemen. At any given time a
ward boss may have several ostensible occupations and a number of secret callings as well. With these qualifications in mind,
Table 4 is presented for what it is worth. During the depression the number of Republican committeemen who were
nothing but professional public-job-holders has fallen from six
to one, and the number of contractors from six to three. On the
other hand, the number of Republican ward bosses who held
minor clerical positions has increased from one to four. In some
parts of the city the Republican party is not getting committeemen of as high economic status now as it did in 1928. On the
other hand, the 1936 Democratic committeemen show some
gains in economic status over their 1928 predecessors. The
number of those engaged in insurance increased from three to
seven, and those in law from four to six. The number of professional public-job-holders has remained the same for this
party—ten in 1928 and eleven in 1936.

Of the 1928 committeemen, fourteen Republicans and only four Democrats were lawyers. (Every ward committeeman who is not a lawyer himself must have some legal talent in his organization to handle the many legal matters that come to a ward headquarters.) Eight years later there were six Democratic and fifteen Republican ward committeemen who were lawyers. Since the legal profession is very closely related to business, finance, and commerce, and since the business leaders tend to be Republican, it is likely that a majority of the lawyers

TABLE 4

PRIVATE OCCUPATIONS OF WARD COMMITTEEMEN IN CHICAGO
BY PARTY, 1928 AND 1936

OCCUPATION	REPUBLICAN		DEMOCRATIC	
	1928	1936	1928	1936
None in addition to political job...........	6	1	10	11
Lawyer................	14	15	4	6
Real estate...........	5	6	9	7
Trade................	7	5	8	6
Insurance.............	3	5	3	7
Contractor............	6	3	5	3
Clerical..............	1	4	2	....
Liquor trade..........	2	3	....	1
Manufacturing........	2	2	1	3
Other professions......	1	....	....	....
No information........	3	6	8	6
Total.............	50	50	50	50

are likewise Republican. Furthermore, the Republican vote is concentrated in areas where there is a large number of persons engaged in professional and commercial pursuits. Consequently, it is natural that there would be more lawyers among the Republican than among the Democratic committeemen. Some of the Republican ward committeemen who are lawyers do not make a profession out of politics. Their main interest is in the law, and politics is a side line for them. On the other hand, a number of Democratic committeemen who started as clerks or saloonkeepers make politics their profession. Many of these

men lack the necessary educational background to go into law.
A few of the Democratic ward bosses who are lawyers belong to
firms which are notorious for their connections with the big
tax-dodgers and the leading figures of the underworld. Several
ward committeemen were members of a law firm which had a
large criminal practice with prominent gangsters as clients and
also a large tax-receivership practice.

Ward committeemen who were interviewed gave a variety
of explanations as to why they entered politics. In quite a few
cases the ward committeemen were urged to run for party
office by some relative. A number had fathers, fathers-in-law,
uncles, or brothers who were aldermen or ward committeemen.
As one of them put it, "My father was a ward committeeman
and one of the original nominators of Carter H. Harrison as
mayor of Chicago. My grandfather was a supreme court judge
in Switzerland. Politics seems to be an inherited trait in our
family."[18] A few entered ward organization politics in order to
promote or protect their business activities. In a Northwest
Side ward, the publisher of several neighborhood newspapers
said, "I entered politics in order to promote the communities
where my business is located."[19] A West Side ward leader made
the comment: "I became a precinct captain in 1915, and I was
selected as a ward leader by the committeemen in 1924. My
interest in politics may be traced to my trade-union connections, as I was an organizer of an electrical union."[20] On the
South Side a veteran committeeman gave a very interesting
account of his entrance into politics: "I started in politics in
1895. I was a member of a group of young men who were
greatly displeased to see all of the offices go to the relatives of
the mayor and the ward committeemen. We organized to
change this; and while unsuccessful for a long time, we finally
won out."[21] There were also committeemen who went into
politics because they thought it would be a help to their legal
practice, their real estate business, or their liquor business.

---

[18] Report of interview.   [20] Report of interview.
[19] Letter.   [21] Report of interview.

Some were practically forced to go into politics by their business and political sponsors. Thus, a judge would force his bailiff to run for ward committeeman, or a gambling operator would give orders to his lieutenant to file for the position. Finally, there were the committeemen who claimed that they sought their positions because of their love of the game of politics.

While the position of ward committeemen carries no salary, it has perquisites. A man who becomes a ward boss expects to improve his economic status. Some of them expect to get rich. It is significant to note the changes that have taken place in the occupations of the 1936 committeemen since they entered politics. To take a few examples, a dentist became a contractor, a professional athlete became a tobacco merchant, a saloonkeeper became an insurance and real estate agent, a machinist became the president of a roofing company, a newsboy became an insurance agent, a trade-union leader became a high-pressure beer salesman, a coal-miner became a barber and then a clerk. Of the 1936 Democratic committeemen, six deserted clerical occupations and six left jobs as liquor-dealers in order to make more money and to enjoy greater prestige as insurance agents, professional public-job-holders, or real estate operators. Mention has already been made of the many secret callings of a highly lucrative nature which ward bosses may have. Ward leaders, in general, cling to their jobs because they find it pays to do so. Of course, there are striking exceptions. In a North Side ward there is a Republican ward committeeman with a private fortune of his own who has found ward politics a drain upon his income.[22] This committeeman has entered politics with the highest ideals, and he has concentrated his private philanthropies in his home community. If there were more of such committeemen, the history of Chicago politics would be different.

The theme of this chapter has been that it is practically impossible to defeat a ward boss in a metropolitan community where the spoils tradition is deeply rooted and where the single-member district system of local representation is employed.

[22] See Mary Hartley, *James Breckinridge Waller* (Chicago, 1931).

Whether a ward committeeman's party wins or loses in general elections, he finds various and sundry devious ways to insure his own re-election on primary days. Tidal waves of public opinion may sweep the city-wide leaders from their posts, but the ward leaders are safe on their little islands. The economic depression may be accompanied by an enormous shift in the party preferences of the voters; but in spite of everything, few changes are registered in the personnel of the city committees of the parties.

CHAPTER III
CHANGING CHARACTER OF PRECINCT CAPTAINS[1]

While ward bosses seem to be able to stick by their jobs through thick and thin, the same cannot be said of the precinct captains or ward heelers. Ward committeemen are tested at

primary elections coming every two years, but a precinct captain has to prove his merit at each election. If a precinct captain belongs to the party in power, he will find the competition very keen. On the other hand, the precinct captains of the losing party are likely to become discouraged and drop out or desert to the opposition.

Precinct captains are the backbone of any metropolitan political organization, since upon them rests the responsibility for seeing and winning the voters. Political machines keep their grip upon the voters because they take pains to establish and maintain face-to-face contacts with individual citizens. An enterprising ward committeeman has to be constantly on the alert to weed out inefficient precinct captains and to discover new ones who will carry their precincts. Consequently, the turnover among precinct captains is usually high. There are some who can hold their positions year after year just as ward bosses do, but they are comparatively rare.

[1] The author is indebted to Miss Sonya Forthal for aid in collecting material regarding the 1928 precinct committeemen and to a number of students for assistance in connection with the 1936 committeemen. Since precinct committeemen had no legal status in the period under discussion, it was difficult to locate them. The private lists of the central headquarters were guarded as trade secrets.

Ward boundaries are changed only once in ten years, but precinct lines are altered after each election. One of the peculiarities of American politics is the smallness of the units reporting election returns.[2] This may be in part the result of the pioneer days, when the number of voters in a rural precinct had to be small because of the difficulties of travel. For the entire country the present average number of voters per precinct is about 400. In the state of Illinois the election precincts are required by law to contain as near as practicable 400 and not more than 600 voters. Thus, a precinct might contain two city blocks or many more, depending upon the density of the population. When the number of voters in a precinct exceeds 600, that precinct is supposed to be subdivided before the next election. In 1934 the average precinct in Chicago had 466 voters, but there were 104 precincts with more than 600 voters and 539 precincts which had under 400 voters.[3] The smallest precinct had only 143 registered votes; and the largest, 1,039. Because of the high mobility of the city population and because of the political pressure for precinct gerrymandering, the law is a difficult one to enforce.

Although the city did not grow as rapidly in the years 1928–36 as it did in the years 1920–28, the number of precincts kept on increasing at a fairly rapid rate. At the time of President Roosevelt's re-election in 1936 the number of precincts was 22 per cent greater than in 1928.[4] The increase was largely the result of a greater interest in voting among all elements of the eligible voting population in 1936. Whereas 76 per cent of the estimated eligible voters in Chicago took part in the Hoover-Smith election, 88 per cent took part in the Roosevelt-Landon

[2] In Great Britain the Parliamentary election returns are compiled by constituencies (average number of voters, 51,000) and not by polling districts.

[3] Figures were obtained from *Public Service Leader*, November 20, 1934. The standard deviation (σ) for the distribution was 71, which may be interpreted as follows: two-thirds of the cases should lie within the distance of σ on either side of the mean, or, in other words, between 395 and 537 registered voters.

[4] The increase in the number of precincts from 1920 to 1928 was 32 per cent.

electoral contest.[5] Precinct captains played an important role in the huge participation of 1936. Nonvoting is no longer as serious a problem as it was in the early twenties.

So burdensome has political work become in the metropolitan communities of the United States that it is not usually undertaken unless some concrete reward in the form of money or a political job is in the offing. These jobs are usually distributed by the party committeemen who have been successful in putting over their candidates at primary elections or in the party conventions. Whenever there is a shift in the fortunes of the two major parties, many precinct committeemen belonging to the losing party desert their party as rats scramble from a sinking ship.

The roster of precinct captains of a typical ward organization in an American city is made up of persons who in some way have demonstrated their ability to win votes. If a man can win votes for one party, then it is reasonable, under American conditions, where the two major parties have not presented widely divergent platforms in local politics, to imagine that he could win votes for the opposing party provided that satisfactory arrangements were made. In England a party agent would not think of changing his party affiliation, no matter how attractive such a change might be. But Chicago is not London or Manchester.

In order to analyze the extent of the changes that have taken place in the character of persons doing precinct work for the parties since 1928, some 300 precinct captains were interviewed

[5] An estimate for the number of adult citizens in Chicago in 1928 was made by interpolation between the 1920 and 1930 census figures. The 1936 estimate was made by extrapolation from the 1930 and 1934 figures, assuming a straight-line trend. The figures were:

Year	Estimated Number of Adult Citizens in Chicago	Number of Registered Voters	Percentage Registered
1928	1,827,000	1,386,631	75.9
1936	2,000,000	1,770,451	88.5

in 1936 along the same lines of the study of 600 precinct captains made in 1928.

Table 5 shows the distribution of Chicago precinct captains by occupation for 1928 and 1936 with some comparative data for New York upstate city committeemen collected by Mosher in 1932.[6] Mosher's figures are based upon a survey of 4,000 party committeemen in eighteen selected cities in the state of New York (not including New York City).

TABLE 5

COMPARISON OF OCCUPATIONS OF CHICAGO AND NEW YORK
PRECINCT COMMITTEEMEN

| OCCUPATIONS | CHICAGO | | | | EIGHTEEN NEW YORK CITIES * | |
| | 1928 | | 1936 | | 1932 | |
	Number	Per Cent	Number	Per Cent	Number	Per Cent
Government employees....	346	59.2	96	48.3	697	19.3
Attorneys...............	22	3.8	12	6.0	186	5.2
Other professions........	35	6.0	10	5.0	145	4.0
Merchants..............	73	12.5	43	21.6	219	6.0
Business executives.......	10	1.7	13	6.5	219	6.0
Clerks, salesmen, laborers, etc....................	98	16.8	25	12.6	2,152	59.5
Total..............	584	100.0	199	100.0	3,618	100.0

* William E. Mosher, "Party and Government Control at the Grass Roots," *National Municipal Review*, XXIV (January, 1935), 15–18, 38.

In Chicago there has been a decrease in the proportion of precinct captains who were government employees. During the eight-year period the ratio of precinct captains who were public-job-holders dropped from about three-fourths to slightly less than one-half. This decrease does not mean that patronage is on the decline in the city. It merely reflects the fact that patronage has been concentrated in the hands of one of the major party organizations. Whereas in 1928 both the Republican and Democratic precinct executives had their hands in the public

[6] W. E. Mosher, "Party and Government Control at the Grass Roots," *National Municipal Review*, XXIV (January, 1935), 16–18.

treasury in large numbers, in 1936 the Democrats had shoved most of their Republican compatriots out of reach of the public monies. In fact, less than one-fifth of the 1936 Republican precinct captains were governmental employees, and these were mostly bipartisan dealers who were very lukewarm about the success of their party.

There was also an increase in the number of precinct captains who classified themselves as merchants and a trend away from what Mosher calls the lesser employments—the clerical, the semiskilled, and the unskilled. While there are no trend figures for the New York cities, it is interesting to note that Chicago committeemen are much more likely to be public-job-holders and they are less likely to be in the "lesser employments" than are the New York committeemen.

From the proportions he found in government service and lesser employment classes, Mosher concluded that a majority of the New York committeemen were docile followers who could be counted on by those in control of the party. He further stated that the party leader, confident of his backing in the official party organization and realizing the average voter's indifference to, if not ignorance of, the function played by primary elections, felt free to ignore the demands of his constituency for long overdue reforms and improvements in government. Because of the great increase in the number of Chicago precinct captains who could be classified as merchants, there has been a trend toward a reduction of the proportion of captains in the docile classes; but the ratio is still about two-thirds.

Comparable data regarding the Philadelphia Republican precinct committeemen (divisional leaders) has been collected by Kurtzman for 1932.[7] Since Kurtzman was dealing with a party organization which at the time held all the local patronage, he found a larger proportion of committeemen on the public pay rolls than did Mosher. In all, 58 per cent of the 3,132 Philadelphia Republican precinct captains studied were holding down public jobs, involving an annual pay roll of over $4,000,-000. Most of the positions were under the county government,

[7] D. H. Kurtzman, *Methods of Controlling Votes in Philadelphia* (Philadelphia, 1935).

but there were many court jobs and a few important elective
state and city posts. In order to obtain a fair basis of comparison, it will be necessary to consider for Chicago the 1936 Democratic precinct committeemen only. Nearly three-fourths of
these were public-job-holders, as contrasted with three-fifths
of the Republicans in Philadelphia. About one-third of the
positions held by Chicago Democratic precinct executives were
furnished by the city hall, one-fourth by the county, one-sixth
by the courts, one-sixth by the state government, one-twelfth
by the sanitary district, and the remaining by miscellaneous
governmental bodies. Only two of the Democratic precinct
captains in Chicago said that they held federal positions. The
depression has brought a great increase in the functions of the
federal government, but the patronage basis of the party machines has remained local. It is also interesting to note that at
a time when it is hard to raise revenues locally to meet the
legitimate expenses of municipal government there is an increase in the amount of prostitution of the public services for
partisan purposes.

The materials on the occupations of Chicago precinct committeemen have been somewhat more elaborately classified than
those of either Kurtzman or Mosher. A subdivision of the so-
called "lesser employments" in Chicago shows that in 1936
there was an increase in the proportion of clerical workers,
housewives, and unemployed persons who entered precinct
work. There were relatively fewer skilled or unskilled laborers
who became precinct captains at the end of the period. In a
very rough manner the roster of precinct captains reflected
employment conditions. There were fewer employed manual
workers to draw upon in 1936 than there had been in 1928.

In his study of New York committeemen Mosher urged that
those who have enjoyed educational advantages are better
equipped to determine the increasingly complex policies of a
modern community than those who have not gone beyond the
grammar-school level.[8] He found that the balance between
the two groups was, in his sample, too heavily weighted in favor

[8] *Op. cit.*, p. 17.

of the latter. Table 6 indicates that in 1928 the situation in Chicago was almost the same as Mosher found it in upstate New York. While 4 per cent more of the Chicago committeemen had had college or professional education than of the New York committeemen, nearly 3 per cent less had gone beyond grammar school. In 1936, however, the balance had tipped in Chicago in favor of the group with more than grade-school edu-

TABLE 6

COMPARISON OF EDUCATIONAL BACKGROUND OF CHICAGO
AND NEW YORK PRECINCT COMMITTEEMEN

EDUCATION	CHICAGO						EIGHTEEN NEW YORK CITIES*	
	Party Committeemen				Total Males Eighteen Years of Age and Over†		Party Committeemen	
	1928		1936		1934		1932	
	Number	Per Cent	Number	Per Cent	Number	Per Cent	Number	Per Cent
Grammar school or less	328	57.6	85	40.1	722,630	61.9	2,212	55.3
High school..........	147	25.8	84	39.6	325,554	27.9	1,320	33.0
College and professional...............	93	16.3	43	20.3	119,056	10.2	467	11.7
Foreign education.....	2	0.3	......	......	......	......	......	......
Total..........	570	100.0	212	100.0	1,167,240	100.0	3,999	100.0

* William E. Mosher, "Party and Government Control at the Grass Roots," *National Municipal Review*, XXIV (January, 1935), 15–18, 38.
† Table 6, Summary Tables for *Census Data of the City of Chicago, 1934.*

cation. In fact, the proportion of college or professional graduates was almost twice that found in New York and 4 per cent greater than the Chicago ratio in 1928. Apparently, the depression resulted in raising the educational level of the Chicago precinct captains.

What do the Chicago materials show about Mosher's thesis that an increase in the educational level of precinct committeemen would result in raising the tone of city politics? Unfortunately, training in political ethics does not seem to be a major

objective of our institutions of higher learning. While there are
some differences between the methods of educated and relatively illiterate committeemen, there are also many striking
similarities.

The relation between education and political morality in certain parts of Chicago may be illustrated by the case of Precinct
Committeeman John Grady.[9] Grady started out as a party
worker at the age of fourteen, when he ran errands for the Republican committeeman of his ward. In 1932, when he saw the
drift was toward the Democratic party, he attached himself to
a candidate for Democratic ward committeeman who had city
hall backing. Grady was a graduate of a private high school
and also of one of the universities in the metropolitan community.

At the time of the 1936 election Grady was one of the prize
precinct captains of his ward. He was going to one of the larger
law schools in the city, working his way through by means of
a pay-roll job, i.e., a position which did not make great inroads
upon the time which he needed for his studies and his political
work. It happened that there was a very large gambling place
in his bailiwick, and in accordance with prevailing custom he
was able to place several of his political workers as employees
of this outlawed business. He also claimed that he was able to
place some of his constituents in public utility jobs, in city
hall jobs, and in hotels, theaters, and business establishments
within the precinct that "worked with the organization." One
of the hotels had a questionable reputation. Pressure was
brought to bear upon the taverns to contribute to all the political benefits. In his canvassing work Grady was a master at
adjusting himself to the peculiarities of the persons addressed.
A tall, handsome young man with a glib tongue, he could fall
into the lingo of the tavern, the dance hall, the gambling den,
the church festival, or the political backroom at will. As far as
could be ascertained, Grady never attempted any direct bribery
of voters by means of money, nor did he engage in any stealing
of votes. With his persuasive manner and thorough canvassing

[9] The name is fictitious.

work, he did not need to stoop to these lowest of all political devices. However, his record is hardly such that one would expect him to take that broad view of the complex community problems to which Mosher refers.

It should not be assumed that all the college-bred precinct captains in Chicago were like Grady. In a neighboring ward, John Jones, a banner Republican precinct committeeman, presented a striking contrast to Grady. Jones was also a graduate of a local university and law school, but he was well established in the practice of law before he entered politics. He has never used his political connections to help his legal business. In fact, his start in politics came in connection with his work in a judicial campaign for the Chicago Bar Association. He did such fine work in this nonpartisan campaign that the secretary of the Republican ward organization introduced him to the ward committeeman.

Since Jones was in sympathy with the general position of the Republican party, he was persuaded to become a precinct captain. In winning votes he never handled or promised any political patronage, he never used any of the indirect methods of bribery such as the furnishing of goods or the securing of special concessions from governmental officials. For the most part, his appeals were of a rational sort. He criticized the policies and acts of the opposition, discussed the relative merits of the candidates, appealed to civic-mindedness, praised the policies and record of his own party, and, where he was known and respected, relied upon friendship and personal influence. He did just as thorough a job of canvassing as Grady and against much greater odds, as his Democratic rival was a job-holder and had many patronage positions to hand out to his workers. Instead of receiving money or favors for his activities, Jones had to make great sacrifices of his own time and money. In connection with the presidential campaign of 1936 he paid $75 out of his own pocket for canvassers and watchers. This, he held, was necessary, as he had to make four complete canvasses of his precinct, which was a very large one. In the rooming-houses in his bailiwick he had to hire special resident canvassers. He would have preferred to use volunteer workers entirely; but he argued that, as one pays a postman for ringing doorbells, why could he not use his own money to pay for similar services.

The case of Joe Czech shows that it is not necessary for a precinct committeeman to have an extensive formal education in order to acquire a social point of view. Joe was a short, stout, rugged, well-spoken Hussite who was born in Bohemia fifty-two years ago. He had very little schooling and spent many of his early years roaming about in Germany and central Europe, where he learned to love the out-of-doors. When he was twenty-one he came to the United States and settled in Chicago as a merchant. Now he is well read, and on his desk appeared the latest copy of the *Atlantic Monthly* and Papini's *Life of Christ*. Joe longed for an out-of-door life, and he went into politics in 1928 in order to get on the forest-preserve staff. Through his friend, Anton J. Cermak, he was able to secure a job as forest-preserve laborer, and he is now the superintendent of a tract of some nine thousand acres. He has a real pride in his work and tries to hire young men or family men who have no other work.

In his precinct Joe's main interest was in seeing what he could do to make life easier for the poor. He started on this topic by saying that in this country we think we have freedom and strength and wealth, but in actuality there is no such thing as freedom except for a favored few. "For the vast majority of workingmen," he added, "the constitutional guaranties of freedom are a mere mockery in the hands of exploiting capitalists. Rufus Dawes is a friend of mine, a damned capitalist, but a nice fellow personally, who might be made into a good Democrat some day." He went on to indicate his bitterness at the existing economic system. His fear was not for the older people, who, he said, no longer really mattered, but for the younger people, who were now coming up without anything to do or any way of earning a living. When "kids" were caught stealing as a result of sheer idleness, he always tried to get them off because he felt they were not really to blame. He worked hard for the Democratic party because he thought that it was doing something to alleviate the youth problem.

Joe's precinct had a large number of relief cases, as nearly one-half of the able-bodied men were unemployed. Rents averaged about $25 a month per family. The persons on relief were the main strength of the party, as they knew they could depend on the Democrats for aid when they were in trouble. His problem was difficult because of the heterogeneous character of the precinct. Over one-half of the inhabitants were foreign-born, with the nationalities ranging in the following order: Czechs, Slovaks, Germans, and Hollanders.[10] Because each group held together closely, it was necessary for him to work with them separately, for the most part through the churches. But so long as he could help them in their troubles, they were with him. Joe passed out food, money for rent, coal, advice on getting hospital care, legal advice, adjusted taxes, and placed men in forest-preserve jobs.

Needless to say, Joe carries his precinct by a comfortable margin. There is no question that many of his constituents felt under obligations to him and may have voted the Democratic ticket on that account. However, as compared with John Grady, whose educational opportunities were vastly superior, Joe was less of an exploiter, and he did not depend upon any underworld connections.

In Chicago much more information was obtained regarding the characteristics of the precinct executives than is yet available regarding New York and Philadelphia party committeemen.[11] Table 7 presents some of these data for the precinct captains of 1928 and those of 1936.

There has undoubtedly been a slight increase in the number of women precinct captains during the past eight years. In the Democratic organization for the Third Ward, a ward inhabited largely by colored people, the complete roster of precinct captains showed that one-fourth were women.[12] This is a much higher ratio than was found in other parts of the city.

The methods of woman precinct captains may be illustrated

[10] *Census Data of Chicago, 1934.*

[11] R. V. Peel has collected materials regarding New York City party committeemen.

[12] See Gosnell, *Negro Politicians*, p. 139.

by the case of Mrs. Smith, an official co-captain of a precinct in the Fifteenth Ward and a veteran of many political battles.[13] This neat, elderly, garrulous woman was responsible for the women's votes only, and left the rest of the work to the male

TABLE 7

CERTAIN CHARACTERISTICS OF PRECINCT CAPTAINS IN CHICAGO

CHARACTERISTIC	1928		1936	
	Total Number Answering Question	Percentage Having Characteristic	Total Number Answering Question	Percentage Having Characteristic
Sex	600	....	300	....
Women	....	5.1	....	11.0
Color	600	....	300	....
Negro	....	3.8	....	11.0
Number under thirty years of age	....	15.0	288	12.2
Birthplace	582	....	218	....
Chicago	....	52.9	....	66.4
Other native American	....	24.4	....	15.9
Foreign	....	22.7	....	17.7
Father's birthplace	563	....	202	....
Chicago	....	5.9	....	19.1
Other native American	....	19.7	....	16.2
Foreign	....	74.4	....	64.7
Church affiliation	550	....	214	....
Protestant	....	33.6	....	34.6
Catholic	....	51.1	....	42.0
Jewish	....	13.3	....	16.4
None	....	....	....	3.3
Married	....	....	273	74.0
Fraternal affiliation	....	....	192	47.4
Military experience	....	....	194	22.2
Thirty years or more in Chicago	573	73.6	211	66.7
Ten years or more in precinct	572	58.4	280	59.3
Ten years or more in political work	552	58.5	284	50.4
Political reason for moving into precinct	568	7.6	251	9.6

captain. For many years she had been an active feminist. In fact, she took part in the agitation for woman suffrage in Illinois before 1913. When partial suffrage was granted after that date, she helped to organize the women and get them out to vote. In those early days, when a woman pleaded she could not vote be-

[13] For a Philadelphia case study of a woman precinct captain, see J. T. Salter, *Boss Rule* (New York, 1935), pp. 193 ff.

cause she was washing or had to look after the baby, Mrs. Smith would help finish the washing or mind the baby. In that way the women became accustomed to vote, and now they do it as a matter of course.

Mrs. Smith was a native of Chicago and so was her father, but there was a heavy concentration of Lithuanians in her precinct. She belonged to the Catholic church, which was influential in her neighborhood. Rents averaged about $40 a month, and there were no relief cases. It was a typical lower-middle-class neighborhood in which the women were not weighted down either by poverty or by a heavy burden of employment outside the home.

A separate women's organization was set up because Mrs. Smith found that a woman could do a lot more to get other women to vote than a man could. Some men even did not like to have the male precinct captain talking to their wives. The women organized card parties and dances. One dance was held at a downtown hotel at which the attendance reached seven hundred. The men always contributed to the expenses of such functions. Mrs. Smith was soon interested in political work for its own sake. She enjoyed getting out and talking to people and thought that many more women would like it if only they once tried it. Women were somewhat limited in what they know about such things because they spent so much time at home and heard of developments only through their men folks. At the card parties the women started to gossip about politics among themselves and thus acquired a desire to have something to say about how things are run. Once women got used to taking an active part, there was no difficulty whatsoever in keeping them interested in seeking ways to be of service.

An examination of the registration figures shows that the ratio of women registered has jumped from 43 per cent of the total in 1928 to 46 per cent in 1936. Undoubtedly, the women party workers are in part responsible for this increased interest in voting on the part of the women in Chicago.

While the ratio of precinct captains born in Chicago was over one-half in 1928 and has been increasing since then, it has al-

ways been the practice of ward committeemen to choose captains who were representative of the predominant nationalistic
groups in their precincts. A consideration of the birthplace of
the fathers of the precinct executives brings out clearly that
these party officials come largely from the second-generation foreign stocks found in the city. In many parts of Chicago there
are still isolated Polish, Italian, Czech, or German communities
where foreign tongues are used extensively.[14] Among the party
workers of foreign stock, those of Irish ancestry made up nearly
one-quarter; those of German parentage, one-seventh; those of
Polish origin, one-seventh; those of Russian ancestry, one-
eighth; while the British, Scandinavian, Italian, and Czech
stocks lagged behind the others in the order given. While in the
entire population the Irish come after the Germans and Poles
in numbers, their political aggressiveness in Chicago has already
been pointed out in connection with the analysis of ward committeemen.

Precinct committeemen are fairly representative of the different religious groups in the city.[15] If anything, they are probably
a little more likely to belong to some church organization than
are some of their constituents. The church furnishes a place for
the party worker to make contacts and to gain respectability.
In some communities the church plays a very important role
in the social life of the inhabitants. A South Chicago Polish
neighborhood was run almost completely by the Catholic priest,
who carried on all the social service activities that in some other
sections would be in the hands of the party workers.

Some of the reasons for the grip of the Irish upon precinct
captaincies in communities where they are no longer the predominant group are illustrated by the case of James Murphy,
a Democratic committeeman in a West Side river ward. Murphy lived in a run-down neighborhood which was overwhelmingly Polish. A steel plant was only a block away, and from the
general character of the district one would expect to find a pre-

---

[14] See map of nationality groups in the city on p. 103.

[15] For a discussion of the Negro churches in politics, see my *Negro Politicians*, pp.
94–100.

cinct captain who was in rather poor circumstances like the rest of his constituents.

It was a great surprise that Murphy turned out to be a most distinguished-looking gentleman, such as one might expect to find in a country club. It was soon clear from his conversation that he had had advantages far superior to those of the people who lived around him. He had traveled widely and was semi-independent. After graduating from high school, he went into the railroad business; but on the advice of his father, who was a precinct captain before him, he got into politics and started a real estate and brokerage business. He was born in the same house where he was then living; and he said that he had no intention of moving in spite of the depreciated character of the neighborhood, because, when he bought a house out in Beverly Hills, his wife refused to move, on the ground that all their friends were in the neighborhood where he had lived all his life.

Murphy was more than willing to talk about his work in politics and about the neighborhood. While he sat on the front steps, people stopped and talked about their difficulties, little and big. The broken English of the Poles presented a sharp contrast to Murphy's cultured voice and accent. But in spite of this difference, the people seemed to like him and to have confidence in what he could do to make their troubles a little easier. One stout Pole had a lot to say about the people who wouldn't give him a job when he needed it, but he admitted that he was on his way to a tavern to spend his bonus check. Murphy handled him with unusual tact, and the man went on his way without the job but satisfied that some one understood his plight.

Although the neighborhood was not very well-to-do, many of the inhabitants owned their own homes. Rentals averaged less than $20 a month per family. Naturally, there had been a relief problem in this area, but it had abated considerably in 1935 and 1936. Murphy said that politics played no part in the granting of relief in his district. The only way to get aid was to go down personally and file an application. He might give some assistance in the form of helping with the directions; but as far as being of any value in actually getting relief, he never pretended that he could do anything.

Murphy had rigged up a small precinct clubroom in the basement of his house where the people could gather at any hour of the day just for a social time. He had found it a most efficacious method of preserving a semblance of unity in the neighborhood. He liked to work with people and to help them when they were in trouble, but he discouraged his son from going into politics because he felt that it was too insecure as a profession. It could only be a matter of time when the party would go out of power, and any man who had been in politics for a number of years would be fitted for nothing else.

Although Murphy was an organization man in good standing, he did not always urge his constituents to vote the organization slate in primaries or the straight ticket in general elections. In the dramatic primary of 1936 he was passive on the gubernatorial issue because he thought Horner was the better man. While he felt he had some influence, he said that the radio and the press had made people much less susceptible to arguments by local politicians.

All the general services that are expected of precinct captains were performed by Murphy. He was not replaced by a Pole in his area because he had the advantage of seniority in the neighborhood, long experience in political work, superior abilities as a talker, and a certain amount of economic independence which enabled him to serve his constituents without exploiting them.

A fairly long period of apprenticeship seems to be necessary for appointment as precinct captain. At least one-half of the 1936 committeemen had been engaged in political work for more than ten years. This means that most of the captains began their duties before the financial crash came in 1929. Nearly two-thirds of the precinct executives had lived in the city for more than thirty years. It appears that one has to become well acclimated to Chicago politics before taking part in it. However, in recent years there has been a slight decrease in the emphasis upon seniority in the selection of minor party executives.

The most common motive for entering politics given by the precinct captains interviewed was that they hoped to obtain some concrete economic reward. The possibility of obtaining a political job by means of precinct work was appealing to those who were in ill health, whose work was seasonal, who had lost their jobs, who wished to escape from heavy manual labor, or who were just starting out in life and found other avenues closed. Persons engaged in certain occupations found that political connections would help them. Thus, many lawyers, tavern-keepers, insurance agents, trucking contractors, plumbing contractors, and real estate agents found that they could mix politics and business. Since the repeal of prohibition, tavern-owners and bartenders have been swarming into politics, particularly in those areas where there has been considerable dry sentiment in the past and where there is some likelihood of a precinct wet-and-dry vote under the local-option provision of the state liquor law.

In a few cases precinct captains were bound to their ward committeemen by personal ties of loyalty which grew out of crisis situations. When a ward boss could dramatically come to the rescue of some man who was in trouble with the police, he could count on that man for steady precinct work from that time on. In one of the roughest wards in the city, Bat Dolan, former hobo, bartender, racketeer union official, and gunman, swore his undying loyalty to his ward committeeman. On two occasions the ward boss had saved him from the clutches of the law-enforcing authorities. The first time he was merely an innocent bystander when a rumpus occurred on West Madison Street, but the police arrested him as a suspect. On this occasion the ward boss saw to his release and spoke to him about securing some political pull in the town. The second charge brought against him was much more serious. In a saloon brawl he shot and killed a man who owed him money and who showed an insolent disregard for his creditors. In fact, his bullying debtor called Bat a "yellow stool pigeon." As in the first case, Bat's political superior saw to his release. The only law that Bat knows or cares about is the law that is laid down by his ward committeeman.

Not all the precinct captains are attracted to political work by considerations which have little place for general interests of the city. We have already cited the case of John Jones, who got into precinct work through his excellent performance in a nonpartisan Bar Association campaign. Scattered throughout the city there are many committeemen, like Jones, who have real political convictions for which they are willing to make personal sacrifices. Some of these precinct captains may have personal ambitions, but their ideals are set higher than those of Grady or Dolan.

The responsibility for the selection of precinct captains is in the hands of the ward committeeman. Successful ward bosses are always looking around for promising assistants. The ideal precinct captain is one who can make friends easily, who works hard and steadily, who gives absolute obedience, who is intelligent but satisfied with a subordinate role, who is not too demanding for himself, and who does not ask too many questions. A precinct captain may be superior in education and economic status to his constituents if he has sufficient tact, but a captain whose education and background is inferior to that of his constituents is likely to cause resentment.

During the upward trend of the business cycle the turnover of the precinct captains is always higher than that of ward committeemen. The precinct lines are far less stable than ward lines, and the selection of precinct committeemen is entirely in the hands of the ward bosses. When a decline in prosperity brings about a shift in the balance of political power, the turnover of the precinct executives is accelerated. The competition for posts in the winning party organization becomes much keener and the ranks of the losing party machine are decimated by desertions. The changes tend to increase the educational level and occupational status of the precinct captains. However, these party officials are still, as a rule, docile followers of the ward bosses. Only an occasional precinct captain has sufficient economic independence and intellectual integrity to choose his own course and to hold to it by conviction.

CHAPTER IV

ACTIVITIES OF PRECINCT CAPTAINS

The precinct captains who constitute the rank and file of a party machine try in every way possible to perform concrete services for the voters which will be remembered on election

JUDGE EDMUND K. JARECKI

day. When a precinct captain is unable by himself to perform a given task, he gets in touch with some one in his party organization who can. In other words, the precinct committeeman is an agent or broker for a great variety of services which are used to cement voters to the party machine.

Whether or not the benevolent services performed by party workers are of real value to the community is a question which has interested social scientists

for some time.[1] The party philanthropist acts in a direct and human fashion which appeals to the individual in distress, but the ultimate effect of the acceptance of the service may be detrimental to the person who receives it. Thus, a voter receives some immediate concrete service in return for which he is willing to support the candidates sponsored by his benefactor. These candidates, however, may be racketeer unionists or gangster-politicians who prey upon the community and who oppose constructive social welfare legislation.

The politicians have great scorn for the so-called "civic minded" and the "pure-souled" reformers. They have no use for

---

[1] Robert Archey Woods, *The City Wilderness* (Boston, 1898), chap. vi; Jane Addams, *Democracy and Social Ethics* (New York, 1902); Lincoln Steffens, *The Autobiography of Lincoln Steffens* (New York, 1931); Frank R. Kent, *The Great Game of Politics* (Garden City, New York, 1923), and *Political Behavior* (New York, 1928); S. Forthal, "Relief and Friendly Service by Political Precinct Leaders," *Social Service Review*, VII (December, 1933), 608–18.

social workers, and they look upon their own party organizations as the real charitable agencies. As a rough and vigorous
precinct captain in one of the slum areas put it:

✱ When anyone gets into trouble with the law—petty thieving, trouble with
a relief investigator—or when he loses his job or is about to be evicted, or
when a kid gets in with a bad gang and starts staying out all night, in cases
like this it is not the relief agency or social welfare agency that the harassed
voter first goes to, but rather to the precinct captain who stands in with the
law, who will not talk down to him but will treat him as a friend in need, and
who is waiting for him in the local tavern or in the ward headquarters, where
there is a full-time secretary who knows just who can handle the situation.

When the interviewer ventured to slip in a word for a near-by
settlement house, the precinct captain interrupted bitterly:

Oh, forget that bunk. You innocent, well-meaning middle-class people
who have never seen a hungry and moneyless family in your life, who have
only a vague idea of how the political and legal and business racket is run,
who don't know the right people to talk to in evictions, or tort cases, you
think you can come in here and help the poor. You can't even talk to them
on their own level, because you're better, you're from the University. I
never graduated from high school, and I'm one of them.[2]

RELIEF AND FRIENDLY ACTIVITIES

In order to investigate the relief and friendly activities of the
party organizations in Chicago, the nine hundred precinct captains interviewed were classified by date of interview and type
of benevolent activity. A number of theories will be put forward as to the effect of the depression upon benevolent activities of the parties. The 1928 and 1936 proportions of precinct
captains who rendered various types of service are indicated
in Table 8.

As in Boston, New York, and Philadelphia, so in Chicago the
precinct captains were ready to distribute material goods to
those of their constituents who were in need.[3] One-half of the
precinct committeemen interviewed in 1928 said that they
handed out food. These party workers were found in the de-

[2] Manuscript report of interview.

[3] Woods, *op. cit.;* Roy V. Peel, *The Political Clubs of New York City* (New York,
1935); John T. Salter, *Boss Rule* (New York, 1935); David Harold Kurtzman, *Methods
of Controlling Votes in Philadelphia* (Philadelphia, 1935).

preciated residential areas of the city, where even in the prosperous twenties employment was irregular. At the beginning

TABLE 8

DISTRIBUTION OF SELECTED CHICAGO PRECINCT CAPTAINS ACCORDING TO
BENEVOLENT SERVICES RENDERED, 1928 AND 1936

TYPES OF BENEVOLENT SERVICES	1928		1936	
	Total Number Answering Question	Percentage Rendering Service	Total Number Answering Question	Percentage Rendering Service
Goods:				
Food..........................	473	49.4	222	69.5
Coal..........................	469	42.8	277	31.8
Rent..........................	466	38.4	219	37.4
Christmas baskets..............	506	55.7	288	39.2
Advice:				
Juvenile guidance..............	460	40.4	276	35.1
Adjusted domestic difficulties.....	450	30.2	276	24.6
Brokerage agency for—				
Local governments:				
Governmental jobs.............	548	54.7	211	50.7
Governmental jobs formerly....			179	43.0
Miscellaneous jobs.............	542	69.1	269	46.5
Streets and alleys..............	451	63.9	274	74.1
Taxes adjusted.................	550	70.4	266	36.1
Permits secured................	532	44.0	265	43.0
Scholarships provided..........			272	9.6
Building and zoning regulations..			254	20.1
Contact with social agency......	533	33.2	279	67.4
Medical aid of some sort........	442	59.2	278	56.6
Public medical agencies.......		47.4		44.2
Relief agencies................			275	65.8
Courts:				
Legal aid.....................	439	64.6	284	62.3
Trouble with law..............	549	38.5	278	53.2
Traffic violations..............	542	52.8	274	26.6
National government:				
Aid in naturalization...........	449	70.9	271	69.4
Veteran's bonus................			231	37.7
H.O.L.C......................			235	51.9
Deference:				
Funerals.......................	455	77.3	279	62.0
Weddings......................	455	51.4	274	52.2

of the depression some of the ward organizations in the poorer sections of the city made valiant efforts to maintain soup kitchens. For a while some of the Italian committeemen bulldozed grocers and butchers into making contributions to Al Capone's famous free-lunch center. In return the merchants' short-weight scales were overlooked by the city sealer.[4] As the economic crisis continued, it became impossible for the political organizations to continue elaborate food-dispensing facilities. In 1936 more of the precinct captains handed out food than in 1928; but they did it, for the most part, in emergency cases. One boss of a slum ward shrewdly remarked that he did not believe in giving food because it was finished off in fifteen minutes and then where was he. Instead he took the six dollars and bought the "kids" outfits, and the parents were always grateful.

A smaller proportion of the party officials distributed coal in 1936 than in 1928. One ward committeeman maintained a coal yard in a blighted area at the beginning of the depression, but he found that he could not continue this part of his business. The demands for free coal were so overwhelming and difficulties in making collections were so great that he had to close his retail business. Coal was distributed by party workers when there was some temporary breakdown in the regular administration of relief.

Since the public welfare agencies did not follow a very consistent policy with reference to the payment of rents, the precinct captains in the most depressed areas were able to provide temporary shelter from time to time for those who were homeless or who were about to be evicted. The depression apparently had no effect upon the proportion of party workers giving this type of aid. However, there is no question that the relation of the party organizations to those who were unable to pay rent had changed. In the boom days of the twenties one prominent politician who was a heavy owner of real estate in a working-class area was accustomed to a lenient policy of collections for those who voted right. After a few of the lean years of the early thirties, this party boss was compelled to bring five hundred eviction suits all at the same time. After the Democrats came to power in the various local governments, some of the Democratic precinct captains became more active than Republicans

[4] *Chicago Daily News*, May 21, 1932; *Chicago Tribune*, May 10, 21, 1932.

in preventing or postponing evictions. Some of the minor parties used the plight of those who had been evicted as a means of gaining an entree into districts where they had never before made any headway.[5] If the regular relief agencies had not begun to pay rent, there might have been more serious eviction riots than occurred in the early thirties.

The practice of distributing Christmas or Passover baskets has continued during the depression period, although to a lessened extent because of the depleted state of the Republican ward treasuries. Democratic ward organizations which were formerly not concerned with this custom have taken it up in recent years. In fact, every ward in the city now has some families which are in a receptive mood for party charity around the holiday season. The Democrats have recently organized their Christmas giving on a grand scale. Teachers of the public and private schools are urged to sell tickets to a championship high-school football game, the proceeds of which are used for the mayor's Christmas fund, which is administered by the ward organizations.[6]

In the foreign-born neighborhoods there are frequently many families in which the relations between the parents and children are strained. The new generation tends to discard the old-world cultural patterns, and the parents have many discipline problems. In an Italian settlement a precinct captain said that one part of his work was the solving of the problem of the "dago kids" who cut school and hung out all night with bad gangs. On the day that I saw him he said that he had placed such a child in a boarding school for a working mother. This same unit official said that he regarded it as very bad policy to interfere in domestic disputes. His comments on this subject were spicy but not printable. One-quarter to one-third of the precinct captains interviewed in 1936 said that they gave advice on domestic and family matters when asked. This was a slightly smaller ratio than was obtained in 1928.

[5] For a description of the South Side eviction riots, see Gosnell, *Negro Politicians* (Chicago, 1935), pp. 329 ff.

[6] Interviews.

Since the political parties in the United States have very
limited financial resources of their own, it is necessary for them
to rely upon the governmental agencies to supply most of the
needs of their constituents who are in want. They act as brokers for the various governmental services filling the gaps left
by the red-tape provisions of the bureaucrats. Party workers
refer their voters to the proper authorities and try to claim as
much credit for themselves as possible.

During a period of large-scale unemployment, precinct committeemen try to function as job brokers. All the different governmental offices—federal, state, county, sanitary district, city,
school, and park—the principal public utility concerns, and
various private companies are approached for jobs. In com-
paring his work with that of a relief agency, one Democratic
precinct captain said:

> Do you think the relief agencies can get jobs for their people with a word
> to the local A. & P. or the National or a restaurant or a tavern? We get jobs
> for some with the city and for others with the utilities. But we can't get as
> many jobs on the public pay roll as you think. We can't touch the fire and
> police services. However, we fill lifeguard jobs at the parks, and there are
> always personal matters that naturally come to a precinct captain in connec-
> tion with a setup like W.P.A.[7]

The voters in the poorer residential areas, many of them of
foreign extraction, take a realistic view of political patronage.
The spoils system was well intrenched in American cities before
the immigrants became important as voters. Political appointments furnished one of the forms of recognition which
came to successful groups in the United States. Furthermore,
the lesser jobs furnished a livelihood to many. In the city alone,
there were one thousand positions exempt from the Civil Service Law, and in addition five times that many temporary appointments available for political distribution. These positions,
and also the state, county, sanitary district, park, school, and
court jobs not filled by competitive examinations, were the
practical monopoly of the Democrats in 1936. In all, there were
over 60,000 employees of the older established governmental

[7] Interview, May 26, 1936.

units located in Chicago, to say nothing of the 75,000 W.P.A. workers.[8] The selection of perhaps a quarter of these was the prerogative of the winning political machine. Precinct captains who rolled up huge votes for the organization candidates were in line for jobs for themselves and their constituents. Political job-holders were assessed 2 per cent of their salaries for the campaign war chest, and in addition they were expected to rally their friends and relatives to the support of the organization slate. When the machine "put the screws" on job-holders and their friends, it was said to be using its "muscle."

Republican precinct captains of the old school have woefully felt the lack of "muscle" in recent years. The repeated Democratic victories have meant that Republican precinct captains have little to offer their constituents in the way of patronage. Only a sprinkling who had made some bipartisan arrangement were able to cling desperately on to a few paltry jobs. The state of mind of those voters who were formerly won over to the Republican cause by means of patronage is illustrated by the case of Leo Posen, a Republican precinct captain of Polish birth who lived in a Polish neighborhood. When he was interviewed, Leo was in a very sour mood. He had been out of work for several years, and not even when the Republicans were in power did they do anything more than promise him a job. To make matters worse, his wife had worked all through the depression. Everybody turned to the Democratic precinct captain, who had worked the precinct ever since Leo was there. Nobody asked Leo whether he could do anything or not. It was just as well, as he was powerless. The Democratic captain wouldn't do any favors for him because he had things so well tied down that he didn't even have to go out and work before election time. He paid others to do his work. Leo complained because the Republicans would not even give him any money to try. They just ignored him; so he decided to ignore them. He hadn't been to the headquarters for several months. There wasn't any use in spending the carfare. In short, Leo was dis-

---

[8] For a listing of public employees located in Chicago, see my *Negro Politicians*, pp. 239, 300, 304, 377–79.

gusted with politics and would have thrown up his job if he hadn't thought that the Democrats might be turned out. Even so, he was not going to work his head off and then get nothing in return. He still had a sneaking suspicion that if he only were given some money he might do something. All that the people were interested in was what they could get out of it. The votes went to the highest bidder. With this, Leo, a disappointed office-seeker himself, not having anything better to do, went down to the corner saloon in order to talk matters over with the boys.[9] Many of the old-line Republicans of Leo's stamp have gone over to the Democratic party.

❋ Party bosses in Chicago have been unscrupulous in the use of public office to build up their political organizations; but from time to time they have been compelled to recognize the larger community interests. When gross inefficiency on the part of the political appointees led to grave scandals, the city bosses were compelled, by the pressure of public opinion, to ignore the recommendations of the ward committeemen and to sacrifice certain political appointees. Thus, after a storm of criticism in the daily press regarding a bad water-tank accident, the machine took more care in the selection of building inspectors.[10] The man who had just inspected the tank which crashed and killed several people was a beer salesman who had no qualifications for the job whatsoever but had been appointed in return for his political activities.

In many sections of the city, precinct committeemen acted as local community agents. About three-quarters of the precinct captains interviewed in 1936 said that they handled complaints regarding rubbish in the streets and alleys. The responsibility for keeping the streets clean lies in the department of public works, but the commissioner in charge of the department is hampered by a ward setup. A ward boss of the party in power will virtually control the superintendent in charge of refuse removal in his district. The local political control of this important function has resulted in inefficiency and waste. What the citizens have a right to demand in return for taxes paid, is

[9] June 24, 1936.   [10] *Chicago Tribune*, May 22, 1934.

meted out to them as a special political favor from the powers that be.

The administration of the tax machinery has presented a dilemma to the political bosses. If taxes are lowered or adjusted too generally, then the total revenues may be inadequate to meet the governmental pay rolls. While the depression has cut the tax-fixing activities of the precinct captains in two, nearly one-half of the Democratic precinct captains interviewed in 1936 said that they still engaged in such practices. Reforms in methods of assessing real estate have greatly reduced the possibilities of political manipulation in this field,[11] but the personal property tax still lends itself to the precinct tax-fixer. Since 1934, when the assessor became an elective officer and his appointees became largely political, precinct captains have again been going the rounds collecting personal-property tax bills and promising to take care of them. In some cases the party agent may merely give advice on the making-out of the schedules; in others, he may encourage his constituents to ignore the schedules or he may take the forms and hand them to an official, who conveniently buries them in his files. The assessor, the board of tax appeals, the county judge, the county treasurer, and the state's attorney all have some responsibility in connection with the assessment and payment of taxes; and it is very easy for a slip to be made somewhere along the line. As long as the state has such an antequated and unworkable tax system as at present, it will be difficult to put tax administration upon a sound basis.

The many city ordinances regulating particular trades may be used by the party workers for political purposes. Since 1928 there has apparently been no change in the proportion of precinct captains who said they were instrumental in securing permits of one sort or another for their constituents. The list would include peddler's, garage, building, milk, and other types of permits. In some cases the zoning regulations present prob-

[11] J. L. Jacobs, *Assessments of Real Estate and Personal Property in Cook County, Illinois* (Chicago, 1934); O. L. Altman, "Chicago's Experiment in Personal Property Taxation, 1931–1936" (Ph.D. thesis, University of Chicago, 1936).

lems that may be solved by recourse to political manipulation. Naturally, in recent years the Democrats have been much more active in securing favors of this sort than the Republicans.

Following the downward trend in the business cycle which started in 1929, party workers have been greatly concerned with the administration of relief. As one prominent public official put it: "Because of the precinct captain's interest in the difficulties of his community and because of his knowledge of the sources of public relief, he is inevitably the means through which a great many needy individuals are brought in contact with the public relief agencies."[12] An efficient, smooth-running ward organization has its own social work secretary, who knows exactly how to cut official red tape and get results from the relief agencies. The number of contacts that precinct captains of both parties make with the organized social service agencies has greatly increased during the past eight years. Whereas only one-half of the precinct captains maintained such contacts in 1928, two-thirds did so in 1936.

As compared with New York, the administration of relief in Chicago has been relatively free from direct political interference.[13] Trained social workers have been employed by the county relief agencies, and the politicians have tried in vain to introduce the spoils system. However, precinct captains have made every effort to claim credit for the services which have been rendered. They have also been highly critical of the professional social workers. One party worker who was a deputy bailiff said that he often came in contact with the social workers and that he opposed them in many things. He declared that much of the trouble came from too much red tape and too personal and inquisitive investigations of the social service agents, most of whom were girls from the University of Chicago who did not "know a damn thing about politics, or relief either."

In an area where juvenile delinquency and crime rates are high, party committeemen are particularly active in helping their constituents who have fallen into the clutches of the law.

---

[12] Forthal, *op. cit.*, p. 617.   [13] Peel, *op. cit.*

Over one-half of the precinct captains interviewed in 1936 said that they gave aid in connection with trouble with the law-enforcing authorities. This was a larger proportion than was found in 1928. Some raised bail or signed bonds; while others merely put in a friendly word to the police, the assistant state's attorney, the court clerk, the bailiff, or the judge himself. The division of responsibility for the enforcement of the criminal law makes it possible for the "fixer" to do his work at a number of different stages during a trial. The police may fail to secure convincing evidence, the state's attorney may fail to prosecute, the court clerk may change the charge, the bailiff may fail to apprehend the defendant who has jumped his bail, and the judge has a variety of ways of mitigating the rigors of the law. In general the methods used for fixing cases in Chicago have been similar to those employed in Philadelphia and New York.[14] As long as judges are nominated and elected by party machines, as long as a considerable portion of the public is educated in the belief that "anything can be fixed," and as long as archaic rules of judicial procedure are retained, the political fixer will be busy at his work.

During the course of a year many precinct captains are called upon to investigate a long list of charges brought against various of their constituents by the law-enforcing authorities. The list furnished by the precinct captains interviewed included disorderly conduct, larceny, gambling, assault with a dangerous weapon, carrying concealed weapons, election offenses, manslaughter, murder, and other charges. The persistency of the political fixers is well illustrated by a larceny case summarized by Martin as follows:

Altogether this defendant achieved nine continuances, two changes of venue, and three bond forfeitures. During the pendency of the case there appeared before Mr. Austin (the person robbed) in behalf of the defendant, whose guilt was unquestioned, two state senators, a member of the lower house (the defendant's attorney, who later was a Democratic candidate for judge of the Municipal Court), a chief clerk of the Appellate Court, two deputy clerks of the Municipal Court, the club president and party committee

[14] Kurtzman, *op. cit.*; Peel, *op. cit.*; V. O. Key, "Techniques of Political Graft in the United States" (Ph.D. thesis, University of Chicago, 1934).

chairman, and six others, citizens of more or less prominence, all of whom urged Mr. Austin to drop the case. In addition, Mr. Austin's principal witness, a youth of fifteen years, was threatened with kidnapping by gangsters, resulting in policemen being assigned to guard his home.[15]

A very common type of fixing, which involves many persons in the better residential areas, is the fixing of traffic slips. In 1928, over one-half of the precinct captains interviewed admitted that they took care of traffic slips for their constituents. Violations of the speeding or parking rules were the most common offenses. In those days a deputy bailiff who was a precinct captain related that he received a handsome sum of money for getting the judge in a good humor to sign a list of discharges without reviewing the cases. The increasing toll of traffic accidents called attention to lax handling of traffic cases. As a result of safety drives and considerable newspaper publicity, the courts have been compelled to tighten up on their procedures. Only one-quarter of the precinct captains interviewed in 1936 said that they had anything to do with traffic cases. One of them said: "Regarding traffic violations, the judges are at present conducting very effective campaigns against fixing, and it is absolutely impossible to have traffic violation cases fixed."[16] However, in a well-to-do precinct a suave party committeeman said: "In cases of smash-ups, where it is very important for the wealthy defendant to have the right court connections before the case should come to trial, the organization has its special lawyers who know the ropes."[17] Thus, a friend in court may be of use to the mighty as well as to the lowly. It is the business of precinct captains to act on this.

The depression has brought the local party agent in closer touch with the federal government. Mention has already been made of the activity of precinct captains as employment brokers for federal-made work jobs. Party committeemen were also active in aiding foreign-born persons who wished to become naturalized, veterans who wished to take advantage of the

[15] E. M. Martin, *The Role of the Bar in Electing the Bench in Chicago* (Chicago, 1936), p. 300.

[16] Interview, May 19, 1936.   [17] Interview, May 26, 1936.

bonus legislation and other laws which gave them a privileged status, and home-owners who wished to avail themselves of the facilities offered by the Home Owners' Loan Corporation. So political did the administration of the latter authority become that the federal authorities in Washington, D.C., were compelled to intervene and clean up the local situation.[18] About one-half of the precinct captains said that they gave advice to their constituents regarding federal loans on homes. It was inevitable that the Democratic party workers would be more active in seeing federal authorities than the Republicans, who were out of power. In some cases the precinct captains worked together in friendly fashion which did not involve bipartisan commitments. The impression left with many voters, however, was that federal activities were more likely to be continued under the Democrats than under the Republicans.

POLITICAL ACTIVITIES

Precinct captains who have put themselves out in many ways to serve their constituents do not have many difficulties in trying to get a hearing when they canvass their districts for votes. Practically all of the committeemen interviewed said that personal house-to-house canvassing was the principal method that they relied upon to reach the voters. Some were well enough off financially to delegate part of the canvassing to assistants, but in the main the precinct captains preferred to do most of the canvassing themselves. About one-half of the captains said that they also sent personal letters to the voters.

Efficient precinct captains saw that a thorough canvass was made before each general or intermediate registration, so that they could be sure that the names of all of their potential supporters were on the books. Considering the high mobility of the population in many areas of the city, this was not an easy task. During a period of economic depression many citizens move in order to find lower rents or to escape paying rent for a while. It is also necessary to guard against attempts of the opposition to pad the registration lists.

---

[18] *Chicago Evening American*, April 3, 1934. A Democratic ward committeeman was involved.

Canvassing techniques must necessarily vary with the type of district. In some of the exclusive high rental areas it is not possible for a political canvasser to get past the doorman or the butler without a proper introduction. A Democratic precinct captain living in an expensive hotel on the "Gold Coast" of Chicago, whom we will call "Tom Collins," said that he spent a good deal of his time every evening hanging around the hotel bar, talking to old acquaintances and making new ones. He was a cynical young bachelor who claimed that he was "too happy to be married." Making contacts was much more important to him than work. "No one," he said, "gets anywhere in politics or business on his merits. He has to have the 'clout' from behind. That is how I got my job." He thought that the main thing was to meet and talk to the voters on a man-to-man basis, e.g., on the prospects of the club and preferably over a Tom Collins. It did not matter where the voters were met—in the ball park, on the rinks, at dances, or at the bar. The main thing was to meet them. Tom did not argue with them on the New Deal. He did not have to, since he was primarily interested in getting them to vote "right" locally. When I mentioned the fact that a Republican precinct captain who lived near by had said that he was against the New Deal because it was ruining the United States, Tom laughed loud and long. "That rich ——— is as smooth as a billiard ball. How the hell do you think he gets his local favors? Our boss sees to that." In this summary fashion Tom disposed of all who vowed that they had political convictions.[19]

About one-half of the precinct captains frankly used the service argument in trying to win votes. They performed favors for their constituents which they hoped would be remembered on election day. Some presented this argument in its baldest form, the so-called "bread-and-butter" plea. The canvasser's job depended upon how many votes he could deliver on primary or election day. "In hard times like the present," one captain said, "you would not vote against my candidates and cause me to lose my job." In Philadelphia this kind of pleading is called

[19] Interview, May 26, 1936.

the "crying-towel" argument.[20] About one-quarter of the party committeemen discussed the merits of the candidates whom they were backing, and the remaining quarter talked about the policies advocated by their party.

In addition to the canvass the politicians employ various social devices in order to establish and maintain contacts with the voters. As in Boston and New York, boys' gangs have been encouraged and fostered by party leaders in the poorest disorganized communities.[21] Out of these gangs the ward bosses hope to develop effective political clubs. In Chicago gangland it has become a tradition that the first source of possible financial aid is the local ward committeeman, who will pay for the headquarters of an athletic club and buy uniforms in the hope that the boys will soon be of use to him on election days. A number of precinct captains and ward bosses have been recruited from political clubs which started as boys' gangs, some of which had semicriminal tendencies. The street corner, the poolroom, or the tavern has been the congregating point for these gangs.

In the more stable, middle-income neighborhoods the politicians were not so likely to encourage the formation of political clubs. To be sure, there were party headquarters of a more or less permanent character in all of the wards; and many of the ward organizations held field days, picnics, boxing shows, benefits, beer parties, card parties, smokers, and dances. However, there were frequently no clubs of a social or athletic character. The attitude of a ward boss in a middle-class area toward political clubs is illustrated by the case of Steve Brody. Steve was a college man who adjusted himself easily to the atmosphere of ward politics. When I asked him about the subject of clubs, he exclaimed:

A political club in this area? Not on your life! It is easier for the big bosses to keep the voters under control when there isn't anything like a club. If the voters got together and formed a club they might begin to get all sorts of

[20] Salter, *op. cit.*, p. 124.

[21] Woods, *op. cit.*, and Peel, *op. cit.* The political activities of boys' gangs in Chicago are discussed by F. M. Thrasher, *The Gang* (Chicago, 1927).

funny ideas. That's one of the first rules of politics. The old politicians don't want the young ones to organize because they always want to change the party. These Young Republican clubs are only a front to keep the young fellows satisfied.[22]

He added that he had parties for his voters from time to time. The ward organization had a party every summer in the forest preserves, and in the fall there was a boxing match in the Armory to raise funds for Christmas baskets.

Among the voters of foreign extraction, the device of the political club was found to be a common one. Thus, the voters of Swedish descent have founded a Swedish-American Republican club, the John Ericsson League, and the Svenska Klubben.[23] Each of these clubs was active in promoting the political recognition of Swedish candidates and in rallying the Swedish vote. The political club was also used as a medium for political education among the Italians. There were at least twenty such clubs organized along the lines of pleasure clubs with monthly dues of fifty cents or a dollar.[24] Such clubs may be paralleled among the numerous other immigrant groups in the city.

For the city as a whole, there is no social organization analogous to Tammany Hall in New York City. In 1936 the chief Democratic club was the Iroquois Club, which had no quarters of its own and which made no point at all of social activities. On the other hand, the Hamilton Club of Chicago has been very active in Republican circles in the past, and it has been a success as a social organization. Many nationally prominent Republicans have addressed the members of this Club from time to time. During the 1936 campaign a huge sunflower banner was hung over the front of the building. On election night a gang of enthusiastic and hilarious Democrats insisted that this sign be removed. Strange to say, the Club itself shortly afterward deleted the word "Republican" from its membership requirements in order to attract a larger clientele.

[22] Interview, June 9, 1936.

[23] Reuel G. Hemdahl, "The Swedes in Illinois Politics" (manuscript, Northwestern University, Evanston, 1932).

[24] Giovanni E. Schiavo, *The Italians in Chicago* (Chicago, 1928), p. 104.

ELECTION ACTIVITIES

Since a precinct captain's success is measured by the votes which he secures for the candidates of his organization, all of his benevolent, political, and social activities are centered toward the day of reckoning, namely, election day. A party committeeman who has canvassed his bailiwick well, who has used rational appeals in so far as possible, and who has rendered legitimate services to his constituents may find all of his work ruined by an opponent who stoops to election trickery and chicanery. On the other hand, the precinct captain who wants to win the prize for having the best precinct in the ward may use all possible honest methods to win votes and also employ ballot thieves to give him the additional boost that he needs to have the highest vote. Under both circumstances, and especially under the latter, it is absolutely necessary for the unit executive of the party to have control over the election machinery in his district.

In connection with the discussion of ward bosses it has already been indicated that the election machinery is practically in the hands of the party organization. At the beginning of the depression the Republican party was the leading party in the city; so its precinct captains were entitled to two of the three judges of election in the odd-numbered precincts and to one in the even-numbered precincts. Eight years later the Democratic party held this position. On both occasions the two major parties divided about evenly the total number of precinct election officials. All through the period, the precinct captain was the one who sent in names for the positions to be filled to his ward committeeman, who in turn transmitted them to the board of election commissioners.

When criticisms have appeared in the daily press regarding the character of judges and clerks of election chosen on the basis of the party submittal lists, Judge Edmund K. Jarecki, who has held the office of county judge since 1922, has always replied that under the present law, which requires partisanship and residence within the precinct, he is not able to get honest and efficient election officials in some parts of the city.[25] The Maguire case showed that many persons with criminal records, some of whom had been convicted of election frauds, were again and again appointed as precinct election officials.[26] Ballot thieves are recruited from the ranks of the pickpockets, card sharks, confidence-game men, and gambling-house operators. These persons have defied the law in other matters and know the sleight-of-hand tricks that are needed to put over ballot-box stuffing, alteration of tally sheets, and ballot erasures. In a game where winning is the main objective, some precinct captains do not hesitate to name election crooks as their candidates for positions on the precinct boards. In 1928 the Republican party had its share of criminals in key electoral positions; but by 1936 many of these underworld characters had drifted over to the Democratic party, which had complete control of the law-enforcing machinery.

Have the number of fraudulent votes increased as the political battles have waxed hotter and hotter in Chicago? Since the depression has not greatly altered the stakes of politics in the city, has the political struggle remained a battle of dollars, bullets, and deceit? As far as certain types of election frauds are concerned, it must be said that the economic crisis has hastened the cleansing of the election process. In the first chapter the background of the fight for permanent registration of voters in Chicago was discussed. This scheme promised a reduction of election expenses and the elimination of the worst abuses in connection with registration. A factional quarrel in the Democratic party plus a contrite spirit in the Republican party as the result of several lean years made it possible for the measure to pass the state legislature. A long period of educational work by various civic organizations, including the League of Women Voters, stamped the measure as one which would be likely to accomplish the purposes of the Horner Democrats and the hun-

[25] *New Election Law Needed*, Citizens' Association of Chicago, Bulletin, No. 75 (1928).

[26] *People* v. *Maguire, Proceedings of the County Court of Cook County*, June 21, 1930 ff. See also review of the case by Professor K. C. Sears (1933), manuscript, University of Chicago Law School.

gry Republicans. There is no question that the new system which went into effect in connection with the November, 1936, general election has greatly reduced such frauds as repeating, impersonation, and false entries on poll lists. After the new law went into operation, it was still possible for election crooks to sign fictitious names in various precincts; but this required the collusion of landlords and of those opposing precinct captains and election clerks who knew their jobs and made complete canvasses. It is significant to note that the October registration fell off, as compared with the March, in the First, Twentieth, Twenty-fourth, and Twenty-seventh wards, indicating very clearly that in these wards under the old registration system padded lists were very common. The greatest discrepancy was found in the Twentieth Ward, where the March registration was over 2,100 in excess of the October registration.[27] The wards in question were inhabited by large numbers of transients, unemployed men, persons on relief, except the Twenty-fourth Ward, which is a center of Russian-Jewish population.

The new system of permanent central registration, with the signature as a means of identification on election day, has marked a great improvement in election administration in the city of Chicago, but it has not solved all the problems in connection with fraudulent voting. Ballots can still be miscounted, altered, or not counted at all. In the Heller-Hasten 1932 election contest for a seat on the municipal court bench 29 per cent of the ballot boxes opened and counted showed evidence of definite or intended fraud.[28] Reports regarding the 1936 primary show that the election crooks have many tricks which they can play during the casting and counting of the ballots.[29] The "endless-chain" fraud may still be used, ballots may be "spilled," and the tally sheets may be changed. Election convictions are most likely to involve irregularities of this sort, since registration frauds were hard to prove before the new sys-

[27] *Chicago Evening American,* March 23, 1936; *Chicago Daily News,* October 11, 1936.

[28] *Chicago Daily News,* January 2, 1934.

[29] *Chicago Evening American,* July 9, 1936; *Chicago Daily News,* July 22, 30, and August 18, 1936.

tem came in. An analysis of the election cases before the
County Court in the period 1922–34 shows that vote frauds
have been most common in the Fourth, Twentieth, Twenty-
fourth, Twenty-seventh, and Forty-second wards.[30] For some
reason the henchmen of "Hinky Dink" and the "Bath" in the
First Ward have enjoyed an extraordinary immunity from
prosecution in connection with election affairs, although evidence of fraud is overwhelming.[31] In addition to the wards
where registration irregularities were common, this list includes
the Forty-second Ward, Botchy Connors' bailiwick.[32] Like the
other River wards, this Gold Coast and slum area includes many
transients and relief cases.

In a district where votes are stolen, it is also possible to in-
timidate the voters by a display or threat of violence. It is not
surprising, then, to find that election murders, kidnapings,
sluggings, and terrorizings are found in the Twentieth, Twenty-
seventh, and Forty-second wards. The famous or infamous
"pineapple" primary of 1928 brought an assassination in the
"bloody" Twentieth and other strong-arm methods in adjoining River wards. While the passing of prohibition has eliminated the gangs which derived their chief source of revenue from
bootlegging, it cannot be said that by 1937 there were no criminal gangs in Chicago who mixed business and politics. In 1936
political killings took place in the Twentieth and Twenty-seventh wards. However, the general police administration of the
city was superior in 1936 to what it had been eight years before,
and election intimidation was less flagrant.

The cynical ward heeler may say that the votes which he
cannot steal or seize by force, he buys. Money plays a very
important role in Chicago elections as well as in the elections
in other large centers of population in the United States.[33] In

[30] *Dishonest Elections and Why We Have Them*, edited from the records of the County
Court (December, 1922—June, 1934) with notes by Women's Civic Council of the
Chicago Area (Mrs. Harriet M. Robertson, editor).

[31] On the Serritella recount, see *Chicago Daily News*, July10, 1936.

[32] "The Kelly-Nash Political Machine," *Fortune*, XIV (August, 1936), 47 ff.

[33] L. Overacker, *Money in Elections* (New York, 1932); C. H. Wooddy, *The Case of
Frank L. Smith* (Chicago, 1931).

the heyday of his power Samuel Insull threatened to buy the entire Democratic organization from Boss Brennan for something over half a million dollars.[34] In 1936 it was estimated that it took just about that much money to oil the regular Democratic machine in the primary election. Together the two major parties spent well over a million dollars for the final general election in the fall of that year.

How is the money spent? Are votes still purchased directly? In some parts of Chicago where poverty and insecurity have robbed men of hope, an election bribe of anywhere from $0.50 to $5.00 or $10.00 looks large and the vote itself, when lost in a sea of 1,700,000 other votes in the city, looks small. Of course, in the long run the bribe-receiver gets the small end of the bargain. He pays in inefficient city administration at points that affect him most; but on election day the breakdown of local relief, of local police protection, and of local sanitation do not seem to be very directly connected with the smiling face and the cheery word of the precinct captain who slips him the coin or the bill. The voter is paid for his "time," and not for his vote. He spends an hour or so standing on the street corner wearing a party badge and passing out a little literature. In some wards even these formalities may not be necessary.

Money is needed for many other persons in addition to "current expenses" and the manning of the polls. The organization which is well supplied with funds can buy newspaper advertising, radio time, literature, cigars, drinks, hotel space for headquarters, halls for meeting places, posters, postage, sound trucks, banners, buttons, tire covers, and the services of clerks, stenographers, radio announcers, canvassers, watchers, bill posters, spellbinders, and advertisers.

The amount of money available for precinct use varies considerably with the election and with the precinct. In the presidential primary of 1936 the precinct captains interviewed said that they received anywhere from less than $25 to over $100 to carry their precincts. The average amount of money spent

[34] Donald Richberg, "Gold-plated Anarchy, An Interpretation of the Fall of the Giants," *Nation*, CXXXVI (April 5, 1933), 368–69.

by the Democratic precinct captains was $60 per precinct; and
that by the Republican captains, $38.

Do precinct captains in Chicago do their jobs so thoroughly
that they can predict the results in their bailiwicks with a fair
degree of accuracy? While we asked the precinct captains before the election whether or not they could carry their precincts,
not all gave us definite answers. Only one-tenth of the Democratic precinct captains who claimed that they could carry their
districts failed to do so, while over four-fifths of the Republican
precinct captains made false claims about their prowess. One-
quarter of the Republican captains were frank to admit that
their cause was a hopeless one. In looking at the record of the
national committees of the two major parties, one might expect
the local committees to come out just about as the national do.[35]
Big Jim Farley was a better predictor than John Hamilton.
Hamilton was not the only one in his organization who did a lot
of wishful thinking before November 2, 1936.

As compared with his 1928 predecessor, the 1936 precinct
committeeman in the city of Chicago was less of an employment
broker, less of a tax-fixer, less of a traffic-slip-adjuster, but more
of a go-between for the relief agencies and the various branches
of the federal government. The 1936 precinct captain was much
more interested in national issues than his brother of the prosperity era. Permanent registration spoiled certain of his election tricks, but it left him free to try other well-known devices.
Money was still essential for his work, but there was a new
crop of Republican party workers who had to volunteer their
services, since the chances of their party's local success seemed
remote. Of course, there were also the bipartisan dealers who
posed as Republicans but worked for the Democratic party.
The depression has brought some improvement in the ethical
standards of the party workers of the city, but these standards
are still pitched at a very low level.

[35] H. F. Gosnell, "How Accurate Were the Polls," *Public Opinion Quarterly*, I (January, 1937), 100.

CHAPTER V

THE VOTERS' RESPONSE[1]

Considering the fact that the city-wide bosses, the ward bosses, and the precinct captains did not change their methods and their philosophy under the impact of the economic crises, we cannot expect to find the voters in the city evincing much originality. There was a big shift from one of the major parties to another; but there were no important third-party movements, as in Wisconsin, no disturbing upheavals in a primary election, as in California, and no city-wide reform movements, as in New York. The voters of Chicago stuck to the old party labels, and throughout the entire period the combined vote of the minor party candidates in the city never exceeded 3.5 per cent of the total vote cast.

The realistic politicians in the city were not concerned with third-party movements. They were interested in the shifts from one major party to another. If our theories regarding the nature of the major party organizations have been correct, then we might expect these shifts to be relatively large. The Democratic party, which was relatively weak in national elections at the beginning of the period, gained one advantage after another. A strong presidential candidate, a powerful organization based on spoils, and an ever weakening opposition swept the voters into the Democratic fold and kept minor party revolts in abeyance.

On the basis of the evidence presented by party workers, it is possible to present a few hypotheses as to the motivation of voters. The appeals made to party history and party heroes in any election campaign clearly indicate that the politicians regard party tradition as an important control. Boss Kelly wants to know how many people he can count on to be loyal to his

[1] The author is indebted to Norman N. Gill and Margaret J. Schmidt for assistance in preparing this chapter.

party year after year. The Republican bosses want to know who will stick to their party in spite of the disastrous reverses in recent elections. If the precinct captain is an efficient one, he will know pretty well who the traditional voters are in his bailiwick. While the findings of precinct workers are not published and the vote itself is secret, the consistency of the voting behavior of individuals can be studied in territorial groups. It is possible to study how nearly alike the responses of the voters in a given area are at different elections. The mobility of the citizens in some areas is much greater than in others, but it is amazing how fixed the general character of a neighborhood may be.

It has already been pointed out that new construction was at a standstill during the period under discussion. This means that there were not great changes in the physical makeup of the various communities studied. Local community research in the city has indicated how close the relationship is between the physical and social elements in city life. If the time elapsed between the elections is not too long, it can be assumed that to some extent the voting responses of the same people are being examined and that to a great extent the behavior of the same type of people is being studied. Besides this, it has been indicated that there have been few changes in the characteristics and activities of the party workers.

In order to study the extent to which the voters in certain areas clung to given parties, it was decided to compare the results of five biennial elections beginning with 1928. The next step in the analysis was to divide the city into units which would be numerous enough to justify the use of statistical techniques and which would not be so minute as to cut across the precinct or census tract lines.[2] Since it was desired to preserve both political and community boundaries, it was finally decided to take the 75 local communities as defined by the census, and

[2] Election returns were obtained from the *Chicago Daily News Almanac and Yearbook*, the *Public Service Leader*, and the records of the board of election commissioners of Chicago; census data, from E. W. Burgess and C. Newcomb (eds.), *Census Data of the City of Chicago, 1930* (Chicago, 1933), and C. Newcomb and R. O. Lang (eds.), *Census Data of Chicago, 1934* (Chicago, 1934).

superimpose them upon the 1921 ward lines for the city.[3] Prior to the 1932 presidential election the 1931 ward boundaries were so new that any changes in ward bosses had little time to be felt. This method produced 166 subdivisions for the entire city, containing, on the average, about 10,000 adult citizens. For reasons to be explained later, 19 of these units were dropped, leaving a total of 147.

For purposes of studying the traditional vote in national elections it was decided to select the percentage of the total vote that the key Democratic candidate received at each election. A start was made with the presidential election of 1928; and the question was asked: "How many votes for each one hundred votes cast did Boss Cermak and his cohorts secure for the 'wet' Alfred E. Smith, a candidate whom they could support with great enthusiasm?" On the Republican side the question was: "How many votes could be kept in line for 'dry' Herbert Hoover?" Two years later the most important election was the senatorial contest in which Boss Cermak and his organization supported James Hamilton Lewis, in the latter's struggle against the "lady," Mrs. Ruth Hanna McCormick. Boss Cermak's last general election was the presidential election of 1932, when he held the boys in line for Franklin D. Roosevelt and made considerable inroads on Herbert Hoover's Chicago strongholds of 1928. In 1934 Bosses Kelly and Nash backed Michael L. Igoe for congressman-at-large against the Republican candidate, C. Wayland Brooks, who two years later won the gubernatorial nomination. The vote for each of the Democratic candidates was expressed as a percentage of the combined Democratic and Republican vote at the particular election. Since the votes received by minor candidates were small, they were neglected. Consequently, the ratios in each area give a picture of the Republican vote as well as the Democratic vote.[4]

The relative success of the party bosses in the elections under consideration is given in Table 9. In the city as a whole, Boss

[3] An attempt was made also to include the 1931 ward lines, but it was discovered that these lines cut across many of the census tracts.

[4] The Republican percentage for any given area can be calculated by subtracting the Democratic percentage from 100.

Cermak fell just short of achieving a majority for Al Smith, as he had bragged he would. However, the Democratic percentage jumped from 49.2 per cent for Smith in 1928 to 59.2 per cent for Roosevelt in 1932. In the nonpresidential years the achievements of the Democratic bosses were even more remarkable. After the New Deal had been in operation over a year and a half, the Democratic vote in the city jumped to 64 per cent, as shown by the Igoe vote in 1934. The figures fail to reveal a steady trend to the Democratic party since the peak of the Democratic popularity appears to have been reached in 1930, when Lewis received 72.1 per cent of the total vote. However, the vote which Lewis received does not represent the true strength of the Democratic party at this election. He ran far ahead of his ticket because his opponent, Mrs. McCormick, the first woman to receive a major party nomination for the office, had incurred the enmity of the Thompson faction of the Republican party and had received unfavorable publicity in connection with the Senate investigation of campaign funds. Mrs. McCormick's slight of well-known Republican leaders, her expenditure of half a million dollars to win the nomination, and the fact that she was a woman made her a vulnerable candidate. A comparison of the votes for congressman-at-large at the four elections shows a more uniform development of the Democratic strength. Starting with 45.4 per cent of the total in 1928, the successive Democratic percentages for the office were 59.3, 57.1, and 64.9.[5] The first eight years of the depression in Chicago

[5] Two congressmen are elected at large from Illinois. The city of Chicago has about one-half of the voters in Illinois. The average vote for this office was found by adding the votes for all Democratic and Republican candidates and dividing by two. The results are given below:

Year	Total Average Vote Cast for Congressmen	Total Average Vote for Democratic Candidates	Percentage Democratic
1924	847,927	257,240	30.3
1926	670,350	293,697	43.8
1928	1,173,425	532,036	45.4
1930	827,751	490,954	59.3
1932	1,269,698	725,456	57.1
1934	1,099,974	712,612	64.8
1936	1,544,069	977,857	63.3

resulted in the Democrats receiving 15–20 per cent more of the
total vote than they received in 1928. This would indicate that
the percentage of the voters who did not change their party
affiliation during the period could not exceed 80.

TABLE 9

VARIABLES USED IN STUDY OF VOTING BEHAVIOR IN CHICAGO*

(N = 147)

Variable	Letter Symbol	Date	Percentage for City	Mean	Lowest Item	Highest Item	Standard Deviation
Smith vote.............	a	1928	49.2	51.7	23.5	88.1	15.0
Lewis vote.............	b	1930	72.1	76.0	42.9	91.5	8.6
Roosevelt vote.........	c	1932	59.2	63.4	29.6	90.0	13.1
Igoe vote..............	n	1934	64.0	66.4	34.4	92.2	12.5
Roosevelt vote.........	v	1936	66.9	70.0	30.6	96.1	12.6
Women voters.........	d	1930	41.8	40.4	8.5	52.5	6.8
Party vote.............	e	1932	58.4	58.4	28.1	87.3	12.0
Bond issue.............	f	1930	58.0	56.6	43.8	85.6	7.7
Wet vote..............	g	1930	78.6	78.4	59.7	93.3	5.7
Voting interest.........	h	1930	66.3	66.8	34.2	104.1	11.0
Foreign birth..........	i	1930	26.9	31.2	13.2	67.3	10.9
Catholic origins........	j	1930	32.4	34.1	4.2	84.6	21.0
Median rental..........	k	1930	($49.56)	($47.50)	($15.22)	($129.40)	18.5
Home-ownership.......	l	1930	31.1	35.8	0.7	82.5	19.1
Unemployment........	m	1931	22.7	28.3	3.7	69.4	12.5
Mobility..............	s	1934	27.6	25.0	11.5	49.0	6.9
Doubling-up...........	t	1934	8.0	6.9	1.8	14.5	2.2
Education.............	u	1934	26.1	24.8	5.5	66.7	15.6
Relief.................	w	1933	11.8	10.6	0.9	30.2	6.2

* All figures are expressed in terms of percentages except median rental, which is given in dollars. For
variables a, b, c, n, and v, the totals used to calculate the percentages were the sums of the Democratic and
Republican votes in each of the 147 areas. For the other variables the bases were: for d, the total number
of registered voters in October, 1930; for e, the total vote cast in November, 1932; for f and g, the total vote
cast on the particular measures; for h and i, the total number of adult citizens; for j, the total population;
for l, the total number of homes; for m, the total number of workers ten years of age and over gainfully employed in 1930; for s and t, the total number of families; for u, the total population eighteen years of age and
over; and for w, the total population, January, 1934.

Election returns were obtained from the Chicago Daily News Almanac and Yearbook, the Public Service
Leader, and the records of the board of election commissioners of Chicago. Census data from Burgess and
Newcomb (eds.), Census Data of the City of Chicago, 1930 (Chicago, 1933), and Newcomb and Lang (eds.),
Census Data of Chicago, 1934 (Chicago, 1934). Relief data through the courtesy of Professor Ernest W.
Burgess.

Since a new era in American politics was definitely started by
the election of 1932, which brought to an end the Republican
dominance of our national government, it was decided to study
the results of this election intensely. To that end Figure 2, a
map, was prepared, giving the proportion of the total vote
received by Roosevelt in 1932 in each of the units selected for
the present study. Those who are familiar with the city can

COMMUNITY AREAS OF CHICAGO

AS ADOPTED BY CENSUS BUREAU, 1930

SHOWING

PERCENTAGE OF ROOSEVELT VOTE TO TOTAL VOTE
1932
(Source: *Public Service Leader*)

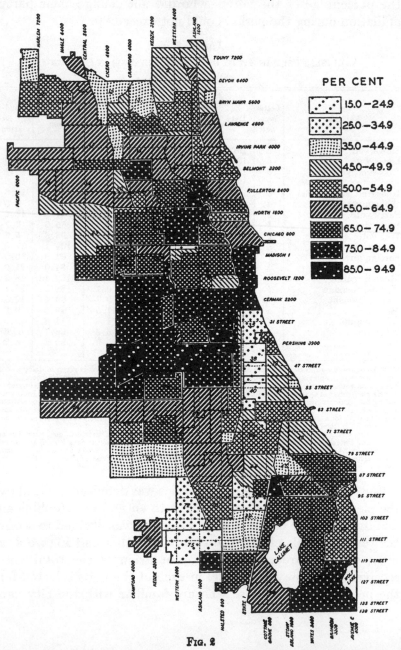

PER CENT

	15.0 – 24.9
	25.0 – 34.9
	35.0 – 44.9
	45.0 – 49.9
	50.0 – 54.9
	55.0 – 64.9
	65.0 – 74.9
	75.0 – 84.9
	85.0 – 94.9

FIG. 2

see at once that the Roosevelt vote was strongest in the areas where rents were lowest, where the proportion of foreign born was highest, where the Catholics were most numerous, where there were more men than women, and where unemployment was most prevalent. Roosevelt's popularity was greatest in the center portions of the city, in and immediately surrounding the business heart of the city, on the banks of the two branches of the Chicago River, and also in two outlying industrial areas— one in South Chicago and the other on the Southwest Side. The most outstanding exception to this generalization is to be found in the areas inhabited largely by Negroes, where the Roosevelt vote was lower than in any other part of the city. Because the distribution of Negroes over the entire city was so uneven and because the behavior of the Negro voters was so atypical, it was decided to consider them separately.[6] Consequently, the areas in which the Negro population was 20 per cent or over were excluded from the general analysis.

Table 9 also gives the means, the extreme cases, and the standard deviations for Democratic percentages in the 147 areas.[7] It is apparent that the exclusion of the districts in which the Negroes were relatively populous results in mean average Democratic percentages which are larger than the Democratic percentages for the city. The relatively small range and standard deviation of the Lewis vote reinforce our comments about the landslide character of this election. All over the city many Republican voters moved away from their candidate toward Lewis. Since our units were kept the same for all five elections, it is possible to use them to trace the shifts in party strength during the period.

[6] See Harold F. Gosnell, *Negro Politicians* (Chicago, 1935).

[7] The standard formulas were used for the calculation of these items. Let us take, for instance, variable c, the Roosevelt vote. The mean, M_c, was calculated by adding the Roosevelt percentages and dividing by 147 (N = the number of cases). $M_c = \Sigma X_c/N$. The standard deviation (σ) was calculated by the formula, $\sigma = \sqrt{\Sigma x^2/N}$, where $x = X_c - M_c$. This measure is sometimes called the root mean square deviation, since it is obtained by finding the square root of the sum of the squares of deviations from the mean divided by the number of cases. The standard deviation shows the extent to which the cases vary from the mean. In general, two-thirds of the cases will be found within the distance of σ below and beyond the mean. See Appendix C.

In addition to studying the relationship between the vote at
different elections, it was decided to study the relationship of
other variables to the voting records. It has been shown elsewhere that in 1920, when separate records were kept in Illinois
for men's and women's votes, in all parts of the state the women
were consistently more in favor of the Republican candidate for
president than the men.[8] No such records have been kept since
that date; and in order to get an indirect measure of the influence of sex upon voting preferences since the depression, the
percentage that the women registered voters were of the total
number of registered voters in 1930 was calculated for each of
the areas. The registration figures by sex showed some interesting variations. In one area, part of Democratic "Hinky
Dink" Kenna's famous bailiwick in the First Ward, only 8.5
per cent of the registered voters were women, while at the other
extreme several areas were found where there were more women
registered than men. These variations tended to follow the sex
ratios found in different parts of the city, but in the foreign-
born neighborhoods the adult women citizens were more indifferent to voting than in the communities which were largely
native.[9] A comparison of the sex ratio map with the map of the
Roosevelt vote shows that the tendency of women to vote
Republican may still be present in the city.[10]

As a measure of the strength of the party organizations, we
chose the percentage that the ballots marked straight were of
the total number of ballots cast in the presidential election of
1932. Since Illinois has the party-column type of ballot, an
elector may vote for all of the candidates of a given party by
putting a cross mark (×) in the appropriate party circle. In
each of the 147 units, the straight Republican and straight
Democratic ballots were combined and expressed as a ratio
of the total vote cast. In the aggregate of these units, the num-

[8] Stuart A. Rice, *Quantitative Methods in Politics* (New York, 1928), pp. 176–80.

[9] C. E. Merriam and H. F. Gosnell, *Non-voting: Causes and Methods of Control*
(Chicago, 1924), pp. 28–32, and H. F. Gosnell, *Getting Out the Vote* (Chicago, 1927),
pp. 81–88, 115–16.

[10] *Census Data, 1934,* map, separately published.

ber of straight Democratic votes exceeded the number of straight Republican votes cast.[11] This means that this variable is a better index of the strength of the Democratic political machine than it is of the strength of the Republican. While from time to time a party boss may surreptitiously urge his helpers to tell the voters to split their tickets, as a rule he makes party regularity and loyalty to the ticket from top to bottom a fetish.[12] The newspapers, the Protestant churches, and the civic organizations are the agencies which encourage independent voting. "Hinky Dink" Kenna's First Ward took the prize for having the largest proportion of straight votes cast; while, at the other extreme, the greatest number of independents was found in Horace G. Lindheimer's home precinct, a swank South Side hotel and apartment area bordering the lake and inhabited by many well-to-do Jews, who split their tickets for Hoover and Horner.

While Illinois does not have the optional referendum, the state constitution provides that state bond issues shall be referred to a popular vote.[13] In order to get an index of the attitude of the Chicago electorate toward public expenditures, the percentage that voted "yes" on a bond issue voted upon November 4, 1930, was used. The title of the measure was: "Shall an act of the General Assembly authorizing the conservation and forest preserves and public recreation grounds go into full force and effect?" This measure was opposed by the Chicago Bureau of Public Efficiency, the *Chicago Tribune*, and the *Chicago Daily News*. It was assumed that the most tax-conscious elements would vote "no." An area inhabited largely by home-owners in the extreme northwestern part of the city registered the most emphatic negative to this proposition, while Democratic River wards indicated that they were in favor of liberal spending.

[11] In the 1932 election, the total number of votes cast was 1,423,074; the total number of straight votes was 831,596, of which 533,801 were Democratic and 297,795 were Republican.

[12] In H. F. Gosnell's *Negro Politicians* a number of examples are given of unswerving party loyalty.

[13] See chap. vi, below.

The attitude of the Chicago voters on the liquor issue was ascertained by the percentage voting "yes" on the following public-policy measure, submitted November 4, 1930: "Shall the Eighteenth Amendment to the Constitution of the United States which among other things prohibits the manufacture, sale, or transportation of intoxicating liquors for beverage purposes within the United States be repealed?" Boss Cermak had always been a dripping wet, and this was his measure. While the vote on it was purely directory and had no legal effect on the status of prohibition in Illinois, it clearly indicated where the wet and dry areas were in the city. The measure was opposed by the *Chicago Daily News*, which had been traditionally dry, and favored by the *Chicago Tribune* and the two Hearst papers, the *Herald and Examiner* and the *Evening American*.[14] The mean shows that the city was pretty wet (78 per cent voted wet). Beverly Hills, in the extreme southwestern corner of the city, a Republican stronghold, was the driest spot; and the wettest was "Hinky Dink" Kenna's bailiwick.

As a measure of the interest shown in voting in the city, the percentage of the adult citizens registered in 1930 was used. The revised October registration figures were employed; and from the census tract tables of population twenty-one years of age and over, the aggregate of the following was obtained: native whites of native white parentage, native whites of foreign or mixed parentage, Negroes, and naturalized citizens.[15] From Table 9 it appears that there were more registered voters in some areas than there were adult citizens. The "bloody" Twentieth and the hobohemia of the First Ward furnished these cases. There was a lapse of nine months between the census-taking data and the registration date. However, it is likely that this alone does not account for the phenomenally high registration mentioned. Other evidence indicates that there was considerable padding of the registration lists in the city.[16] The

[14] Issues of November 3, 1930.

[15] Burgess and Newcomb, *op. cit.*, pp. 299–326.

[16] Women's Civic Council, *A Partial Record of the Conduct of Elections in Chicago and Cook County from December, 1922, to June, 1934* (Chicago, 1934).

variable under consideration, therefore, represents the element of fraudulent registration, padded lists, phantom voters, as well as interest in voting. The variables described so far have all concerned the political behavior of citizens in Chicago. It was also of interest to relate the political variables to measures of social and economic conditions. The city has a large proportion of foreign-born persons (26.9 per cent), whose presence has had an important influence upon local politics. At every election a great deal of attention is paid by the party managers and party candidates to the different nationalistic and racial elements in the city. Special efforts are made to cultivate the foreign-language press, and the political orators try to appeal to the different immigrant elements. Headquarters are established for the Irish-Americans, German-Americans, Polish National Alliance, Italian-Americans, and like groups. As a measure of the influence of foreign birth upon politics, the percentage of the adult naturalized citizens to the total number of adult citizens was calculated for each area from the figures available in the 1930 census. This measure conceals the striking differences between foreign-born groups as to length of residence in this country, religion, language, and economic status; but it furnishes a guide to the neighborhoods where there is a concentration of foreign-born elements. In Chicago the most numerous groups among the adult naturalized citizens were the Germans, the Poles, the Russians and Russian-Jews, the Scandinavians, the Irish, the Italians, and the Czechs.[17]

Figure 3, a map, shows the parts of the city where various

[17] The 1930 census gives the following distribution of foreign-born naturalized adults in Chicago by country of birth: Poland, 86,934; Germany, 76,725; Russia, 51,544; Sweden, 43,103; Italy, 42,050; Ireland, 39,161; Czechoslovakia, 32,650; and other countries, 141,349. If the native whites of foreign or mixed parentage fifteen years of age or over in 1930 are added to the foreign-born naturalized adults, then the size of the nationalistic groups in Chicago by country of origin becomes: Germany, 316,909; Poland, 219,241; Ireland, 155,578; Sweden, 103,097; Russia, 102,937; Italy, 92,137; Czechoslovakia, 82,417; other countries, 976,877. When first- and second-generation immigrants are taken together, the importance of the Irish and Germans becomes apparent. Those who were fifteen years of age in 1930 would be of voting age by 1936. The figures were calculated from *Fifteenth Census of the United States, 1930*, Vol. II.

foreign-born groups are concentrated.[18] A comparison between this map and the map for the 1932 Roosevelt vote shows that in the sections of the city where each of the following groups was concentrated, the Democratic vote was high: Czechs, Irish, Poles, Italians, Russians and Russian-Jews, and Lithuanians. Except for the Irish, these groups belong to the newer immigration. The Irish first joined the Democratic party in the time of Thomas Jefferson and spread from New York and Philadelphia to the middle-western cities. Tammany Hall, a Democratic society in New York, welcomed the Irish in 1800 in spite of their poverty, illiteracy, menial occupations, and Catholic faith. In Chicago the Irish have dominated the Democratic party for many decades. One needs but to mention the list of Democratic city bosses—Sullivan, Brennan, Nash, Kelly—to say nothing of the ward bosses—Kenna, Connors, Powers, Ryan, Brady, and O'Brien—and the rival factions led by Courtney and Igoe. Of the Democratic groups of foreign extraction, the Irish stand next to the Poles in numbers; and they have the great advantage of having English as a mother-tongue and a long period of residence. However, the rise of such ward bosses as Zintak, Konkowski, and Rostenkowski shows that the Irish are being challenged. The period when Cermak, a Czech, was the city boss was the most trying to the Irish. Since the newer immigrants were largely Catholics, it was natural for them to be attracted by the Democratic party.

Where the Germans or Swedes were concentrated, the margin between the Roosevelt and the Hoover vote was close, with Hoover in the lead in several places. It is probable that the initial adherence of the Germans and Swedes to the Republican party was the result of their immigration at the time of the Civil War and their antipathy to slavery and the financial policies of the Republican opposition. In Chicago, a Lueder, a Lehr, a Hoellen, a Nelson, a Lundin, a Brekke, and an Olson have figured prominently in Republican politics.

[18] *Census Data, 1930*, pp. 669–87, maps 5–14. The concentration of the different groups varies. All range from 10 to 34 per cent of the total population, except the Irish, who range from 10 to 14; the Germans, who range from 10 to 24; and the Negroes, who range from 10 to 99.

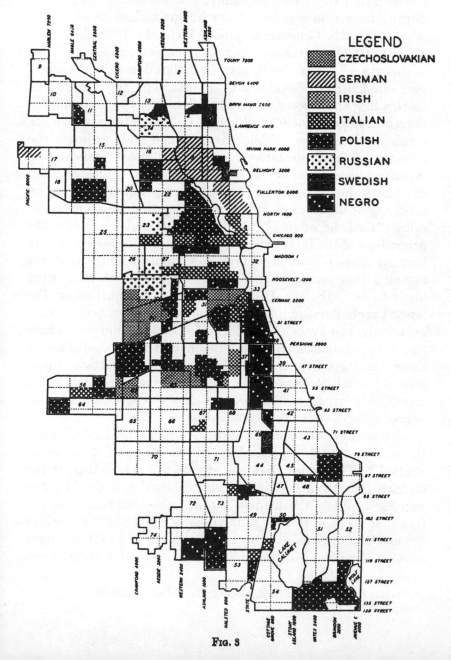

COMMUNITY AREAS OF CHICAGO

AS ADOPTED BY CENSUS BUREAU, 1930
SHOWING
NATIONALITY AND RACIAL GROUPS
1930
(Source: *Census Data of Chicago*)

LEGEND

CZECHOSLOVAKIAN

GERMAN

IRISH

ITALIAN

POLISH

RUSSIAN

SWEDISH

NEGRO

FIG. 3

It has already been indicated that in Chicago politics religious affiliations have played an important role, particularly in the Democratic party. Unfortunately, it is impossible to get any direct information regarding the religious affiliations of voters. According to the Census of Religious Bodies for 1926, there were about 1,000,000 church members thirteen years of age and over in the city, of whom the Roman Catholics constituted slightly over one-half, the Jews about one-fifth, and the Protestants (both white and colored) the remainder.[19] In the total population the number of nonchurch members is slightly less than the number of members. While these figures underestimate the influence of the Protestant churches, they clearly indicate the superior organization of the Roman Catholics. Unfortunately, the census does not furnish church-membership figures for any subdivisions of the city. It was necessary to devise a measure, called "Catholic origins," which was obtained by finding the percentage of the total population composed of those who were born, or whose parents were born, in Catholic countries. It was assumed that immigrants from the following countries were likely to be Catholics: Irish Free State, Belgium, France, Poland, Czechoslovakia, Austria, Hungary, Yugoslavia, Lithuania, Italy, and French Canada.[20] This measure did not include the native white Roman Catholics of native parentage, of whom there was a goodly number. However, the proportion of persons of Catholic origins for the city was about one-third, which was slightly larger than the proportion of Catholic church members of all ages to the total population.

As a measure of economic status it was decided to calculate the median rental, expressed in dollars, for each of the areas studied.[21] This index does not divide the population of the districts into two mutually exclusive categories, as do the other variables. While the median rental values may conceal the fact that there were wide differences in rents paid by families living within a given district, such as the Gold Coast and slum area on the Near North Side, such sharp contrasts were not

---

[19] I, 389-91.

[20] *Census Data, 1930*, pp. 191-233, 245-98.   [21] *Ibid.*, pp. 567-94.

common all over the city. It has also been shown that median rents are fairly closely related to incomes.[22] A comparison of the map showing median rentals with the map of the 1932 Roosevelt vote indicates that, in general, Roosevelt got his highest vote in the low-rental areas and his lowest vote in the high-rental areas.[23]

Five other social measures were taken from census data on the theory that they would show some relationship to party preferences and to changes in voting behavior. These were: home-ownership, as shown by the percentage that the owned homes were of the total number of homes; unemployment, as shown by the percentage unemployed in 1931 of the gainful workers ten years of age and over as listed in 1930;[24] mobility, as indicated by the percentage of the total families that had lived less than one year at present address; doubling-up, as shown by the percentage of total families with one or more subheads, and education, as indicated by the percentage of the population, eighteen years of age and over, which had completed more than ten grades in school.[25] In a large metropolitan community like Chicago, home-ownership is not a good index to economic status, as some of the wealthiest people live in high-class apartments and many working class people with very limited incomes own their own cheap frame houses, but it does select the elements which are tax conscious. The unemployment index was far from perfect; but it picked out the areas of greatest concentration of unemployed, thus indicating where the depression was hitting hardest and where the relief problem was most serious. Doubling-up was not as useful a measure as

[22] William F. Ogburn, "A Study of Rents in Various Cities," *Monthly Labor Review*, VIII (September, 1919), 617–38.

[23] *Census Data, 1930*, Map 2.

[24] The unemployment figures for 1931 were secured through the courtesy of Joseph F. Veseley.

[25] A number of different indexes could have been selected from the 1934 educational data. The median grade completed or the proportion of the population that had completed less than five grades could have been used. For a discussion of these various indexes, see R. O. Lang, "The Relation of Educational Status to Economic Status in the City of Chicago by Census Tracts, 1934" (University of Chicago doctoral dissertation, 1936).

unemployment, because it affected a smaller proportion of the population and the variations were slight. Because of the residence requirements for voting and the interest in literacy tests for voting in some states, the measures of mobility and education were of particular interest. The last three variables were taken from the 1934 Census of Chicago, which furnished, for the first time, information on these topics.

1932 PRESIDENTIAL VOTE

A comparison of the map of the 1932 Roosevelt vote with the maps showing the geographical distribution of the other variables will show the general character of the relationships but not in a precise fashion, because large class intervals must be used. In a scatter diagram or dot chart the exact values for paired observations of two variables may be plotted and examined. Figure 4 gives values of the 1932 Roosevelt vote on the Y-axis plotted against the corresponding values for the 1928 Smith vote on the X-axis. Thus, the dot in the lower left-hand corner of the chart represents census community 72 (Beverly Hills), where the Smith vote was 23.7 per cent and the Roosevelt vote 29.6 per cent. The dot in the upper right-hand corner of the chart stands for a section of census community 60 (a Polish area), in which the Smith vote was 88.1 per cent and the Roosevelt vote 90.0 per cent. In similar fashion each of the points plotted represents the paired values of the Democratic percentages at the two presidential elections for a given area. It is clear that the points tend to follow a straight-line pathway which is almost at a 45° angle to the horizontal axis. By the method of least squares a straight line may be fitted to these points which expresses the Roosevelt vote as a function of the Smith vote. This line is called the regression line of X_c on X_a, and it is expressed in algebraic form by the equation, $X_c = 20.92 + 0.8221 X_a$. The equation shows that, on the average, Roosevelt got a high vote in the area where Smith received a high vote (82 per cent of Smith's votes) plus a diminishing number of other voters as one passes from those areas where Smith's vote was small to those where it was large. Where the Smith vote was relatively low, the average gains made by Roosevelt over the Smith vote were greatest; and where the Smith vote was high, Roosevelt's average gains were least. It was found

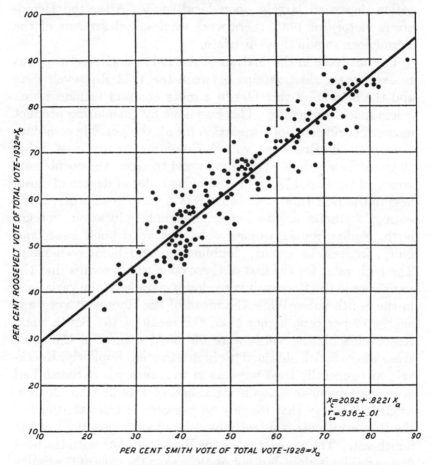

Fig. 4.—Scatter diagram showing relationship between 1932 Roosevelt vote and 1928 Smith vote in 147 selected areas in Chicago.

that the areas where the Roosevelt vote was about the same as the Smith vote (those below the regression line) contained a large Catholic population, which was already strongly Democratic in 1928. A few of these areas also contained a strong Republican machine which was more active in 1932 for the

Republican candidate for governor than it was in 1928. The areas in which the shift to Roosevelt was most marked (those above the line) were territories in which the Republican organization depended largely upon local spoils. After the Democratic victory of 1930, there were wholesale desertions of the Republican ship in these districts.

The next step in the analysis of the 1932 election returns was to express the relationships between the 1932 Roosevelt vote and the remaining variables in a more abstract fashion which is less space-consuming. This was done by calculating product moment coefficients of correlation for all the possible combinations with the Roosevelt vote.[26] Column c, or row c, of Table 10 gives these values. Without regard to signs, the coefficients arranged the variables in the following order of degree of closeness to the 1932 Roosevelt vote: Smith vote, Lewis vote, party voting, Catholic origins, unemployment, education, foreign birth, median rental, woman vote, wet vote, bond issue, mobility, interest in voting, doubling-up, and home-ownership. The high value for the first of these coefficients means that the variations in the Roosevelt vote closely paralleled the variations in the Smith vote. While the mean of the Roosevelt vote was nearly 12 per cent higher than the mean of the Smith vote, Roosevelt's highest votes were obtained mainly in the same areas where Smith obtained his highest votes. Similarly, Roosevelt was generally least popular in the areas where Smith had been least popular. Another method of interpreting this coefficient is to say that roughly 88 per cent of the variations of the Roosevelt vote is directly associated with variations of the Smith vote. The association of the Roosevelt vote with the next five variables is close, but not as close as in the case of the Smith vote. The negative sign for the correlation between the Roosevelt vote and median rental means that the relationship is inverse. In other words, the Roosevelt vote was generally high in those areas where the rents were low, and vice versa. The

---

[26] For a discussion of correlation, see M. Ezekiel, *Methods of Correlation Analysis* (New York, 1930). See Appendix C, p. 210, for a discussion of the methods used to check all calculations for the present study.

TABLE 10

Correlation Matrix: Intercorrelations of Variables Related to Voting Behavior in Chicago, 1930–36

	Letter Symbol	Smith (a)	Lewis (b)	Roosevelt 1932 (c)	Igoe (n)	Roosevelt 1936 (v)	Women (d)	Party Voting (e)	Bond Issue (f)	Wet Vote (g)	Interest in Voting (h)	Foreign Birth (i)	Catholic Origins (j)	Median Rental (k)	Home-Owners (l)	Unemployment (m)	Mobility (s)	Doubling-up (t)	Education (u)
Smith	a		.78	.94	.91	.88	-.57	.79	.46	.68	.35	.64	.78	-.62	-.15	-.69	-.31	-.18	-.62
Lewis	b	.78		.84	.80	.81	-.55	.62	.17	.64	.21	.60	.57	-.53	-.03	-.57	-.33	-.10	-.63
Roosevelt, 1932	c	.94	.84		.96	.96	-.66	.84	.40	.65	.27	.73	.78	-.68	-.05	-.76	-.35	-.11	-.73
Igoe	n	.91	.80	.96		.94	-.66	.84	.44	.61	.27	.71	.76	-.64	-.05	-.72	-.36	-.06	-.70
Roosevelt, 1936	v	.88	.81	.96	.94		-.61	.81	.39	.61	.26	.81	.75	-.68	-.07	-.75	-.34	-.03	-.75
Women	d	-.57	-.55	-.66	-.66	-.61		-.68	.37	-.49	.21	.51	.54	-.58	.07	-.68	.42	.14	-.65
Party voting	e	.79	.62	.84	.84	.81	-.68		.42	.47	.48	.66	.75	-.76	.08	-.81	-.51	-.01	-.81
Bond issue	f	.46	.17	.40	.44	.39	.37	.42		.58	.08	.14	.20	-.12	.57	.25	.20	.02	-.05
Wet vote	g	.68	.64	.65	.61	.61	-.49	.47	.58		.17	.34	.34	-.27	.38	-.37	.02	.29	-.30
Interest in voting	h	.35	.21	.27	.27	.26	.21	.48	.08	.17		.32	.32	-.43	.18	-.32	-.49	.16	-.44
Foreign birth	i	.64	.60	.73	.71	.81	.51	.66	.14	.34	.32		.72	-.66	.16	-.70	.48	.14	-.74
Catholic origins	j	.78	.57	.78	.76	.75	.54	.75	.20	.34	.32	.72		-.58	.15	-.52	.52	.17	-.73
Median rental	k	-.62	-.53	-.68	-.64	-.68	-.58	-.76	-.12	-.27	-.43	-.66	-.58		.25	-.80	.62	.01	.88
Home-owners	l	-.15	-.03	-.05	-.05	-.07	.07	.08	.57	.38	.18	.16	.15	.25		.25	.72	-.40	.36
Unemployment	m	-.69	-.57	-.76	-.72	-.75	-.68	-.81	.25	-.37	-.32	-.70	-.52	-.80	.25		.58	.01	-.84
Mobility	s	-.31	-.33	-.35	-.36	-.34	.42	-.51	.20	.02	-.49	.48	.52	.62	.72	.58		.19	.68
Doubling-up	t	-.18	-.10	-.11	-.06	-.03	.14	-.01	-.02	.29	.16	.14	.17	.01	-.40	.01	.19		-.14
Education	u	-.62	-.63	-.73	-.70	-.75	-.65	-.81	-.05	-.30	-.44	-.74	-.73	.88	.36	-.84	.68	-.14	

relationships between the Roosevelt vote and the woman vote and between the Roosevelt vote and educational level may be interpreted in the same fashion. Much smaller in size are the coefficients involving the covariation of the Roosevelt vote and the last five measures, namely, bond issue, mobility, interest in voting, doubling-up, and home-ownership. We can say that the Roosevelt vote has no apparent relationship to the presence or absence of home-owners, and that it has a loose positive association with the affirmative votes on the bond issue and an even looser association with interest in voting.

An examination of the scatter diagrams throws some light on the question of why certain variables were not more closely related to the Roosevelt vote.[26a] While the association of the Roosevelt vote with the measure of Catholic origins was close, there were certain non-Catholic areas which voted overwhelmingly for Roosevelt. A sampling of some of these areas showed that many of them had a large Jewish population. The Democratic candidate for governor was a Jew and undoubtedly helped all his running-mates in areas where the people of his group were numerous.[27] In a few of the areas where the ratio of persons of Catholic origins was high, the Roosevelt vote was not quite as high as one might expect. It was found that one of the Republican factions was particularly strong in these areas. The Republican candidate for governor was a member of this faction, and he ran ahead of his ticket in these districts.

A priori, one might have expected to find a closer correlation between the Roosevelt vote and the measures of economic status. What were some of the influences which were reducing the closeness of this association? The scatter diagram, a map of the Roosevelt vote, and the interviews with ward committeemen indicated that in the outlying residential areas of the city there were voters who were paying modest rentals who still adhered to the Republican party. As one ward committeeman put it, "This ward is strongly conservative and Republican.

[26a] Unpublished charts.

[27] This was especially true in the Twenty-fourth Ward, which roughly coincides with census community 30. It was true also in the Fifth and Forty-sixth wards.

It is made up of Yankee, Protestant, dry home-owners. Regardless of the depression, they supported Hoover."[28] Since there were a large number of home-owners in these areas, the median rental figures were somewhat misleading. The most prosperous residents of these areas did not pay rent; and those who paid, did not live in the most attractive dwelling places. On the other hand, there were parts of the city where the rentals were high and the Roosevelt vote was also higher than might have been expected. For the most part, these districts were found in those hotel areas where the Democrats were fairly well organized.

In his study of the 1928 presidential election in certain northern counties of the United States, Ogburn found that the prohibition issue was of primary importance.[29] In the present study the zero-order coefficients place the wet vote below many other measures. While most of the wets in Chicago were Democrats, it was found that in a number of bright-light areas, such as the North Side, Uptown, and Lake View communities, there were clusters of wet Republicans.[29a] It is surprising that there were not more of these clusters, considering the fact that the *Chicago Tribune* had waged a vigorous campaign to get the Republican party to adopt a wet stand. There were also some relatively dry areas which showed a higher Democratic vote in 1932 than one might expect. Included in this group were the areas where there were persons owning their own homes, or paying modest rentals, who were hit particularly hard by the economic depression. Before 1930 most of the voters in these districts had voted dry and for the Republican party, but in 1932 they shifted over to the Democratic party without changing their stand on the prohibition issue.

It is clear from the foregoing discussion that the Roosevelt vote was closely related to a number of variables. How can a more complete picture of the total situation be presented? One

[28] Report of interview.

[29] W. F. Ogburn and N. S. Talbot, "A Measurement of the Factors in the Presidential Election of 1928," *Social Forces*, VIII (December, 1929), 175–83.

[29a] See Fig. 5 for location of areas.

method is to analyze the ratios in small and more or less homogeneous communities. In a Polish community where Roosevelt's vote was 20 per cent above his city average, there were relatively more unemployed, more persons of Catholic origins, more foreign-born, and more straight-ticket voters than in the city at large.[30] In a section where the Roosevelt vote was less than his city average, the opposite conditions were found, i.e., relatively speaking, unemployment was less, rents were higher, the ratio of women registered was higher, and there was a greater proportion of native white Protestants.[31] The following general view of the situation was given by a Republican ward committeeman:

> The vote was due to Roosevelt's personal popularity; to a strong Democratic organization with plenty of patronage; a grudge vote against Hoover; and to a demand for a new deal and some Messiah to lead the way out of the depression. Unemployment was by far the most important factor in the 1932 election. The wet issue also played a role The Democratic party was only the instrument for the people to express their grudge vote against the previous Administration, not the cause of victory as such.[32]

The close association of the Roosevelt vote with so many variables raises a number of questions. Are not some of these variables measuring the same thing? What are the intercorrelations of these measures? Do the coefficients tend to group themselves in clusters? What is the net effect of changes in one variable upon the Roosevelt vote when the influence of other variables is kept constant? The statistical device of partial correlation is useful in answering some of these questions. In order to solve the equations involved in this technique, it is necessary to have all of the intercorrelations. These are presented in Table 10.

Since the calculations involved in partial correlation become increasingly complicated as new variables are added, it was decided to select five independent variables for this step in the analysis. Which variables should be eliminated? It was decided to eliminate those which we believed had the least bearing

[30] Census community 24.
[31] Census communities 1, 39, 41, 75.   [32] In a near West Side ward.

on the problem. In this group came the bond issue, interest in voting, and home-ownership. It was decided also to eliminate one of every set of variables that appeared to be measuring the same thing. Since the resemblance between the Smith vote and the Lewis vote was close, it was decided to drop the Lewis vote. The relationships of two variables, foreign birth and Catholic origins, with all of the other variables tended to be very similar; so foreign birth was not included in the calculations of the partial coefficients. According to the zero-order coefficients, the higher the level of education, the lower was the Roosevelt vote. This would seem to indicate that the illiterates voted for Roosevelt while the college graduates largely supported Hoover. However, a closer examination of these figures shows that education is very closely related to economic status. The same observation applied to women, median rental, and unemployment. While unemployment had signs which were opposite to the other two variables, all three are measures of economic status. Of the three, unemployment was chosen because it is more closely related to the Roosevelt vote.

Keeping religion, unemployment, the wet-vote, and the party-vote variables constant, the partial correlation between the Roosevelt vote and the Smith vote remains high.[32a] In other words, after making allowances for the other influences mentioned, the traditional Democratic vote still remains close to the Roosevelt vote in Chicago.

The partials between the other variables and the Roosevelt vote are much lower. Although the zero-order coefficient between the Roosevelt vote and Catholic origins is fairly high, when the Smith vote, unemployment, the wet vote, and the party vote are kept constant, the partial becomes insignificant. This is largely because the Smith vote and Catholic origins are so closely related to each other. Another way of expressing this relationship would be to say that, if areas could be found where the Smith vote, the unemployment ratio, the wet vote, and the party vote did not change, such variations as occurred in the ratio of persons of Catholic origins would show no marked asso-

[32a] See Appendix C, equations for chap. v, p. 211.

ciation with the Roosevelt vote. To take an extreme illustration, imagine a group of areas where the Smith vote was very low, most of the men were employed in 1931, a relatively large proportion of the voters were dry, and comparatively few straight ballots were cast in 1932. In these areas, the ratios of persons of Catholic origins would be low, and such slight variations as took place in them would show no definite relationship to the Roosevelt vote.

Another surprising relationship revealed by the coefficients of partial correlation is the fact that the unemployment variable is not close to the Roosevelt vote when the Smith vote, Catholic origins, the wet vote, and straight party voting are held constant. Certainly the average increase of 12 per cent in the Democratic vote over the entire city between 1928 and 1932 can be attributed largely to economic considerations. However, when we come to examine a map of the city we find that the greatest increases did not always occur in the areas where unemployment was greatest. In the areas where employment was still high, the voters were suffering various deprivations. Bank failures and the collapse of security values involved radical changes in the standard of living of many. The resultant tensions fomented a reaction against the Republican regime. Regardless of the social and economic characteristics of a given ward, every political expert interviewed was firmly of the belief that the most significant "cause" of the election turnover was the economic one.[33]

The net correlations of the Roosevelt vote with the wet vote and with party voting were not as close as might have been expected. According to one study, the net correlation of the Smith vote with the wet vote was high in 1928.[34] In Chicago, however, the relation of the Smith vote and the wet vote was not high. The second highest of all the partials is that between the Roosevelt vote and party voting, keeping constant the Smith vote, Catholic origins, unemployment, and the wet

[33] Economic influences were referred to as "depression psychology," "anti-Hoover" sentiment, a "craze "to throw out the "ins."

[34] Ogburn and Talbot, *op. cit.*

vote. This means that party organization came second after party tradition in explaining the variations in the Roosevelt vote as between the different districts in Chicago.

It is also of interest to examine the way in which the Roosevelt vote changes when these five other variables change. This can be done by means of an equation of net regression which describes the relationship between the Roosevelt vote as a dependent variable and the others as independent variables. This equation may be interpreted as meaning that the average change in the Roosevelt vote for a unit change in the Smith vote, keeping the other variables constant, was of first importance; the average change in the Roosevelt vote for unit change in straight party voting was of much less importance, keeping the other variables constant; the same held true for the wet vote; and the average change in the Roosevelt vote for unit changes in Catholic origins and unemployment, keeping the remaining variables constant, was insignificant. In other words, this equation places the variables in the same order of importance in determining the 1932 Roosevelt vote as do the coefficients of partial correlation.

On the basis of the statistical method employed, it has been shown that the net relationship between variations in the Roosevelt vote and variations in economic status was not very close in Chicago. This is a rather surprising result in view of the fact that it is obvious that economic insecurity resulted in a large turnover of the votes. One of the reasons for this lack of relationship is to be found in the nature of the measures employed. The areas where unemployment hit the hardest were those which were already strongly Democratic in 1928. To increase the Democratic vote in these areas was a difficult task, since there were some Republicans who could not be moved from their party allegiance even by economic adversity. If the difference between the 1928 and the 1932 votes (expressed by per cents) is given as a ratio of the percentage of non-Democratic in 1928, the resulting measure makes some allowance for this situation. The correlation of this measure with unemployment was .40. In other words, there were many exceptions to the general tendency for poor people to swing more decidedly than the rich in the direction of the Democratic party in 1932.

All economic groups were affected adversely by the economic crisis which started in 1929. The higher income groups were injured by bank failures, loss of interest, loss of equities; whereas the lowest income groups were hit by unemployment and actual want. All levels relieved some of their tensions by voting against the party in power.

1934 CONGRESSIONAL VOTE IN CHICAGO

The 1934 election returns give the first clear indication as to what the new Tammany machine was doing to the voting behavior of the citizens of Chicago. In the twentieth century one of the "laws" of American politics has been that a president loses some of his House support in the congressional elections which come in the middle of his term. This principle did not hold for the congressional elections of 1934, however. President Franklin Roosevelt increased his grip on Congress following these elections. How did he do it? As far as the state of Illinois is concerned, he was able to do it because of the strength of the Kelly-Nash machine. Downstate there was a falling-off in the percentage of the Democratic vote for congressman-at-large. This was offset by an increased Democratic percentage in the city of Chicago.[35] Whereas in 1932 there was not much difference between the voting behavior of the citizens of Chicago and those of downstate, in 1934 there was a spread of some 15 per cent. The downstaters reacted to the mid-term congressional elections in the normal American fashion; the citizens of Chicago did not. Let us now turn to a closer examination of the Igoe vote in the city.

[35] The relevant percentages are:

PERCENTAGE OF MAJOR PARTY VOTE RECEIVED BY DEMOCRATIC CANDIDATES FOR CONGRESSMEN-AT-LARGE

Year	Chicago	Country Towns in Cook County Outside of Chicago	Downstate
1932	57.1	45.8	52.9
1934	64.8	49.3	50.2

What elements of the voting population of the city were attracted or repelled by the experiments of the first part of the Roosevelt administration? The *Literary Digest* poll of 1934 indicated clearly that there was a shift in the party preference of many voters after the character of the New Deal policies became generally known. An analysis was next made of the traits of the voters who shifted from one party to the other after one and a half year's experience with a Democratic administration. This was done by using the Igoe vote as a starting-point.

While the Igoe vote was, on the average, 3 per cent higher than the Roosevelt vote in the various sections of the city, the coefficients show that there was a close relationship between votes for the two candidates. In fact, the Igoe vote was most highly associated with the Roosevelt vote, as the coefficient of .960 indicates. In other words, party tradition and party organization appeared to account for most of the variations in the Igoe vote. Where Roosevelt has been strong, Igoe was also strong; and vice versa. However, it is also clear that there were some shifts in the Democratic support. Most of these can be accounted for on the theory that in 1932 the Republican support came largely from the Protestant, employed, well-educated, native-born, relatively prosperous groups that tended to be drier than other groups and which had a larger proportion of women registered as voters. The Democratic gains of 1934 were made among people who had been formerly Republican. Consequently, the relation between the Igoe vote and political, social, and economic variables should logically be slightly less close than the relationship between the Roosevelt vote and these variables. This was the case for every variable except the following: party voting, women, bond issue, and mobility. The differences between the Igoe and the Roosevelt votes are so slight as to be of little significance; but if an explanation is wanted, it would emphasize the fact that all of these variables were closely related to the measure of party voting. Since the Democrats had more patronage in 1934 than in 1932, we might expect the Igoe vote to be more highly correlated with organi-

zational influences than the Roosevelt vote. A relatively large
difference was found between the coefficients involving the wet
vote and the Igoe and Roosevelt votes. This may be due to the
fact that the repeal of prohibition had become a dead issue. As
in the case of the Roosevelt vote, the Igoe vote has no apparent
relationship to the variables of doubling-up and home-ownership.

The fact that the variations of the Igoe vote as between the
different areas so nearly paralleled the variations of many other
measures raises a number of questions. If some of the variables
are closely related to each other, does not this mean that they
are measuring the same thing?

A detailed comparison could be made between the intercorrelations of the Igoe vote and those of each of the other variables. However, such a procedure would leave a confused impression. The correlation matrix may be subjected to a more
minute examination by means of the net regression technique
which has already been applied to the Roosevelt vote.[36] A logical starting-point is the Roosevelt vote, since it is so highly
correlated with the Igoe vote, which should now be regarded as
the dependent variable.[36a]

The regression equation for the Igoe vote as a function of the
Roosevelt vote shows that, on the average, Igoe got a high
percentage of the Roosevelt vote plus a diminishing number of
other voters as the Roosevelt vote increased. Where the Roosevelt vote was relatively low, the average gains made by Igoe
over the Roosevelt vote were greatest; and where the Roosevelt
vote was high, Igoe's average gains were least. In fact, in the
areas where the Roosevelt vote equaled or excelled 88 per cent,
one might expect to find an Igoe vote which was equal to or less
than the Roosevelt vote. Actually, the scatter diagram shows
that there were no such cases. The points which are not close
to the regression line indicate some of the influences which

[36] See H. F. Gosnell and M. J. Schmidt, "Factorial and Correlational Analysis of
the 1934 Vote in Chicago," *Journal of American Statistical Association*, XXXI (September, 1936), 507–18.

[36a] See Appendix C.

account for the 1934 shifts in the Democratic vote. In certain Republican areas which were relatively dry in 1932 there were marked shifts to the Democratic side two years later. Other areas which were strongly Democratic in 1932 did not show any increases in Democratic strength two years later.

Would the addition of other variables to the equation materially increase the closeness of the fit to the Igoe vote? In order to answer this question, the following variables were selected: the wet vote, percentage foreign born, and median rental. An examination of Table 10 will show that these variables are not highly intercorrelated with each other. The equation of regression which describes the relationship between the Igoe vote as a dependent variable and the others as independent variables may be interpreted as meaning that the average change in the Igoe vote for a unit change in the Roosevelt vote, keeping the other variables constant, was very high, whereas the average change in the Igoe vote for a unit change in each of the other variables, keeping the Roosevelt vote and the remaining variables constant, was relatively insignificant. It is interesting to note that there is reversal of signs for the wet vote, meaning that, keeping the Roosevelt vote, foreign birth, and median rental constant, the net relationship between the Igoe vote and the wet vote was low and inverse. As we have already seen, Igoe won votes among dry Republicans, and he did not run quite as well as expected in certain wet Democratic areas.

Since the Igoe vote and the Roosevelt vote are so closely related, the question may be raised as to how the Igoe vote may be explained without reference to party tradition, as measured by previous voting behavior. In other words, what sort of people have acquired the habit of voting Democratic in Chicago? Leaving out the Roosevelt vote, the equation indicates that the average change in the Igoe vote for a unit change in the wet vote, keeping the other variables constant, was fairly high. The coefficient of net regression for the percentage of foreign born was lower but significant. On the other hand, economic status as measured by median rental did not add greatly to the accuracy of the estimated Igoe vote, when the other variables were held constant. It is interesting to note that signs for the coefficients of net regression in this equation are the same as those for the original zero-order coefficients. This means that, when the Roosevelt vote is eliminated, we cannot perceive the slight shift of voters in relatively dry areas to Igoe.

When viewed closely, the Igoe vote does not appear to have introduced many new elements into the pattern of voting behavior in Chicago. The greatest shift toward the Democratic party was found in the wards inhabited largely by Negroes, which were not made the subject for special analysis in this study. The important thing to remember regarding the Igoe vote is that there was an increase in the Democratic ratio; whereas in other parts of the state there was a decrease, and at other mid-term elections in Chicago, when the balance between the parties in the city was more even, there had been decreases in the percentage of the vote received by the candidates belonging to the same party as the occupant of the White House.

1936 PRESIDENTIAL VOTE

The 1934 congressional vote foreshadowed what would happen in the presidential election of 1936. As compared with the 1932 election, President Roosevelt's popularity fell off down state, but in the city of Chicago it increased. During the campaign, the *Literary Digest* poll, the Crossley poll, and the Gallup poll failed to catch this trend in Chicago; but the Chicago *Daily Times* poll indicated that Roosevelt would pile up a bigger vote against Landon than he did against Hoover.[37] The *Times* poll evidently reached, better than the other polls, those elements which go to make up the popular basis of the Kelly-Nash machine.

A comparison of Figures 2 and 5, maps which give the 1932 and the 1936 Roosevelt votes for the different areas of the city of Chicago, shows that there has been a general shift away from the Republican party. Particularly in the so-called "Black Belt" there has been an enormous decline in the popularity of

[37] See H. F. Gosnell, "How Accurate Were the Polls?" *Public Opinion Quarterly*, I (January, 1937), 97–105.

COMMUNITY AREAS OF CHICAGO

AS ADOPTED BY CENSUS BUREAU, 1930
SHOWING
PERCENTAGE OF ROOSEVELT VOTE TO TOTAL VOTE
1936
(Source: *Public Service Leader*)

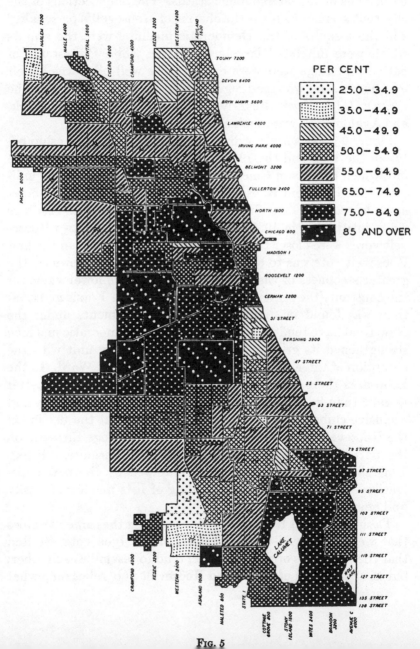

PER CENT

	25.0 – 34.9
	35.0 – 44.9
	45.0 – 49.9
	50.0 – 54.9
	55.0 – 64.9
	65.0 – 74.9
	75.0 – 84.9
	85 AND OVER

Fig. 5

Republican candidates. The areas inhabited largely by Negroes are rapidly being whipped into line with other areas inhabited by persons of similar economic status. The only sections of the city that seemed to resist the charms of Roosevelt's personality and the assaults of the Democratic machine were those units which were inhabited largely by native white Protestants of native parentage who were comfortably well off, owned their own homes, and who read regularly the *Chicago Tribune* and the *Chicago Daily News*. Beverly Hills, West Ridge, Edison Park, and Avalon Park were such areas.[38]

Figure 6 gives a scatter diagram showing the relationship between the 1932 and the 1936 Roosevelt votes by the 147 units into which the city of Chicago was divided. This dot chart indicates that President Roosevelt lost only 6 of these units, whereas he lost 26 in 1932. On the average, the Roosevelt vote was 6.6 points higher in 1936 than it was in 1932. The two Roosevelt votes were closer to each other in all respects than the first Roosevelt vote was to the Al Smith vote. This is shown by the greater steepness of the regression line and the lower value for the constant (the regression line intercepts the Y-axis at 12.08) than was found in Figure 4. Political alignments under the New Deal have tended to crystallize. The Democratic machine strengthened its grip on the electorate in every unit with the exception of three, two of which were in the First Ward. In the Loop area there were two districts where Roosevelt did better in 1932 than he did in 1936. Since there were many hotels and exclusive clubs in these units, it is probable that the decline in the Roosevelt percentage was the result of a huge turn-out on the part of the Republican residents. Furthermore, "Hinky Dink's" methods were somewhat cramped by the new registration law, which made the padding of lists much more risky and onerous.

Taking the 1936 Roosevelt vote and using the same variables that were employed in the analysis of the Igoe vote, we find that the equations of net regression tend to resemble each other; but the prediction of the second Roosevelt vote relies somewhat

[38] See Figure 5 for location of areas.

less upon the 1932 vote and somewhat more upon the ratio of foreign born.[39] The new equation may be interpreted as meaning that the average change in the 1936 Roosevelt vote for a unit change in the 1932 vote, keeping the other variables con-

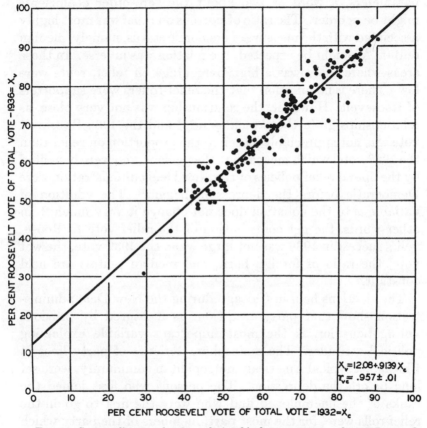

FIG. 6.—Scatter diagram showing relationship between 1932 and 1936 Roosevelt votes in 147 selected areas in Chicago.

stant, was high; whereas the average change in the 1936 vote for unit change in each of the other variables, keeping the 1932 vote and the remaining variables constant, was insignificant except in the case of the percentage of foreign born.

In order to test certain hypotheses regarding the influence of

[39] See Appendix C.

the relief vote upon the 1936 election results, it was decided to add to the foregoing equation variable w, which is the percentage of total persons who were on relief in October, 1933.[40] Before discussing the effect that this addition had upon the parameters, a word or two about the zero-order coefficients might be in order. The ratio of persons on relief was most highly associated with the measure of economic status, namely, median rental. As might be expected, the relation was inverse. In those areas where there was a high percentage on relief, rents were low. There is no question that the relief-rollers were supporters of Roosevelt. However, the relationship was not very close, as relationships go in the present study; and the 1936 Roosevelt vote was not appreciably closer to the proportion on relief than the 1932 vote, which means that the persons who were benefited by the liberal relief policies of the New Deal administration were Democratic before the depression began.[41] The addition of variable w to the equation does not change it very much.[42] In other words, the net contribution of the relief vote to Roosevelt's success in 1936 was not large when the 1932 vote, the wet vote, the ratio of foreign born, and median rentals are held constant.

The elections held in Chicago during the New Deal administration show that party tradition, as measured by previous voting behavior, is the most important variable explaining political attitudes. The main characteristics of party lines in Chicago, a typical American metropolitan community, were set long before the depression. The persons who first joined the ranks of the unemployed and who were the first to go on the relief rolls were, for the most part, members of the party which the economic crisis swept into power nationally.

Looking at the Chicago figures from a broader point of view, we can say that, if the city electorate is in any way typical of

---

[40] This information by census tracts was furnished by the courtesy of Professor Ernest W. Burgess, of the University of Chicago, who supervised the sorting of the 385,000 original cases.

[41] Using the same notation as in Table 10, the zero-order coefficients are: $r_{cw} = .536$; $r_{gw} = .314$; $r_{lw} = .516$; $r_{kw} = -.795$; $r_{vw} = .558$.

[42] See Appendix C.

the national electorate, the present study shows that in a democratic country having a two-party system, that party which
enjoys the least success nationally over a period of years which
are characterized in general by economic prosperity and a laissez
faire governmental policy tends to attract to it those elements
which have the least social prestige and economic security. In
the period from 1860 to 1932, the Republican party was the
party which normally held the reins of government at Washington, and the period was one which had no depressions comparable to the one which started in 1929. The men of wealth,
the scions of the older Protestant families, the women with
money and leisure, were attracted to the Republican party except in the South. On the other hand, the foreign born, those
who happened to emigrate recently from Catholic countries,
those who had difficulty in getting jobs in this country, those
who settled in the poorest sections of the great cities, naturally
gravitated to the Democratic party, which in the northern
cities has usually listened to the pleas of the submerged groups.

There is no question that the 1932 election brought in a new
era in American politics. As in other parts of the United States,
an increase in economic insecurity in the second largest city of
the country brought a reaction against the party in power.
However, this reaction was more pronounced in the city than
in the rural parts of the state of Illinois, and it was much more
pronounced in some sections of the metropolis than in others.
Greatest shifts were noted in the outlying lower-middle-class
areas, where there were many foreclosures or threatened foreclosures; and the smallest shifts were found in high-class hotel
areas and in the sections having many Protestant home-owners
who weathered the depression with comparatively little difficulty. The adjustment of political attitudes to changing economic conditions depends upon the economic and social status
of the individuals concerned, upon their social conditioning,
and upon the agencies of mass impression which are active in
the situation.

CHAPTER VI

CONDUCT OF PROPOSITION VOTING[1]

Proposition elections have been the battleground for many economic and political struggles in the city of Chicago. The issues voted upon have reflected the vital interests of important

MAYOR WILLIAM HALE ("BIG BILL") THOMPSON

pressure groups and agencies of mass impression. Thus, the following organizations have been among those which have taken a decided stand for or against particular measures: the Civic Federation, the Chicago Bureau of Public Efficiency, the daily newspapers, City Planning Commission, the Woman's Club, the Chicago Medical Society, the traction companies, the organized "wets" and "drys," the real estate boards, the labor organizations, the Chicago Association of Commerce, and the political par-

ties. For many years Insull and the other traction barons waged a bitter fight against the advocates of municipal ownership of local transportation systems. Edward F. Dunne, mayor and later governor, was one of the leaders of the movement for public ownership. The Democratic bosses, Brennan and Cermak, were in the front of the battle against prohibition, working in close harmony with the liquor-dealers, the *Chicago Tribune*, and the liberal elements in the city. On all questions involving public expenditures, the Chicago Bureau of Public Efficiency has been most alert, studying each question carefully from the

[1] The author is indebted to D. M. Maynard's "The Operation of the Referendum in Chicago" (University of Chicago doctoral dissertation, 1930) for part of the materials upon which this chapter is based. See also C. O. Gardner, *The Referendum in Chicago* (Philadelphia: University of Pennsylvania, 1920).

standpoint of the taxpayer and spreading its views by means of press releases and circulars.

The voters in the city of Chicago have been called upon to pass judgment upon propositions submitted to them since the middle of the nineteenth century. All state and city bond issues, all propositions providing for the annexation of territory by the city of Chicago, all modifications of the form of city government, all amendments to the state banking laws, all questions relating to the Illinois and Michigan Canal, and all state constitutional amendments must be submitted to the voters.[2] The state legislature has, from time to time, by special act, submitted other measures to a popular vote.[3] In addition, a Public Policy Act passed by the legislature in 1901 provides for the submission of any question of public policy upon the receipt of a petition signed by 25 per cent of the voters of any city or 10 per cent of the voters of the state. It is thus apparent that the voters of the city are required to act upon a narrow range of municipal and state matters, and they may act upon a much wider range of topics brought up either under the amending clause of the state constitution or under the Public Policy Act. In fact, however, the number of constitutional amendments voted upon has been extremely limited, and the high petition requirements for public-policy measures and their lack of any legal effect have kept the submission of such proposals to a minimum. As compared with a city in a state which has the optional referendum and the initiative in full force, the city of Chicago has only a truncated system of popular law-making.[4] Nevertheless, some of the questions voted upon have

[2] The Illinois constitution requires the presentation of state bond issues (Art. IV, par. 18), local bond issues, annexation proposals, modifications of city government (Art. IV, sec. 34), amendments to state banking laws (Art. XII, par. 5), laws relating to Illinois and Michigan Canal (separate section 4), and amendments to the state constitution (Art. XIV).

[3] Examples of such optional legislation are the so-called "Mueller Law" of 1903, which authorized cities to purchase and operate street railways after the law had been accepted by a popular vote, and the Boxing Law of 1925(?).

[4] Although the city council does not have the power to submit measures as it wishes, it has, in a few instances, submitted questions without any express authority. On November 2, 1926, the question as to the advisability of retaining daylight saving was pre-

been of considerable importance, and the reaction of various portions of the Chicago electorate on these issues throws light upon the character of urban democracy in the United States.

Since the adoption of the constitution of 1848, nearly 400 measures have been submitted to the voters of Chicago. All but 50 of these have been presented since 1900. In the first part of the twentieth century the perfection of the electric railway, the need for better roads as the automobile industry developed, the growing strength of the prohibition movement in the country at large, and the great faith in competency of the electorate which characterized the Progressive era brought the use of the referendum into much more general use in Chicago, as well as in other parts of the country. The high point was reached in 1928 during Mayor Thompson's administration, when 49 measures were presented to the Chicago voters, most of which involved the approval of road bonds and bond issues for other public works. Since 1930 there has been a very rapid falling-off in the number of propositions submitted. Except for two emergency-relief bond issues, no bond issues whatsoever appeared on the ballot in the years 1932–36. The number of other propositions presented has likewise been very small. The depression has so adversely affected the credit of the various governmental bodies in the city of Chicago that financing of long-term improvements has been handled largely by loans or gifts from the federal government rather than by local bond issues, which depend upon popular ratification by the voters. The number of public-opinion measures voted upon has been greatly reduced by repeal of the Prohibition Amendment and by stalemate on the traction issue.

FRAUD AND ERROR IN REFERENDUM RETURNS

While the number of measures voted upon recently has declined sharply, the problem of handling the referendum returns has remained a serious one. Particularly with reference to those

---

sented to the voters. Regarding this action, Leon Hornstein, first assistant corporation counsel, said: "The city council has no authority to place such measures on the ballot. The act of the city council was illegal; but as no one challenged it, the measure appeared on the ballot."

measures where a political party or a powerful economic group has a great deal at stake, it is difficult in Chicago to insure an honest and accurate count of the ballots. Because of the overburdening of the candidate ballot and because of defects in the election procedure, carelessness, and corruption on the part of the election officials, gross errors have crept into the official referendum returns. Since 1900, practically all local measures have been presented on separate proposition ballots. The counting of these ballots by the precinct election officials has been highly inefficient and unsatisfactory, to say the least.[5] A number of bond issues have been challenged on the ground that they did not pass as shown on the face of the returns.[6]

"Who gives a d—— about the referendum ballot?" was the cynical comment of a city hall employee, not the remark of one of the notorious River ward bosses.[7] It was based upon years of practical experience in Chicago politics.

An examination of the books at the election commissioners' office for a number of years shows a most extraordinary state of affairs. The following types of suspicious returns in various precincts have been discovered: a larger total cast on the propositions than there were registered voters; a complete failure to record any negative votes, although adjoining precincts showed a considerable body of opinion unfavorable to the measures; an identical number of "yes" and "no" votes on all measures in a much larger number of precincts than would be possible according to the laws of probability; a large number of precincts with the referendum votes ending in round numbers. An intensive analysis of the official figures for one "little ballot" containing sixteen measures showed that about one-quarter of the returns were questionable. Below are some of the actual figures found on the books. These furnish very clear presumptive evidence of fraud as well as carelessness. An actual recount made of the

[5] D. M. Maynard, "Fraud and Error in Chicago Referendum Returns," *National Municipal Review*, Vol. XIX (March, 1930).

[6] *Mac Guidwin* v. *South Park Commissioners*, 333 Ill. (1928), 58; *Chicago Daily News*, July 25, 1931.

[7] Maynard, "Fraud and Error in Chicago Referendum Returns," *op. cit.*

proposition votes in selected precincts showed that the errors were not compensating but cumulative. In these precincts the ballot thieves had stolen nearly 10 per cent of the total number of votes recorded for their favorite measures.[8]

For many years student watchers have been sent to the polls to investigate election practices, and on a number of occasions they were instructed to look out particularly for the way in which the "little ballots" were handled. In every precinct it was reported that many voters leave their proposition ballots on the floor of the voting booths. A party official who has been instructed to turn in a big vote for a given measure runs little risk in picking up and marking these discarded ballots. In a number of places it was discovered that referendum ballots are "weighed," not counted. One official divided the "yes" and "no" ballots on the first question into two piles and estimated the result. Another official carefully counted the marks for the first question and carried over the identical figures for the remaining questions. The way in which the proposition ballots are marked and counted tends, in many cases, to exaggerate the size of the vote, and in others actually to change the result.

POPULAR INTEREST IN VOTING ON REFERENDA

Political scientists generally agree that too great a burden has been placed upon the American voter. Part of this burden is in the form of proposition voting. To what extent have the principles of the short ballot been violated by overloading the "little ballot" voted upon in Chicago? What have been the responses of the Chicago electors when they have been called upon to do too much in the way of issue voting?

[8] *Ibid.*

PERCENTAGE IN FAVOR OF THE MEASURES IN THE 56 SAMPLE PRECINCTS

	Volstead Modification	Illinois and Michigan Canal	Constitutional Amendments	Road Bonds	Jail Bonds	Daylight Saving
Official count......	72.3	73.3	54.7	59.0	61.0	65.3
Recount..........	71.7	74.7	50.8	50.5	51.9	61.3
Difference........	.6	1.4	3.9	8.5	9.1	4.0

In the period from 1924 to 1936 the largest number of propositions voted upon at any one time was 32, the number submitted at the primary election of April 10, 1928. On another occasion (November 4, 1930) as many as 20 measures were voted upon, and at a third election (April 13, 1926) 19 measures were presented. In all, there were five occasions when 10 or more measures were brought before the voters at the same election. Figure 7 shows the tendency of the voters to overlook certain measures when the ballot is overweighted.

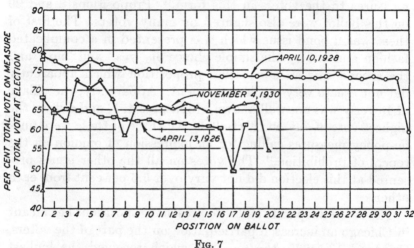

SIZE OF PROPOSITION VOTE AND POSITION ON BALLOT

PER CENT TOTAL VOTE ON MEASURE OF TOTAL VOTE AT ELECTION

POSITION ON BALLOT

FIG. 7

It is apparent from Figure 7 that there is considerable variation in the interest of the voter in measures presented on the same ballot. The way in which a measure is submitted and its position on the ballot explain some of these variations. When a "little ballot" contains 18 or more measures, there is some tendency for the interest of the voter to decline toward the end. This tendency, which we might call the "fatigue curve of voting," is most evident in the 1928 proposition elections presented in the chart. At this election, nearly 20 per cent of the voters who indicated their choice on the first measure slighted the thirty-second measure. However, there are many notable exceptions to the fatigue rule. Even in 1928 the thirty-first meas-

ure was only 5 per cent under the first. The last measure on this
ballot was an amendment to the Municipal Court Act, which
was presented in a confusing fashion.[9] The interest curve for
November 4, 1930, shows several exceptions to the rule. It is
worth while to consider the reasons for the reversal of the rule
upon that date. The first measure voted upon at this election
was an amendment to the Banking Act, which was worded in
a very technical fashion, as the accompanying sample ballot
(Fig. 8) shows. It is impossible to tell from the ballot title
what this measure was about. There is no excuse for presenting
measures to the voters in this form.[10] Propositions 8 and 20
on this ballot were also slighted by many voters. The first of
these was a bond issue which was presented in a complicated
fashion and not by the simple choice of "yes" and "no," and
the second was an annexation proposition which apparently
did not create very much excitement. Apparently, the village
of Beverly was not well known. Measures 4, 5, and 6 drew the
highest vote of any on this ballot. All three of these were public-policy measures calling for an expression of opinion on the
repeal of prohibition.[11] The votes on all the other issues presented at this election did not vary over 5.6 per cent from each
other.

The use of a separate ballot to present propositions has meant
in Chicago an increased participation on the part of the voters.
On April 13, 1926, the measure which received the highest

[9] The title read: "For or against consenting to 'An act to add Sec. 2-A' to 'An act
in relation to a Municipal court in the city of Chicago,' whereby court procedure
would authorize transfer of causes filed in the first class to the fourth class, and vice
versa, to avoid dismissal of causes erroneously filed in the wrong class."

[10] An extreme case of this type was the annexation proposal submitted on April 5,
1927. It read: "Proposition for annexation of certain property described as follows,
to wit: The Northeast Quarter (N.E. ¼) of Section Twenty-Three (23) Township Forty
(40) North, Range Twelve (12) East of the Third Principal Meridian; and all of the
Southeast Quarter (S.E. ¼) of Section Twenty-Three (23), Township Forty (40) North,
Range Twelve (12) East of the Third Principal Meridian, lying North of the Indian
Boundary line; and all of Section Twenty-Four (24), Township Forty (40) North,
Range Twelve (12) East of the Third Principal Meridian; and the North Half (N. ½)
of the Northeast Quarter (N.E. ¼) of Section Twenty-Five (25) Township Forty (40)
North Range Twelve (12) East of the Third Principal Meridian, all said property
situated in Cook County, Illinois."

[11] See below, pp. 144–50.

Issued by the Board of Election Commissioners of the City of Chicago, and ex-officio of the Cities of Chicago Heights and Berwyn, the Town of Cicero and the Villages of Summit and Evergreen Park. Election Tuesday, November 4, 1930.

For Use in All the Precincts of the City of Chicago.

Edmund K. Jarecki,
COUNTY JUDGE

SPECIMEN PROPOSITION BALLOT

BANKING LAW BALLOT

1
FOR "An Act to amend sections 1, 2, 4, 5, 7, 8, 9, 10, 11, 12, 13, 14, 15, and 15½ of 'An Act to revise the law with relation to banks and banking,' approved June 23, 1919, as amended, and to add to said Act a new section, to be known as section 11½."

AGAINST "An Act to amend sections 1, 2, 4, 5, 7, 8, 9, 10, 11, 12, 13, 14, 15, and 15½ of 'An Act to revise the law with relation to banks and banking,' approved June 23, 1919, as amended, and to add to said Act a new section, to be known as section 11½."

TO AMEND AN ACT CONCERNING JURORS

2
Shall an Act to amend "An Act concerning jurors, and to repeal certain Acts therein named," providing that women legal voters shall have the right to serve on juries and for certain exemptions from jury service, be adopted?

| YES | |
| NO | |

TO AMEND AN ACT AUTHORIZING THE APPOINTMENT OF JURY COMMISSIONERS AND THE PREPARATION OF JURY LISTS

3
Shall an Act to amend "An Act to authorize judges of courts of record to appoint jury commissioners and prescribing their powers and duties," providing for preparations by the jury commissioners of jury lists of both sexes, be adopted?

| YES | |
| NO | |

QUESTION OF PUBLIC POLICY
EIGHTEENTH AMENDMENT TO UNITED STATES CONSTITUTION

4
"Shall the Eighteenth Amendment to the Constitution of the United States, which among other things prohibits the manufacture, sale or transportation of intoxicating liquors for beverage purposes within the United States, be repealed."

| YES | |
| NO | |

QUESTION OF PUBLIC POLICY
MODIFICATION OF NATIONAL PROHIBITION ACT

5
"Shall the Congress of the United States modify the National Prohibition Act to enforce the Eighteenth Amendment to the Constitution of the United States (commonly known as the Volstead Act) so that the same shall not prohibit the manufacture, sale or transportation of beverages which are not in fact intoxicating, as determined in accordance with the laws of the respective states."

| YES | |
| NO | |

QUESTION OF PUBLIC POLICY
REPEAL OF ILLINOIS PROHIBITION ACT

6
"Shall the Illinois Prohibition Act be repealed?"

| YES | |
| NO | |

BONDS FOR FOREST PRESERVE DISTRICT, $2,500,000.00

7
Shall the bonds of the Forest Preserve District of Cook County, Illinois, in the amount of Two Million Five Hundred Thousand Dollars ($2,500,000) maturing serially Five Hundred Thousand Dollars ($500,000) one year after date and Five Hundred Thousand Dollars ($500,000) each year thereafter, in denominations of One Thousand Dollars ($1,000) and bearing interest at the rate of four (4) per centum per annum, be issued by the Forest Preserve District of Cook County, Illinois, for the purpose of building comfort stations, shelter houses and other improvements and facilities as authorized by law in the Forest Preserves of said District?

| YES | |
| NO | |

BONDS FOR COOK COUNTY HOSPITAL NURSES' DORMITORY
$2,350,000.00

8
Proposition to issue the bonds of Cook County, Illinois, to the amount of $2,350,000.00 for the purpose of providing a new Cook County Hospital Nurses' Dormitory as an addition to the present County Hospital in and for said County of Cook, and the necessary land and equipment therefor, and the levying of a tax of not to exceed three-quarters (¾) of a cent on each $100.00 of the valuation of all taxable property in said County for each of the years 1931 to 1950, both inclusive, for the purpose of paying the principal and interest of said bonds, said annual tax to be in excess of the statutory limit of thirty-two cents (32c) for the even numbered years and twenty-eight cents (28c) for the odd numbered years per One Hundred Dollars ($100.00) valuation.

FOR BONDS AND ADDITIONAL TAX in excess of the statutory limit of thirty-two cents (32c) for the even numbered years and twenty-eight cents (28c) for the odd numbered years per One Hundred Dollars ($100.00) valuation.

AGAINST BONDS AND ADDITIONAL TAX in excess of the statutory limits of thirty-two cents (32c) for the even numbered years and twenty-eight cents (28c) for the odd numbered years per One Hundred Dollars ($100.00) valuation.

BONDS FOR BRIDGE IN NORTH STATE STREET, $3,500,000.00

9
Shall bonds or obligations for the purpose of providing funds for the payment by the City of Chicago of the cost of the construction of a bridge in North State Street and approaches thereto, including the acquisition of necessary land in connection therewith, to the amount of three million five hundred ($3,500,000.00) dollars be issued by the City Council of the City of Chicago?

| YES | |
| NO | |

BONDS FOR OGDEN AVENUE IMPROVEMENT, $5,460,000.00

10 Shall bonds or obligations for the purpose of providing funds for the payment by the City of Chicago of that portion of the cost and expenses to be borne by the City of Chicago which has now accrued and may hereafter accrue in the matter of the improvement of Ogden Avenue to the amount of five million four hundred and sixty thousand ($5,460,000.00) dollars be issued by the City Council of the City of Chicago?

YES	
NO	

BONDS FOR BRIDGE IN SOUTH HALSTED STREET, $2,700,000.00

11 Shall bonds or obligations for the purpose of providing funds for the payment by the City of Chicago of the cost of the construction of a bridge in South Halsted Street and approaches thereto to the amount of two million seven hundred thousand ($2,700,000.00) dollars be issued by the City Council of the City of Chicago?

YES	
NO	

BONDS FOR RECONSTRUCTION OF VARIOUS EXISTING BRIDGES, $1,000,000.00

12 Shall bonds or obligations for the purpose of providing funds for the payment by the City of Chicago of the cost of the reconstruction of existing bridges in West Chicago Avenue, North Dearborn Street, West Division Street, (Canal), West Eighteenth Street, West Grand Avenue, North Halsted Street (Canal), West Harrison Street, East Ninety-second Street and West Van Buren Street to the amount of one million ($1,000,000.00) dollars be issued by the City Council of the City of Chicago?

YES	
NO	

BONDS FOR TRAFFIC SIGNALS, $500,000.00

13 Shall bonds or obligations for the purpose of providing funds for the payment by the City of Chicago of the cost of the construction and installation of traffic control signals to the amount of five hundred thousand ($500,000.00) dollars be issued by the City Council of the City of Chicago?

YES	
NO	

BONDS FOR ELECTRIC LIGHTING SYSTEM, $2,000,000.00

14 Shall bonds or obligations for the purpose of providing funds for the payment by the City of Chicago of the cost of the extension of the electric street lighting system of the City of Chicago to the amount of two million ($2,000,000.00) dollars be issued by the City Council of the City of Chicago?

YES	
NO	

BONDS FOR EAST FORTY-SEVENTH STREET VIADUCT, $300,000.00

15 Shall bonds or obligations for the purpose of providing funds for the payment by the City of Chicago of the cost of the real estate necessary to be acquired to construct the West approach to East Forty-seventh Street subway under the Illinois Central Railroad tracks to the amount of three hundred thousand ($300,000.00) dollars be issued by the City Council of the City of Chicago?

YES	
NO	

BONDS FOR EXTENDING INDIANAPOLIS AVENUE, $400,000.00

16 Shall bonds or obligations for the purpose of providing funds for the payment by the City of Chicago of the cost of the opening and extension of Indianapolis Avenue from Ewing Avenue to East One Hundredth Street to the amount of four hundred thousand ($400,000.00) dollars be issued by the City Council of the City of Chicago?

YES	
NO	

BONDS FOR PLAYGROUNDS AND RAINBOW PARK IMPROVEMENT, $500,000.00

17 Shall bonds or obligations for the purpose of providing funds for the payment by the City of Chicago of the cost of the construction and equipment of playgrounds, and the payment of the cost of the land necessary to be acquired therefor, including the improvement of Rainbow Park from East 75th Street to East 79th Street, to the amount of five hundred thousand ($500,000.00) dollars, be issued by the City Council of the City of Chicago?

YES	
NO	

BONDS FOR PUBLIC BENEFITS FOR STREET WIDENINGS AND IMPROVEMENTS, $4,310,000.00

18 Shall bonds or obligations for the purpose of providing funds for the payment by the City of Chicago of the amount of public benefits now due or to become due in connection with the widening and improvement of North and South Ashland Avenue, North and South Western Avenue, North LaSalle Street, and for the payment of the amount of public benefits now due or to become due during 1931 in connection with the widening and improvement of Peterson and Ridge Avenues, South Halsted Street, West Ninety-fifth Street, South Desplaines Street and Milwaukee Avenue, to the amount of four million three hundred and ten thousand ($4,310,000.00) dollars be issued by the City Council of the City of Chicago?

YES	
NO	

QUESTION OF PUBLIC POLICY
FILTRATION OF CHICAGO'S WATER SUPPLY

19 "Shall the City Council pass an ordinance providing for the filtration of Chicago's Water Supply in the interest of public health?"

YES	
NO	

ANNEXATION PROPOSITION

20	
FOR the annexation of the Village of Beverly to the City of Chicago.	
AGAINST the annexation of the Village of Beverly to the City of Chicago.	

FIG. 8

vote was the proposition to adopt the optional boxing bill, which was placed on a separate ballot.[12] At the November election of 1930 the highest vote was cast for the $14,000,000 state-wide conservation bond issue, which likewise appeared in a little ballot of its own.[13] To put it in other terms, the placing of a measure on the huge candidate ballot leads to its slighting by many voters. Before the Separate Ballot Law of 1899 went into effect, all measures were presented on the blanket ballot. In the nineties, one-half or more of the voters who marked their ballots for candidates neglected to indicate their views on the propositions. In the twentieth century, all but a few measures have been presented on separate, or so-called "little," ballots. Recent deviations from this rule have brought an enormous falling-off in the vote. Governor Emmerson was anxious to have passed a constitutional amendment which liberalized the Illinois taxation system. The question of participation is enormously important in the case of constitutional amendments, as a majority of all those voting at the election is required for the passage of an amendment. A voter who comes to the polls and marks his choices for candidates but fails to vote on a proposed contitutional amendment is in effect voting "no." Governor Emmerson thought that, if the amendment was placed on the candidate ballot, more voters would pay attention to it. How mistaken he was in this notion is shown by the fact that the constitutional amendment got 40 per cent less of the total vote cast than a measure which appeared on a separate ballot.

The problem of popular indifference to proposition voting may be approached from another angle. What variation in interest is there according to the way in which the measure gets on the ballot? Do bond issues bring a bigger vote than annexation or public-policy proposals? Some light on these questions is thrown by Table 11, which gives the percentage of the vote on measures of the total vote cast at the election for the period 1924–35 by type of submission.

[12] Percentage of the vote cast at the election, 77.5.

[13] Percentage of the vote cast at the election, 79.2.

According to the measuring-rod presented in this table, the greatest interest has been shown in special local referenda and in occasional bond issues. However, it happens that the special local referenda were presented at special local elections, at which they were major issues. Consequently, it is necessary also to consider the ratio of the total registered vote cast on the measures. These data are presented in Table 12, which gives the percentage of the total registered vote cast on measures by type of submission. In this table it is clear that the special local

TABLE 11

PERCENTAGE OF VOTE ON MEASURE OF TOTAL VOTE AT ELECTION, 1924–35

Type of Submission	30–39	40–49	50–59	60–69	70–79	80–89	90–100	Total
Bond issues, state					1	3		4
Bond issues, local			6	64	41	2	1	114
Public policy, state					4			4
Public policy, local				1	4			5
Annexation		3	4	1		2		10
Modification of city government		1	6	4		2		13
Banking laws	1	2			1			4
Constitutional amendments	2	1	2		2			7
Illinois and Michigan Canal				1	1			2
Special, local				4	1		3	8
Special, state				2				2
Total number of measures	3	7	18	77	58	9	4	173

referenda do not stand out as challenging the greatest attention of the voters. However, selected bond issues are still at the top, as far as popular interest is concerned.

These two tables show that the problem of amending the Illinois constitution is a serious one. According to both the criteria presented, it is apparent that many voters are slighting constitutional amendments.

Table 12 shows that there is a challenging situation with respect to certain bond issues. Important decisions as to the expenditures of money have on eight occasions attracted less than 30 per cent of the registered voters and on thirty-seven occasions less than 40 per cent. The rule of the majority, as far as propositions are concerned, means the rule of a minority of the registered voters. Changes in banking laws are likewise seriously neglected by many voters.

The record of the Chicago electorate on proposition voting has been about the same as in the country at large.[14] This does not mean the efficiency of the Chicago voters has been particularly high, as in some sections of the country the lack of interest on proposition voting is enormous. The best record ever achieved in Chicago was the vote on the soldier's bonus bonds

TABLE 12

PERCENTAGE OF VOTE ON MEASURE OF TOTAL REGISTRATION, 1924–35

Type of Submission	10–19	20–29	30–39	40–49	50–59	60–69	70–79	Total
Bond issues, state					1		3	4
Bond issues, local	4	4	29	48	27	2		114
Public policy, state					3	1		4
Public policy, local	3			1		1		5
Annexation	2	3	1	2	2			10
Modification of city government	1	3	5	2		2		13
Banking laws			2	1		1		4
Constitutional amendments		1	3	1	2			7
Illinois and Michigan Canal						2		2
Special, local	2	2	1	1	2			8
Special, state				2				2
Total number of measures	12	13	41	59	37	9	3	173

presented at the November election of 1922. On this measure 84 per cent of the registered vote was cast and 92 per cent of the vote recorded at the election.

In Chicago the handling of proposition voting has been seriously defective. Not only have fraud and error crept into the counting of the ballots, but obscure and confusing titles and an overloading of the ballot have led to a large amount of indifference on a number of occasions.

[14] Considering the some 1,299 state-wide measures voted upon during the period 1924–35, the author found that the mean of the percentage of the total vote on measure of the total vote cast at the election was 60.8 per cent, as compared with 62 per cent for Chicago; and that the mean of the percentage of the total vote on measure of total registration (429 cases) was 48 per cent as compared with 46.7 per cent in Chicago.

CHAPTER VII

ACTION ON TYPICAL MEASURES

There have been conflicting theories about the nonrational tendencies of the behavior of the voters in marking proposition ballots. One contention is that the voters are required to pass

SAMUEL INSULL

upon technical questions which are beyond their comprehension and that they follow the precept: when in doubt, vote "no."[1] Another view is that on measures like local bond issues the people can be depended on to vote "yes" indiscriminately because borrowing money means shifting burdens to future generations that have the bills to pay.[2] Which of these hypotheses is in accordance with the Chicago experience with the referendum?

Since the present study has emphasized the effect of the depression upon the attitudes of the voters, the propositions submitted during the past twelve years are of particular interest. The first half of this period (1924–29) was one of relative prosperity, while the last half (1930–35) was one of economic distress. During the entire period 174 measures were submitted, on 115 of which a majority of the voters voting on the measure voted "yes." The action of the voters on these measures, classified according to the way in which the measures came before them, is given in Table 13.

BOND ISSUES

As shown in Table 13, local bond issues have far exceeded in numbers any other type of measure voted upon in Chicago.

[1] W. Schumaker, "People's Rule in Oregon," *Political Science Quarterly*, XLVII (June, 1932), 242–58.

[2] E. P. Oberholtzer, *The Referendum in America* (New York, 1912), p. 503.

When the period as a whole is considered, it is apparent that there is no tendency in Chicago for the voters to approve bond issues indiscriminately on the ground that future generations will bear the burden of the expenditures. The experience of earlier periods shows the same situation.[3] When such agencies as the press, the Bureau of Public Efficiency, the Citizens' Association, the Association of Commerce, and the real estate boards conduct a vigorous campaign against a given bond issue or set of bond issues, a large number of voters follow their advice.

TABLE 13

ACTION ON MEASURES BY FORM OF SUBMISSION, 1924–35

Measures	Majority Voting "Yes"	Majority Voting "No"	Number of Measures Submitted
Bond issues, state.......	4		4
Bond issues, local.......	66	48	114
Public policy, state......	4	....	4
Public policy, local......	5	....	5
Annexation............	10	....	10
Modification of city government..............	9	4	13
Banking laws...........	4	....	4
State constitutional amendment...........	6	1	7
Illinois and Michigan Canal.................	2	....	2
Special, state...........	2	....	2
Special, local..........	6	2	8
Total.............	118	55	173

An examination of the number of bond issues that passed each year shows that the voters were favorable to borrowing for public improvements except in 1928 and 1929. The city and county bond issues which were presented in the years 1924–27 included a variety of street improvements suggested by the Chicago Plan Commission, the building of a new county court and jail, the improvement of street-lighting, and the development of parks. All of the proposals were adopted. In 1928, however, the Chicago Plan Commission, the city government, and the county board overreached themselves. At the April

[3] Gardner, *The Referendum in Chicago* (Philadelphia, 1920), pp. 11–13.

election, 31 bond issues were proposed which aggregated to over $77,000,000. Besides being the largest amount ever submitted to the Chicago voters at any time, the total was greater than the city's entire bonded debt at the time. Mayor Thompson, "Mike" Faherty, the head of the board of local improvements, and the Democratic city council were responsible for ten of the propositions, which asked for an aggregate of $48,500,000 to complete street improvements already started. James Simpson, then the head of Marshall Field and Company and the chairman of the Chicago Plan Commission, urged the submission of bonds for new street improvements, and, according to one account, promised that all the newspapers would support the issues.[4] The 1928 primary was a very unfavorable occasion for such staggering financial proposals to be made, since the city administration was then under severe fire. Thompson and Faherty were being sued for money paid to the real estate experts hired by the city in connection with street improvements authorized by bond issues passed during a prior Thompson administration. In addition the city administration was being vigorously attacked on account of its Insull traction "deals" and its handling of the crime situation. Because of the assassination of one anti-Thompson ward boss and the bombing of the homes of two anti-Thompson leaders, Deneen and Swanson, the primary was called the "pineapple primary." The public was at last aroused. Scare headlines in the press drove home the more sedate recommendations of civic organizations such as the Chicago Bureau of Public Efficiency and the Citizens' Association.[5] All of the bond issues were overwhelmingly defeated.

In the fall of 1928 a much more modest attempt was made to

[4] William H. Stuart, *The 20 Incredible Years* (Chicago, 1935), p. 361.

[5] Chicago Bureau of Public Efficiency, *The Bond Issues To Be Voted upon April 10, 1928* (pamphlet, 1928), said in part: "Not only is it an excessively long proposition ballot containing 32 measures most of which were bond issues, but it was built up by logrolling methods and by the offensive use of political and other pressure. The defeat of all the pending city bond issues would help to discourage the unbridled and wasteful expenditure of bond funds and would also have the wholesome effect of making officials more careful and straightforward in presenting future projects to the voters."

win approval for street-improvement bonds. The proposals aggregated to $24,500,000, about one-third of the amount voted on at the April election. While the Bureau of Public Efficiency recognized that "bond issues furnished a most fruitful source of extravagance, waste, and other abuses during the prior incumbency of the present city officials," it recommended the passage of the measures because of the private interests involved.[6] However, the public still manifested its lack of confidence in the city administration. In the summer the Circuit Court had rendered a judgment of close to $3,000,000 against Thompson, Harding, and Faherty in the expert fee case, a judgment which was immediately appealed to a higher court. All of the newspapers, except the *Chicago Evening American*, demanded the resignation of Faherty as president of the board of local improvements; but Thompson and his lieutenant stood firm. The unfavorable attitude of the press and the continued distrust of the Thompson machine led to another defeat of the bond issues on the proposition ballot.

After the fall election of 1928 a series of investigations of the Sanitary District and the county board were started which resulted in discrediting a number of Democratic, as well as Republican, party leaders. Serious charges of graft and extravagance were made in connection with the construction work of the Sanitary District, the building of the new county jail building, and the purchase of lands for the county park system. In addition the reassessment made many voters tax conscious. When the county board, the city council, and the Lincoln Park District brought bond issues aggregating to $47,700,000 before the voters at a special election held in the fall of 1929, all three of these governmental bodies were repulsed. Although the vote was closer than it had been the preceding year, the negative, distrusting mood of the electorate persisted.

Not until the spring of 1930 was the attitude of the voters changed toward the authorization of bond issues. By this time, unemployment began to be a very serious problem and the pas-

[6] Chicago Bureau of Public Efficiency, *The Bond Issues To Be Voted upon November 6, 1928* (pamphlet, 1928).

sage of the measures was urged as a means of providing work.
In the April election all of the bond issues which concerned
the payment of judgments rendered in condemnation proceedings passed; but the Ogden Avenue proposition, which called
for new construction work, was defeated. Finally, in the fall of
1930, when the third Thompson administration was nearing a
close, the Ogden Avenue and other street improvements were
supported by the voters.

In a preceding chapter, use was made of a November, 1930,
bond issue as a measure of the public's willingness to accept
governmental expenditures.[7] The measure selected was the
$14,000,000 state conservation and forest preserves and public
recreation ground bond issue, which was opposed by an evening
and a morning paper and by the Bureau of Public Efficiency.
In the present connection it is of interest to discuss the relationship of the vote on this bond issue to the other variables
studied in the 147 areas into which the city was divided. The
closest relationship was an inverse one with the variable indicating the percentage of home-owners.[8] In other words, in those
sections of the city where there was a large proportion of home-
owners, the affirmative vote for this bond issue was usually low;
and in those sections of the city where there were few home-
owners, the affirmative vote tended to be high. However, there
were some exceptions to the latter tendency in the high-class
apartment house areas on the North Side, where the ratio of
home-owners was low and the proportion of "yes" votes on the
bond issue was also relatively low. Affirmative votes on the
bond issue tended to be positively associated with affirmative
votes on the wet issue, straight-ticket voting, and also with
votes for Democratic candidates at different elections. Surprising as it may seem, there was not a very close relationship between economic status, as measured by median rental, and
votes on the bond issue. One would expect that those who paid
higher rents would tend to vote against the bond issue because
of the resulting tax burden, and that those who paid low rents

[7] See above, p. 99.   [8] $r_{fl} = -.57$.

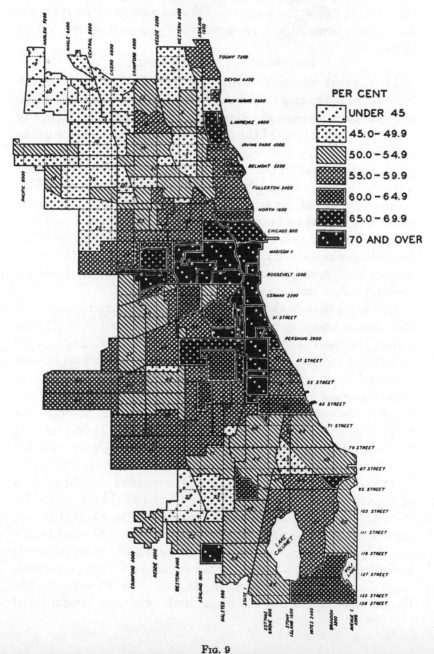

COMMUNITY AREAS OF CHICAGO

AS ADOPTED BY CENSUS BUREAU, 1930
SHOWING

PERCENTAGE VOTING "YES" ON 1930 BOND ISSUE

(Source: Board of Election Commissioners)

PER CENT

UNDER 45

45.0 - 49.9

50.0 - 54.9

55.0 - 59.9

60.0 - 64.9

65.0 - 69.9

70 AND OVER

FIG. 9

would vote for the issue since it might mean more work for laboring-class people. There was only a slight tendency for the areas to follow this pattern. Persons who pay high rents are not always conscious of their indirect payment of real estate taxes.

THE TRANSPORTATION QUESTION

At frequent intervals during the past thirty-five years the traction issue has come before the Chicago voters. One solution after another has been indorsed, but the city is still far from any permanent settlement of the problem. In the first decade of the twentieth century the voters expressed their preference for municipal ownership; but when the crucial measure was voted upon in 1906, the three-fifths majority was not attained. Following this defeat for the advocates of municipal ownership, the forces in favor of private ownership have gained steadily. The 1907 ordinance which was adopted by the voters provided for a temporary solution of the traction problem, as far as the surface lines were concerned; but it left the consideration of a comprehensive traction scheme for the future.

A number of mayors in succession tried their hand at solving the traction problem but met with failure in each case. Mayor Carter Harrison II supported a grandiose plan called the "comprehensive scheme of 1914." The press was unanimous in condemning it, and the voters would have none of it. The city council proposed an elaborate plan in 1918 which provided for a municipally constructed, but privately operated, subway system. This scheme met the opposition of Mayor Thompson and the labor groups and was defeated. Mayor Dever and his Democratic colleagues brought forward a scheme in 1925 which had the approval of Boss Brennan. It provided a novel method of financing by traction certificates which could be acquired by the city. While the surface lines supported it, Samuel Insull, representing the elevated lines, was opposed to it because he felt the valuations were too low. For various and sundry reasons, including complaints regarding the excessively high valuations, three former mayors—Harrison, Dunne, and Thompson—the Hearst newspapers, and the Municipal Ownership League lined up against the proposal. It was defeated by a three-to-two vote and marked a serious setback for the Brennan Democratic organization.

No other traction ordinance came before the voters until 1930. This plan represented the united efforts of the City Council Committee on Local Transportation and its subcommittee, aided by the Citizens' Traction Settlement Committee, headed by James Simpson. It provided for a comprehensive, unified local transportation system, operated under a terminable permit by one corporate management and subject to the control of a local commission of three members. During the first ten years of its existence the company was to spend $200,000,000 for extensions, equipment, additions, and improvements; and the city was to build a subway system, the cost of which was to be met by use of the city traction fund and by special assessments levied upon property especially benefited.

Mayor Thompson favored the plan; and in his speech made on the occasion of the signing of the ordinance, he stressed the employment which the extensions would create. Samuel Insull also came out publicly in favor of the plan in a speech at the annual banquet of the Chicago Stock Exchange.[9] The force of the depression was not fully felt as yet; and Insull, apparently at the height of his power, could talk of a coming boom. Blindly optimistic, he had no intimation of the forces which were soon to sweep him off his high pinacle. At the time, business groups, labor organizations, all the daily newspapers except one, and many civic organizations were carried along by the swelling tide in favor of the ordinance.

The opposition to the plan was led by such men as Harold Ickes, former Mayor Carter Harrison, Donald Richberg, and William Holly. Quixotic crusaders, voices crying in the wilderness, they nevertheless kept up their efforts until the end. Ickes attacked the ordinance on the ground that it failed to include a forfeiture clause, that the valuations fixed were excessive, that the return allowed to the city was inadequate, that it provided no means of enforcing the duty of the transit company

[9] *Chicago Tribune*, May 13, 1930.

with respect to betterments and extensions, and that it was in effect a perpetual franchise.[10] The efforts of the Citizens' Committee against the traction ordinance were futile. However, it is interesting to note that the above-mentioned leaders of the opposition were chosen to fill important positions in President Roosevelt's New Deal administration. Their counsel was rejected at home but they were looked to for national leadership.

The final vote on the measure at the special July election was as follows: 325,837 for the ordinance and 56,690 against it. The people were sick of the traction mess and thought that something might be done.

Insull, the bankers, the real estate men, the labor unions, the steel industry, the car manufacturers, and the general public were destined never to reap any benefits from this victory. Before the new company could be organized, Insull found himself in financial and other difficulties. Legal obstacles were placed in the way of the subway by Loop real estate interests. Extension after extension of the acceptance date was voted by the city council; but finally, in 1934, Mayor Kelly urged the council not to grant another extension and the ordinance passed into history as another futile attempt to solve the traction problem. Mayor Kelly gave as his ostensible reason for scrapping the plan the opinion that the valuations were far too high under the existing circumstances. The view was also expressed that an accounting of the city transit fund might have proved embarrassing at the time.

THE PROHIBITION ISSUE

Now that the Eighteenth Amendment to the United States Constitution has been repealed, it is of historical interest to trace the steps by which sentiment unfavorable to prohibition was fostered. While the prominent dry leaders scoffed at polls taken of public sentiment on this issue during the prohibition era, the events of the past few years have clearly shown how shortsighted these gentlemen were. The *Literary Digest* national polls on this issue conducted in the years 1922, 1930, and

[10] *Ibid.*, June 5, 1930.

1932 showed a tremendous increase in wet sentiment.[11] These
polls had been boycotted by the drys, and the results were characterized as preposterous. Not until the eve of repeal did the
dry organizations like the Anti-saloon League and the Women's
Christian Temperance Union wake up to the fact that they had
been lulled to sleep by the supposed security of a constitutional
amendment.

In the city of Chicago there were four public-opinion votes on
the liquor question during the prohibition era. An analysis of
the influences at work at each of these votings throws some
light upon what was happening to public sentiment on this

TABLE 14

COMPARISON OF RETURNS ON PROHIBITION REFERENDA

Year	Number Voting "Wet" (1)	Number Voting "Dry" (2)	Total Number Voting on Measure (3)	Total Vote at Election (4)	Total Registration (5)	Percentage of Vote on Measure of Total Vote at Election (3 of 4)	Percentage of Registered Vote Cast on Measure (3 of 5)	Percentage Voting Wet (1 of 3)
1919, April 1, men.......	276,817	70,165	346,982	440,069	500,064	82.4	69.4	79.8
1919, April 1, women....	129,373	77,014	206,387	258,851	306,920	61.9	67.3	62.7
1919, April 1, total......	406,190	147,179	553,369	698,920	806,984	75.0	68.5	74.5
1922, Nov. 7, total......	500,757	110,707	611,464	736,617	804,648	84.0	76.0	81.9
1926, Nov. 2, total......	426,966	165,885	592,851	756,652	876,509	78.4	67.6	72.0
1930, Nov. 4, total......	535,071	145,401	680,472	937,097	1,264,234	72.6	53.8	78.6
1933, June 5, ratification of Twenty-first Amendment, total..........	604,664	52,459	657,123	695,445	1,498,314	94.5	43.8	92.0

much-debated question in a typical metropolitan community.
The *Literary Digest* poll for the state of Illinois showed a steady
increase of opinion favorable to repeal, but the public-policy
measures show fluctuations in the wet and dry sentiment. Table
14 presents some comparative figures on the issue. The question was not presented in exactly the same form at each of these
elections, but the wording was sufficiently similar to separate
the wets from the drys.

The wet and dry question appeared for the first time in April,
1919, as a local public-policy measure under the title, "Shall
Chicago Become Anti-saloon Territory?" Phillip I. Yarrow,
the head of the Chicago Dry Federation, was active in starting

[11] C. E. Robinson, *Straw Votes* (New York, 1932), pp. 147 ff.

the circulation of the petitions for this measure late in 1917.
Within a short time a petition with nearly 150,000 names on it
was presented; but this was challenged by the wets, and a court
order compelling the placing of the question on the ballot was
not obtained until 1919.[12] By that time the issue was of no
immediate importance, as national wartime prohibition was
soon to go into effect. The dry leaders were completely indifferent regarding the fate of the measure which they had sponsored. On the eve of the election Yarrow said, "We haven't
spent a cent or wasted a postage stamp in soliciting votes at the
coming election."[13] On the other hand, the wets, led by Anton
J. Cermak, who was then bailiff of the Municipal Court, were
extremely active and spent large sums on newspaper advertising. The *Chicago Tribune*[14] advised a negative vote on the
ground that prohibition was an infringement of personal lib-
erty. Three-fourths of those who voted on the measure voted
wet.

In 1922 Boss Brennan and his lieutenant Cermak were active
in placing on the ballot a public-policy measure calling for an
expression of opinion on the modification of the Volstead Prohibition Act which defined intoxicating beverages at one-half
of 1 per cent. The proposition was backed by the local branch
of the National Association Opposed to the Prohibition Amendment, which spent money on newspaper advertisements. The
dry organizations again felt that it was useless for them to rally
a big vote against the measure, and they merely advised their
own members to vote "no." Appearing first on the proposition
ballot was the soldier's bonus measure, which attracted most of
the publicity. However, the *Chicago Tribune*[15] continued its
editorials against prohibition. The fact that the percentage of
the registered vote cast on the question was much higher in 1922
than in 1919 was undoubtedly the result of the great interest
aroused in the bonus issue. More attention was paid to the

[12] *Chicago Herald and Examiner*, March 30, 1919.

[13] *Chicago Tribune*, March 31, 1919.

[14] March 27, 1919.   [15] November 3, 1922.

little ballots than at any previous election. The returns indicated a marked increase in wet sentiment.

By 1926 the city had been under the prohibition regime for seven years. The Brennan-Cermak wet forces secured the submission of a state-wide public-policy measure at the November election which again raised the question of modifying the Volstead Act. While the Women's Christian Temperance Union advised its members to ignore the wet referendum, and the Anti-saloon League characterized the measure as a "fake referendum inspired by outlawed liquor interests," a local women's organization vigorously urged the defeat of the proposition. The dry organizations were aware of the movement directed toward the repeal of the Eighteenth Amendment, but they felt so secure that they scoffed at this movement. "Why should we go out and retake a frontier which we already occupy?" was the question raised in the *American Issue*, the official organ of the Anti-saloon League. In an editorial replying to this position, the *Chicago Evening Post*[16] said, "Don't heed the craven, stupid urging of the Anti-saloon League to ignore the Brennan referendum vote number." On the other hand, the wet forces were not quite as active as they had been on previous occasions. "Those who were opposed to Volsteadism will vote 'yes' on the proposition," was the editorial comment of the *Chicago Tribune*, which upheld the measure as a fair test of public sentiment. However, the organized wets were either discouraged or waiting their time. As compared with the 1922 poll, fewer people voted upon the measure; and of those who did vote, 10 per cent more were on the dry side.

The 1930 referendum on the repeal of the Eighteenth Amendment clearly showed that the 1926 poll gave a false view of the trend of public sentiment in Chicago on the prohibition question. The city was not becoming drier but, if anything, a little wetter. In the 1928 presidential election campaign, Al Smith, standing on a wet platform, nearly carried the city, which normally gave the Republican candidate for president 70 per cent of the total vote. With reference to the 1930 referendum, Boss

[16] October 27, 1926.

Cermak and the Thompson and Harding factions of the Republican party found themselves together against the drys. In addition, the Hearst papers came out for repeal in this year. The offensive was clearly in the hands of the wets, who copied the techniques of the drys of the preprohibition era. Before the Eighteenth Amendment was passed, the drys blamed the iniquitous "saloon" for a multitude of social ills, such as waywardness, prostitution, crime, poverty, and corruption. After a few years' experience under the dry regime, the wets began to blame prohibition for bootlegging, lawlessness, crime corruption, and poison-liquor deaths.[17] One of the editors of a leading daily boasted to the author about the role of his paper in discrediting prohibition. When the question came up in 1933 as to the election of wet or dry delegates to the state convention to consider the repeal of the Eighteenth Amendment, 91 per cent of the Chicago voters who took part in the election voted for the wet delegates.

It is now of interest to consider the character of the voters who voted wet in contrast to those who were on the dry side. At the time of the 1919 referendum on the liquor question the votes of the men and the women were kept separate in Illinois. As Table 14 indicates, the men opposed prohibition at this time by a vote of four to one, whereas the women opposed it by less than two to one. In six of the thirty-five wards into which the city was then divided, the women actually voted dry.[18] In all the other wards the women were drier than the men, but there was considerable spread between the differences. The vote of the men and women was nearest alike in the lower West Side, inhabited largely by Czechs, Jews, and Poles;[19] while the greatest spread (about one-quarter of the women voted drier than the men) was found in the communities of Hyde Park, Woodlawn, Englewood, and Beverly Hills on the South Side and in Rogers Park and Uptown on the North Side. In general, the

[17] P. H. Odegard, *The American Public Mind* (New York, 1930), p. 180.

[18] Wards 6, 7, 9, 25, 32, and 33 (1911 ward lines). These roughly correspond to census communities 41, 42, 67–75, 1, and 2.

[19] Ward 10, which roughly corresponds to census community 31.

dry vote was found in the higher rental areas where the native white of native parentage pedominated.

Since 1920 the votes of men and women have not been kept separately in Illinois. However, in connection with the 1930 election an attempt was made to study the influence of women's votes indirectly. The methods used and the basic figures have already been presented in a preceding chapter.[20] It was found that in those areas where the ratio of women registered voters to total registered was high, there the ratio of dry votes was also high.[21] It may be inferred from this that in 1930 the women in Chicago were still much drier than the men.

The relation of the wet vote to the other variables studied is also of interest. A comparison of Figure 10 showing the wet and dry vote in 1930 with the maps for the Roosevelt vote shows a close resemblance (omitting the areas of Negro concentration). The wet vote was also closely associated with the Smith vote. In those areas where Al Smith polled a large vote, the proportion of wet voters was high. However, there was a loosening of the relationship between the wet vote and Democratic vote in 1934, owing no doubt to the fact that the repeal issue had been settled by this time and the attention of the voter was attracted by other considerations. The study also shows that the Catholics, the foreign born, the unemployed, the persons who pay the lowest rents, and the non-home-owners tend to be wet. Inversely, the Protestants, the native whites of native parentage, the employed, the persons paying the highest rents, the home-owners, and the persons with superior educational attainments tend to be drier than the average for the city. Persons who vote dry also tend to be more independent of party ties and constitute an important bloc in the body of split-ticket voters who follow the recommendations of the churches, civic organizations, and the press.

TAX-AMENDMENT VOTES

Among the most important questions voted upon by the Chicago electorate are amendments to the Illinois constitution.

[20] See above, pp. 98.   [21] See Table 10, above, p. 109.

COMMUNITY AREAS OF CHICAGO

AS ADOPTED BY CENSUS BUREAU, 1930
SHOWING

PERCENTAGE VOTING "WET" ON 1930 REPEAL REFERENDUM
(Source: Board of Election Commissioners)

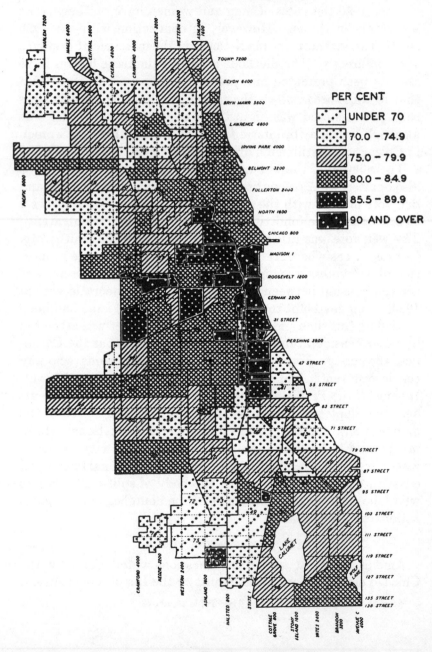

PER CENT

UNDER 70
70.0 – 74.9
75.0 – 79.9
80.0 – 84.9
85.5 – 89.9
90 AND OVER

FIG. 10

Since the amending clause requires that proposed amendments shall be approved by a majority of the electors voting at the general election, the size of the vote cast on the measure is a matter of great importance. A person who comes to the polls at a general election and fails to vote on an amendment which is being proposed is in effect voting no. Cook County now has over one-half of the total population of the state, and an amendment which did not carry the county would ordinarily have little chance of passing.

Of the constitutional questions which have been voted upon in Illinois during the past twenty years, the tax amendments have been of leading significance. There is no division of informed opinion that the present system of collecting revenue for state and local governments in Illinois is so fundamentally unsound, obsolete, unfair, and ineffective as to result in an unbearable situation. Rates have been excessively increased, and yet the city and the board of education has been unable to obtain adequate revenue from the general property tax, upon which they must chiefly rely. This tax is inequitable and discriminatory as between individuals, localities, and classes of property. Reference has already been made to the corruption which grew out of this system.[22]

Tax-amendment proposals were brought before the voters in 1916, 1926, and 1930. These amendments were not the same in all three cases, but the differences were minor. The purpose of each proposal was to allow more discretion to the Illinois general assembly regarding taxation. In effect they abrogated the clause of the constitution regarding uniformity and permitted the newer forms of taxation, such as the income tax. The votes on these measures are presented in Table 15.

This table reveals a remarkable shift in public opinion on this issue. In 1930, when the local governments were never in such desperate need for new sources of revenue, the voters overwhelmingly turned down the possibility of constitutional relief. What were some of the influences which caused the voters to act in such an apparently irrational fashion?

[22] See above, pp. 7, 77.

At the election of 1916 the tax-amendment proposal was unanimously indorsed by all of the Chicago newspapers. The *Chicago Tribune*[23] declared in an editorial: "Decent opinion is not divided. No fair argument against it has been presented." "There was no opposition to the measure," declared the *Chicago Daily News*,[24] "since the sound arguments are all in its favor." The Hearst papers likewise came out in favor of the amendment. In addition the Democratic and Republican parties both gave their workers orders to call attention to the amendment on the little ballot. The measure carried Chicago but lost downstate.

TABLE 15

NUMBER AND PERCENTAGE OF VOTERS IN CHICAGO FAVORING
TAX AMENDMENTS, 1916, 1926, AND 1930

Year	Total Registration	Total Vote at Election	Vote For	Vote Against	Total Vote on Measure	Percentage of Vote on Measure to Total Vote at Election	Percentage of Vote on Measure to Total Registration	Percentage of Vote in Favor of Measure to Total Vote on Measure	Percentage of Vote in Favor to Total Voting at Election
(1)	(2)	(3)	(4)	(5)	(6)	(7)	(8)	(9)	(10)
1916..........	504,674	487,210	244,006	117,305	361,311	74.1	71.7	67.5	50.2
1926..........	876,509	756,652	244,708	201,961	446,669	59.0	51.0	54.8	32.3
1930..........	1,264,234	937,097	146,044	217,735	363,779	39.8	28.7	40.2	15.6

Ten years later the measure was again proposed at a general congressional election in substantially the same form. However, this time the papers were divided in their support of the measure. The Hearst papers, the *Post*, and the *News* were in favor of the amendment; but the *Tribune* (in true form) reversed itself and found a new definition for "decent" opinion. "We must clean up the state government before we alter the legislature's taxing powers," ran a *Tribune*[25] editorial. "Those who produce the wealth of the state will vote against the amendment unless they are willing to see their welfare become a pawn in a game of political control" continued the argument of the paper. Here is perhaps a real clue to the situation. In 1916 Joseph Patterson,

[23] November 6, 1916.   [24] November 2, 1916.   [25] October 28, 1926.

a man with liberal tendencies, had some voice in determining the policies of the paper, while in 1926 he had relinquished the control to his cousin, Colonel Robert R. McCormick, who was opposed to heavy taxation of the higher incomes.[26]

The amendment had been drafted by a committee representing the co-operation of numerous state-wide organizations, including such diverse groups as the bankers, the labor unions, the farmers, the teachers, the real estate operators, and civic organizations. The Illinois Chamber of Commerce and the Illinois Manufacturers' Association worked hard to defeat the measure. While a majority of those Chicagoans voting on the measure were in favor of it, the vote fell far short of reaching a majority of those voting at the election.

In 1930 the general assembly, urged on by Governor Emmerson and various civic groups, again brought a tax amendment before the voters. This time the forces opposing the amendment were augmented by several important newspapers. The Hearst papers and the *Daily News* joined the *Tribune* in fighting the amendment. For some time Hearst had been losing his earlier liberal ideas, and he was becoming more outspoken in his opposition to taxes which might place a burden on his properties.[27] Victor Lawson, the liberal proprietor of the *News*, died in 1925; and his paper came more and more under the sway of interests that opposed tax reform. The Chicago papers were opposed to the amendment in part because they felt that it would bring an income tax and other forms of taxation which would be imposed by downstate at the expense of the inhabitants of the city.[28]

The enormous falling-off in the popular interest in voting on this measure was in part due to mechanical factors. Governor Emmerson thought that by putting the amendment on the general candidate ballot it would get a larger poll. It is apparent from column 7 of Table 15 that this was a very much mistaken conception. The percentage of the vote on the measure

[26] "The Chicago Tribune," *Fortune*, IX (May, 1934), 101–13.

[27] F. Lundberg, *Imperial Hearst* (New York, 1936), pp. 265 ff.

[28] *Chicago Tribune*, May 16, 1930.

to total registration dropped from 51 to 28 per cent by this change in the method of presentation. While in other states the depression seemed to make the voters more willing to accept tax reform, it did not have this effect in Illinois.

What has been the nature of the response of various elements of the electorate to the tax amendments? An analysis of the detailed returns shows that the behavior of the voters has not been as consistent on this issue as on the wet and dry issue. Taxation is a technical subject which is difficult for the layman to understand. It seems almost impossible to overcome the indifference of the citizen who cannot visualize what an antiquated tax system does to him. When such a citizen does happen to glance at newspaper articles on the subject, he is likely to find conflicting views and become more confused.

On the eve of one of the tax-amendment elections, 600 registered voters, scattered over 70 precincts, were interviewed by field investigators in order to determine their attitude toward the question.[29] While the proportion of those interviewed who expected to vote in favor of the measure was higher than the actual percentage in the city at large who voted for the measure, the sample showed some interesting variations as between different social groups. The expectancy not to vote on the measure was most pronounced among the younger citizens, the women, the persons with little or no schooling, the foreign born, the Negroes, and those who paid low rentals. Ignorance of the specific question caused many abstentions, although one-half of those who admitted that they knew nothing of the question expected to vote anyway. Those who had read the measure were much more interested in voting on it than those who had not. Those who expected to vote in favor of the measure were relatively more numerous among the young voters, the women, the persons with high-school or college education, the native whites, the Negroes, and those who paid moderate rentals. About one-fifth of those interviewed said that they relied upon the press for information and guidance on such matters. Almost

[29] D. M. Maynard, "The Operation of the Referendum in Chicago" (University of Chicago doctoral thesis, 1930).

one-third trusted their own judgment. The remainder relied upon friends, business associates, and civic organizations.

The official returns in general bear out the findings of the field investigation. Affirmative votes on tax-amendment propositions were relatively more numerous in neighborhoods where there were larger numbers of women voters, higher proportions of high-school graduates, a preponderant number of native whites, and where median rentals were slightly above the average. However, there were certain striking exceptions. In the River wards immediately surrounding the Loop, where property was depreciated for residential purposes, there was a relatively large proportion of favorable votes. These wards are among the so-called "controllable wards," and it is likely that the result was the product of intimidation and election corruption.

SUMMARY

The experience of the voters in Chicago with the referendum shows that there is no general tendency for them to accept or reject measures blindly. In other words, discrimination of some sort has been exercised. Bond issues have been accepted when backed by the press, business, and civic organizations, and they have been rejected when unfavorable publicity has undermined the confidence of the public in the efficiency and honesty of the spending authorities. On such technical questions as the traction issue and the taxation system the voters have sometimes floundered in a sea of conflicting claims and interpretations. Because of the character of the Chicago agencies of mass impression, the voters have been unable, as yet, to solve these problems. Tax reform in particular has been blocked by a hostile press and an indifferent public.

CHAPTER VIII

RELATION OF THE PRESS TO VOTING[1]

One of the paradoxes of Chicago politics during the New Deal administration has been the increase in Roosevelt's popularity, as shown by the 1936 vote, in spite of the overwhelming opposition of the press during the preceding two years. The combined city circulation of the opposition newspapers was over a million and a half, while the daily paper which supported Roosevelt had about one-third of a million readers. It is said in a number of places that the city of Chicago was the best illustration in 1936 of the declining political power of the press.[2]

COLONEL FRANK KNOX OF THE
CHICAGO DAILY NEWS

The present chapter will demonstrate that the situation was not as simple as it appeared to many observers. A closer examination shows that the press has been more powerful during the Roosevelt administration than the superficial commentators think. The application of some well-known statistical techniques reveals this in a striking fashion.

Another one of the paradoxes of Chicago politics was the great political vitality of Mayor Thompson during the prosperous twenties in the face of a highly unfavorable press. It was said that a machine did not need newspaper support and could defy public opinion with impunity for long periods of time. In the pages that follow, an endeavor will be made to show

[1] The author is indebted to Miss Margaret Schmidt for assistance in preparing this chapter.

[2] "The Press Loses the Election," *New Republic*, LXXXIX (November 18, 1936), 63.

how the press eliminated the strong Thompson machine. The daily newspapers may not be the most powerful of all agencies of mass impression, but they are still to be reckoned with by all realistic politicians. They may be able to swing a section of the electorate which holds the balance of power upon crucial occasions.

The present study of the role of the press in a metropolitan community of the United States holds no brief for the Chicago newspapers. It merely endeavors, in as objective and scientific manner as possible, to present the situation and to draw such conclusions and generalizations as seem warranted.

There are many difficulties confronting any attempt to estimate the role of the press in the democratic process. Are the newspapers molders or followers of public opinion? How can the incidence of the policies of the press be separated from the many other complex variables which are woven together in a complicated pattern?

NEWSPAPER HOME COVERAGE

At first sight the task looks like an impossible one; but a combination of events in Chicago led the author to be bold enough to make an attempt. The breaking-up of census data into small units called "census tracts" makes it possible to relate certain social and economic variables to voting behavior.[3] The taking of a newspaper home-coverage census by the *Chicago Daily News* in 1933–34 furnished a quantitative index for the different Chicago newspapers which could be fitted to the same electoral and census units.[4]

Before discussing the statistical analysis it will be necessary to describe in more detail the character of the different variables involved. The daily-newspaper home-coverage study made by the *Chicago Daily News* was designed to help the advertising

---

[3] E. W. Burgess and C. Newcomb (eds.), *Census Data of the City of Chicago 1930* (Chicago, 1933). Election returns were obtained from the *Chicago Daily News Almanac and Yearbook*, the *Public Service Leader*, and the records of the board of election commissioners of Chicago.

[4] Chicago Daily News, *Daily Newspaper Home Coverage in Metropolitan Chicago* (Chicago, 1934).

department of that paper. The methods employed in conducting this survey were not ideal for our purposes. In the final report of this survey the following definition was given of "home-coverage":

A newspaper was credited as having home coverage if it regularly (at least three times a week) entered and stayed in the home. The test of morning-paper home coverage was whether the paper regularly entered the home during the morning and remained during the day. A family receiving a morning paper which was taken away by some member of the household (in the morning) was not considered as receiving home coverage in the morning-paper field. The number of such cases was less than 2 per cent of the families interviewed.[5]

This method does not give the total circulation figures for the daily papers, but it furnishes an index as to the relative popularity of the different newspapers in a given area. There is no special reason to suppose that the underestimation of the circulation of the morning papers which results from this method would be any greater in one area than in another. The procedure gives a useful guide to the variability of newspaper circulation as between different districts.[6]

It was found that the ratio of families receiving no regular daily newspaper coverage ranged from 2 per cent in some localities to as high as 57 per cent in others. In the scatter diagrams which were constructed for the different pairs of variables the areas in which there were large numbers of persons who took no newspapers proved to be atypical. Sometimes these units exaggerated, and at other times they concealed, the character of relationships. The people in Chicago who read no daily paper published in English tended to vote in blocs.

Difficulties were also presented by the districts in which Negroes constituted a large proportion of the population. These

[5] *Ibid.*, Part VII.

[6] In 1931 the Chicago Tribune issued a *Book of Facts*, which gives a geographical distribution of the *Tribune* circulation for 48 city districts. The Tribune's figures included news stand sales as well as home deliveries. Consequently, the figures would not be comparable to the home-coverage data of the *News*. However, it was assumed that there should be some relationship. The coefficient of correlation between the Tribune's own figures and the figures for the *Tribune* given in the home-coverage study is .72 ($n = 23$).

units had opposite political tendencies to those inhabited by whites of similar economic status. Not until after 1932 was there any indication that the Negroes were affected by the city-wide drift to the Democratic party. The areas in which there were large numbers of colored voters were so far out of line politically that it was thought advisable to omit them altogether.[7] The findings of the study apply to a sample of the white population of the city of Chicago.

The home-coverage newspaper survey was made under the supervision of Professor James L. Palmer, of the University of Chicago; and a former assistant of his was employed by the *Chicago Daily News* to supervise the details of field work, editing, and tabulation. The investigators were, for the most part, university-trained men; and at least 10 per cent of the persons interviewed by each man were rechecked by supervisors. For purposes of the present study, 47 areas were selected from all parts of the city. Figure 11, which shows the percentage of home-coverage of the *Daily News*, gives the geographical distribution of these areas. In these regions there were 195,919 families, of which 94,391 were interviewed in connection with the newspaper home-coverage project. The total number of registered voters in the areas was 279,054, which was 22 per cent of the registration for the entire city. Two morning newspapers—the *Tribune* and the *Herald and Examiner*—and three evening papers—the *News*, the *American*, and the *Times*—were chosen because of their size and importance.[8] In the areas taken, the *News* had the highest average home-coverage and also the greatest amount of variation; next came the *Tribune* and the *American*; while the *Herald and Examiner* and the *Times* lagged far behind these two.

Since the 1929 crash the position of the older Chicago newspapers, as far as their city circulation is concerned, has re-

[7] Four units in which the Negro population was 20 per cent or over were dropped. For an analysis of the voting behavior of Negroes in Chicago, see H. F. Gosnell, *Negro Politicians* (Chicago, 1935), pp. 15–92.

[8] There is one other daily published in Chicago which is printed in English, the *Journal of Commerce*, but it was not included in the home-coverage survey. The areas left blank on the map were not covered in the present study.

COMMUNITY AREAS OF CHICAGO

AS ADOPTED BY CENSUS BUREAU, 1930
SHOWING

PERCENTAGE OF FAMILIES INTERVIEWED HAVING
CHICAGO DAILY NEWS HOME-COVERAGE
1933

(Source: *Chicago Daily News*)

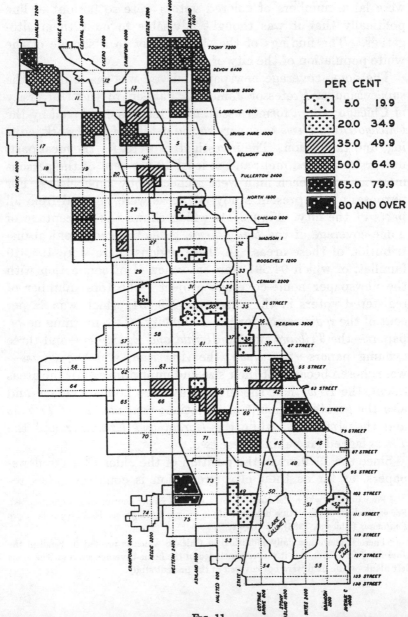

FIG. 11

mained about constant. The *Tribune* has lost in circulation to some extent. The high point of its circulation was September, 1929. One of the most striking events in Chicago journalism during the past eight years has been the rise in the circulation of the Chicago *Times,* a tabloid sheet which was established in March, 1930, on the remains of the old *Chicago Journal.* From a struggling sheet of about 100,000 circulation, the *Times* has

TABLE 16*

TOTAL 1931 CITY CIRCULATION AND 1933 HOME-COVERAGE
OF FIVE CHICAGO DAILIES

NEWSPAPER	LETTER SYM-BOL	TOTAL CITY CIRCU-LATION 1931†	PERCENT-AGE FOR CITY†	HOME-COVERAGE, 47 AREAS OF CITY, 1933‡			
				Mean	Lowest Item	Highest Item	Standard Deviation
News............	a	390,000	47	46.5	8.3	82.6	18.6
Tribune..........	b	470,000	56	37.4	14.1	66.1	14.7
American........	c	450,000	55	37.8	19.9	50.1	7.1
Herald and Examin-							
er.............	d	280,000	34	11.5	5.4	18.5	3.3
Times..........	x	165,000	20	10.6	4.4	17.3	2.9

* Each variable has been assigned a letter, by which it is identified. For a discussion of the technica l terms used, see page 97 above and Appendix C below, page 210.
† Information taken from the Chicago Tribune, *op. cit.,* p. 8.
‡ Information from the *Daily Newspaper Home Coverage in Metropolitan Chicago* (Chicago, 1934).

risen steadily, until at the end of 1936 it could boast a circulation of 340,000, larger than the morning Hearst paper.

CANDIDATES AND THE PRESS

The attitude of a newspaper toward a candidate may take several different forms. In accordance with the well-known slogan of politics, "Bad publicity is better than none,"[9] an editor may decide to ignore completely a candidate. If this policy is not followed, the opposition to a given candidate may become a great moral crusade in which the editorial columns, the news columns, the photograph department, and the cartoons are devoted to demolishing the undesired candidate. The opposition to a candidate may take much more mild expressions.

[9] Frank Kent, *Political Behavior* (New York, 1928), p. 252.

Comparatively little space may be devoted to defeating the candidate when the editor feels that there is not much real choice between the candidates running. The indorsement of candidates may also be indicated in a variety of ways. The indorsement may appear only on the eve of the election in the shape of a marked ballot. A paper may also run a series of editorials on the merits of the candidate which it supports.The Chicago newspapers have also devoted their news columns to publicity favorable to certain candidates. The influence of a paper upon a given election varies not only with the circulation of that paper but also with the intensity and duration of the campaign the paper has waged for or against the personalities involved in the election. It is extremely difficult to ascertain the intensity of a press campaign concerning a given candidate, since the pulling power of the language used is not known and the election news is always a mixture of materials on candidates and issues.

Since it is very difficult to isolate the news items that refer to particular candidates in an election where many offices are to be filled, it was decided to study intensively the editorials and cartoons which appeared in the five weeks preceding each election. An attempt was made to ascertain roughly the column-inches devoted in each paper to editorial and cartoon indorsements given candidates. Subjective considerations necessarily entered into the selection of articles that were counted as being for or against a given candidate. The main purpose of Table 17 is to give a rough indication of the approximate position of each newspaper regarding the candidates concerned.

Since the newspaper home-coverage study was made in 1933 and 1934, it was thought desirable to select elections as near to these years as possible. No election was considered which antedated the primary election of April 8, 1930, and the general election of November 3, 1936, was the last one studied.[10]

---

[10] The 1932 primary was not included in the analysis because the newspapers did not take clear-cut positions on any of the candidates involved. Only candidates who were running in the Republican primaries of 1930 and 1931 were selected, because there were no contests in the Democratic primaries of those years.

A brief review of the elections concerned is necessary in order to get the setting of the problem.[11] In the Republican primary of 1930, Senator Charles S. Deneen, a candidate for renomination, was opposed by Mrs. Ruth Hanna McCormick and New-

TABLE 17

COLUMN-INCHES OF EDITORIALS, CARTOONS, AND MARKED BALLOTS FOR CANDIDATES, 1930–36

	Republican Primary 1930		Election 1930	Republican Primary 1931			City Election 1931	General Election 1932		Election 1934	Election 1936
	Mc-Cormick	Deneen	Lewis	Thompson	Albert	Lyle	Cermak	Roosevelt	Horner	Igoe	Roosevelt
News:	oppos.	indors.	indors.	oppos.*	indors.†	incon-sistent‡	indors.	oppos.	indors.	oppos.	oppos.
Marked ballot	......	88	88	......	8	......	7	118	118	....	.....
Editorials....	......	94	58	281	170	111	149	550	120	61	410
Cartoons.....	......	00	22	154	21	133	181	372	44	10	344
Tribune:	indors.		oppos.	oppos.*	incon-sistent§	indors.||	indors.	oppos.	indors.	oppos.	oppos.
Marked ballot	61	......	102	......	......	15	22	......	54	88	.....
Editorials....	106	......	84	275	38	238	106	312	146	134	983
Cartoons.....	14	......	45	617	279	338	297	235	22	23	827
American:	indors.		indors.	indors.				indors.			oppos.
Marked ballot	13	......									
Editorials....	450	......	40	20				74			300
Cartoons.....	40	......						708			38
Herald and Examiner:	indors.		indors.	**				oppos.	indors.	indors.		oppos.
Marked ballot	......		91								
Editorials....	1,552		146					1,604	319		1,758
Cartoons.....	222		31				25	1,390			52
Daily Times:								indors.	indors.	indors.††	indors.
Editorials....								202	108	12	570
Cartoons.....										11	73

* Total column-inches—against Thompson.
† Column-inches favoring Albert.
‡ Editorials against Thompson but not favoring Albert specifically.
§ Column-inches against Thompson but not favoring Lyle specifically.
\|\| Column-inches favoring Lyle.
** Editorial support for Thompson, indirectly.
†† New Deal congressman referred to; no specific mention of Igoe.

ton Jenkins. Mrs. McCormick was the most serious contender since, as congressman-at-large, she had built up a state-wide organization and had shown a willingness to spend her own money freely for campaign purposes. Deneen had backing him

[11] The following summaries are based upon newspaper clippings, accounts of political meetings, and a collection of campaign materials. See chaps. i and v.

the pro–World Court elements, a few labor organizations, his own Republican faction, the Anti-saloon League, and some business groups. Mrs. McCormick's victorious campaign was based on the support of the anti–World Court movement, a large number of trade-unions, the Mayor Thompson city hall machine, a number of prominent World War veterans, and some of the wet groups.[12] The *News* indorsed Deneen, and the *Tribune* indorsed Mrs. McCormick, while both the Hearst papers indorsed Mrs. McCormick. According to the measuring rod used, the *Herald and Examiner* was the most enthusiastic of all the papers in its support of the primary candidate, since it ran over 1,500 column-inches in editorials backing Mrs. McCormick.

In the fall election Mrs. McCormick was opposed by James Hamilton Lewis on the Democratic ticket. Lewis had served a term in the United States Senate during the Wilson administration and had been defeated for re-election in 1918 by Mrs. McCormick's husband. Normally the Republican nomination for United States senator was equivalent to election in Illinois, barring a split such as occurred in 1912. However, the economic depression caused many voters to shift from the Republican to the Democratic party. Flushed with a brilliant primary victory, Mrs. McCormick failed to notice this change in sentiment. She incurred the enmity of the Thompson organization by boldly slighting its contribution to her cause. The conspicuous display of her wealth before the Senate committee investigating campaign funds injured her cause. The vote for Lewis, the successful candidate, was correlated with the regular Democratic vote, the wet vote, the proportion of men registered, and the amount of unemployment.[13] Although the *News* ordinarily had Republican leanings in national elections, it indorsed Lewis. The Hearst papers also backed the Democratic candidate, but the *American* did not assert itself on Lewis' behalf. Mrs. McCormick had the support of the *Tribune*; but Colonel R. R. McCormick, proprietor of the *Tribune*

[12] For statistical corroboration of this, see Table 20, below, columns *e* and *f*.

[13] Consult column *g* of Table 20.

and brother of her late husband, was rather restrained in his indorsement of her candidacy.

The 1931 Republican mayoralty primary was a desperate struggle between rival factions.[14] Early in the preceding fall, Mayor Thompson had decided to seek a fourth term. His factional opponents could not unite on a candidate to run against him; and in the meantime Municipal Judge John H. Lyle, who had been much publicized by his attacks on gangsters, announced his intention to run. All of the anti-Thompson Republican leaders flocked to Lyle except Deneen, who entered a candidate of his own, Alderman Arthur F. Albert. Mayor Thompson had the support of the city hall machine, some of the labor groups, and a very efficient publicity staff. In a three-cornered contest which has been rarely equaled in the annals of American politics for bitterness and vulgarity, Thompson won by a plurality vote. His support came largely from the wet elements, the foreign-born neighborhoods, and the poorer residential areas.[15] The press was one of the principal issues of this picturesque campaign. "Big Bill" denounced Lyle, "the nutty judge," as the candidate of the Tribune, and "Li'll Arthur" as the candidate of the News. On the platform he would appear with two halters. He charged Lyle with wearing the Tribune halter and Albert with wearing the News halter. He, "Big Bill," wore no man's halter but was "guided by the will of the people." Naturally the News and the Tribune were the most vigorous in their opposition to Thompson. The News took a rather inconsistent attitude toward Lyle, since it was more interested in defeating Thompson than in nominating its own candidate.

A different situation confronted Thompson in the final election. All opposing candidates except Anton J. Cermak, the Democratic nominee, withdrew or were eliminated. Thompson could not count upon a united Republican organization; and Cermak was supported by independents, business men's groups,

[14] C. H. Wooddy, "Jubilee in Chicago," National Municipal Review, XX (June, 1931), 321–25.

[15] Consult column h of Table 20.

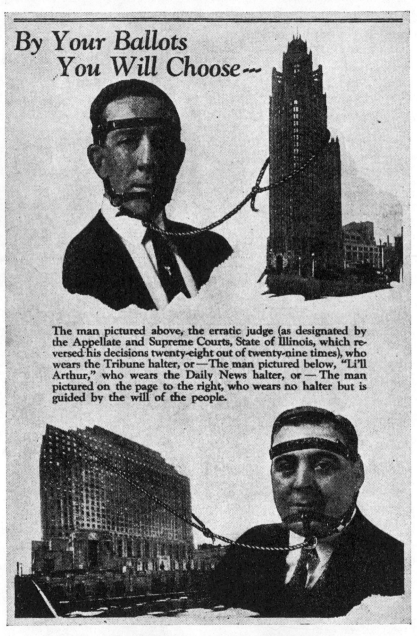

By Your Ballots
You Will Choose —

The man pictured above, the erratic judge (as designated by the Appellate and Supreme Courts, State of Illinois, which reversed his decisions twenty-eight out of twenty-nine times), who wears the Tribune halter, or —The man pictured below, "Li'll Arthur," who wears the Daily News halter, or — The man pictured on the page to the right, who wears no halter but is guided by the will of the people.

MAYOR THOMPSON'S HALTER CAMPAIGN

women's organizations, the wet interests, foreign-born groups, and a powerful Democratic machine. While Thompson used all of his ballyhoo techniques, he found that he could make little impression upon the discontent arising from the economic crisis, the desire of the business man to improve the reputation of the city, the sulkiness of some of the Republican leaders, the new technique of ridicule which was being used against him, and the confidence of the Democrats. The *Tribune* and *News* continued their fight against Thompson and indorsed Cermak. The Hearst papers did not take any stand in this election, although the *Herald and Examiner* ran some cartoons which were critical of Cermak. Cermak was swept into office with the largest majority on record.

When the general election came in 1932, the Republicans were still divided into warring camps. At the primary, Len Small, member of the Thompson faction, won the Republican nomination for governor in a divided field. For governor, the Democrats nominated Henry Horner, who had made an excellent record as probate judge. The lines of division in the gubernatorial contest were somewhat similar to those in the mayoralty election of the preceding year. In addition to the regular Democratic organization support, Horner received considerable assistance from the independent Republicans. True to their recent stand in national politics, the *News* and the *Tribune* opposed Roosevelt and urged the election of Herbert Hoover. On the other hand, the Hearst papers in 1932 indorsed Roosevelt. The *Times* was a consistent supporter of Roosevelt right from the beginning of the campaign. Horner was indorsed by all the Chicago newspapers. The final vote indicated that he ran ahead of the ticket.

In 1934 came a test of the popularity of the New Deal policies and the strength of the Democratic organization in the city of Chicago. Unfortunately, this year did not call for the election of a United States senator in the state of Illinois; so it is difficult to get a basis for comparison with the 1930 election. However, the state still selected two congressmen-at-large, and the vote for the candidates for one of these posts was taken as the measure of Democratic strength. Michael Igoe was the outstanding Democratic candidate for congressman-at-large, and his leading Republican opponent was C. Wayland Brooks. Igoe's vote was expressed as a percentage of the combined vote received by Igoe and Brooks. The line-up of the papers had changed somewhat by this time. While the *News* and the *Tribune* were still strongly Republican in national affairs, the Hearst papers were no longer active in supporting the New Deal administration. The *Times* was the sole daily newspaper which was wholeheartedly praising President Roosevelt.

In 1936 some of the daily newspaper proprietors in Chicago found themselves in embarrassing positions. Colonel McCormick of the *Tribune* had warmly supported the local Democratic administration headed by Mayor Kelly, but he was one of the most uncompromising of the New Deal critics. Would the local machine cut the national ticket in order to please a metropolitan newspaper proprietor? As the campaign wore on, it became apparent that President Roosevelt had more to offer Mayor Kelly than had Colonel McCormick. The hostility manifested toward the *Tribune* photographers at the great Roosevelt rally in the Chicago Stadium must have convinced Kelly that his cohorts were with Roosevelt. Secretary Ickes' attack upon Colonel McCormick and the *Tribune* was well received, even on the North Side, where the *Tribune* is relatively more popular.

The *News* has had a long-standing reputation for independence in politics. It has also rendered signal service in collecting information regarding candidates for the guidance of the voters. With its proprietor, Colonel Frank Knox, as vice-presidential candidate on the Republican ticket, the *News* could not function as it had in the past. When Colonel Knox took over the paper in 1932, it became more partisan than it had been before. In 1936 it reached the peak of its partisanship.

During the 1936 presidential campaign, William Randolph Hearst, reversing his 1932 position, took the lead for the red-baiters, tax-dodgers, calamity-howlers, ultra-nationalists, and the self-appointed defenders of constitutionalism and American liberties. His two Chicago newspapers followed his dictates faithfully and printed vigorous editorials, news articles, and cartoons designed to discredit the New Deal.

Only the tabloid *Daily Times* presented the full case of the Democratic party in the campaign. Following the lead of the *New York Daily News*, the *Times* presented one-half a page to the two national committees each day. The circulation of the *Times* increased by leaps and bounds. During the campaign it conducted an Illinois straw poll which came closer to predicting the result in the state than any of the nation-wide polls.[16]

When the results came in showing a two-to-one victory for Roosevelt in Chicago, the resentment against the older newspapers took overt form. Some copies of the *Tribune* were burned, and a window in the *Tribune* service bureau was smashed. Several commentators have said that the election was an indication of the weakness of the press as a propaganda agency. Although the big circulation newspapers stood four to one against Roosevelt, the election results told quite a different story.

Eleven candidates were chosen from the elections which have been mentioned, and their votes were expressed as percentages of the total vote cast in each of the 47 areas. Table 18 gives certain relevant figures regarding the distributions of these percentages, and it also gives the results in the city at large. It can be seen that the sample is not a perfect one, since it was drawn more heavily from the Republican and independent sections of the city; but this is not serious, for enough strong Democratic areas were included to give the range of variation found in the city.

The problem of estimating the influence of the press upon voting behavior in an urban community like Chicago may be impossible to solve with the existing techniques. Reading a newspaper and marking a ballot in a particular way are isolated

---

[16] Illinois poll taken by:

	Percentage Democratic
Chicago Daily Times	58
Crossley	54
Gallup	51
Literary Digest	39
Final returns	59

bits of complicated patterns of social behavior. If either of these acts is removed from its social, political, economic, and psychological context, it becomes a meaningless procedure. Therefore, the relation between voting and newspaper circulation must be considered in the light of the total situation in which these variables are found. It has already been pointed out that variations in voting behavior can be explained in terms of many influences other than the attitude of newspapers. In order to

TABLE 18

PERCENTAGE OF TOTAL VOTE RECEIVED BY SPECIFIED CANDIDATES

CANDIDATE	ELECTION	LETTER SYMBOL	PERCENTAGE OF TOTAL VOTE IN ENTIRE CITY	PERCENTAGE OF TOTAL VOTE IN 47 SELECTED AREAS			
				Mean	Highest Item	Lowest Item	Standard Deviation
McCormick.......	April, 1930	e	59.5	56.6	68.1	40.7	5.9
Deneen..........	April, 1930	f	30.4	33.3	52.3	21.0	6.6
Lewis............	November, 1930	g	72.1	70.5	92.0	46.2	9.5
Thompson........	February, 1931	h	46.6	36.2	82.6	14.2	15.3
Albert...........	February, 1931	i	15.6	18.3	27.6	9.2	4.4
Lyle.............	February, 1931	j	35.9	43.7	67.5	6.2	14.0
Cermak..........	April, 1931	k	58.5	63.2	91.4	45.3	8.4
Roosevelt........	November, 1932	l	59.2	55.3	90.8	26.2	14.1
Horner..........	November, 1932	m	64.0	66.4	87.0	47.5	8.8
Igoe.............	November, 1934	n	64.0	57.1	94.0	30.0	14.2
Roosevelt........	November, 1936	z	66.9	61.8	92.8	29.3	14.3

throw as much light as possible upon the total situation, the variables given in Table 19 were added.

Of the variables listed in this table, the following had a more or less political nature: interest in voting, as measured by the percentage of the adult citizens registered in 1930; party voting, as measured by the percentage of all ballots marked straight in 1932; willingness to support public expenditures, as measured by the percentage which voted "yes" on a 1930 bond issue condemned by civic organizations; and wet sentiment, as measured by the percentage which voted "yes" on a 1930 public-policy referendum calling for the repeal of the Eighteenth Amendment.[17]

[17] The data for these variables are described above, chap. v.

An examination of the original data and the scatter diagrams made from them showed that the readers of the *News* and the *Tribune* were found in greatest numbers in those areas where straight-party voting, affirmative votes on the bond issue, and wet votes were least prevalent. Except for the fact that the *Tribune* opposed prohibition,[18] these tendencies agree with the general stand taken by these newspapers.[19] The readers of the *Examiner* were relatively more numerous in the areas which

TABLE 19

EIGHT VARIABLES DESCRIBING 47 SELECTED AREAS IN CHICAGO

Variable	Date	Letter Symbol	Percentage for City	Mean	Lowest Item	Highest Item	Standard Deviation
Voting interest.........	1930	*o*	66.3	65.3	41.6	93.4	10.4
Party voting............	1932	*p*	58.4	51.5	27.9	84.3	12.9
Bond issue.............	1930	*q*	58.0	54.5	41.0	80.0	8.0
Wet vote...............	1930	*r*	78.6	75.2	56.4	90.4	6.7
Women.................	1930	*s*	41.8	44.8	31.9	54.0	5.2
Catholic origins........	1930	*t*	32.4	26.9	7.9	81.5	20.1
Unemployment.........	1931	*u*	22.7	21.9	4.3	63.5	13.1
Median rental..........	1930*	*v*	49.6	57.7	20.8	124.7	20.1
Taking no newspaper....	1933	*w*	17.7†	16.0	2.3	56.9	14.2

* Expressed in dollars.
† Percentage for sample of selected areas.

voted wettest and which were most strongly in favor of the bond issue. The Hearst *American* did not show marked tendencies in either direction, partly because of the disturbing effect of the units in which there were many persons who read no newspapers.[20]

Table 19 gives the following variables selected from the voting records, census data, and the home-coverage survey: percentage of the total registered voters who were women; percentage of the total population who were born, or whose parents were born, in Catholic countries; percentage unemployed in

[18] In October, 1930, the *Tribune* ran a sample ballot marked for repeal six times, and it ran 91 column-inches of editorials and 17 column-inches of cartoons in favor of repeal.

[19] The *News* ran a marked ballot against repeal and 26 column-inches of editorials.

[20] The Hearst papers were emphatically wetter than the *Tribune*, each running between 450 and 500 column-inches of editorials and cartoons in favor of repeal.

1931 of gainful workers ten years of age and over; median rental; and percentage of families interviewed that took no daily newspaper printed in English. The circulations of the *News* and the *Tribune* tended to vary directly with the ratio of women registered and with median rental, while they varied inversely with the measures of religious affiliation, indifference to the press, and unemployment. Thus, in those areas, like Beverly Hills, where the proportion of women registered was high, the proportion taking no newspapers was low, and where rents were high, the home coverage of these two papers was high; but in a Polish area where there were many Catholics and a large number of unemployed, and many taking no newspapers, it was low. In the case of the Hearst papers, no such marked tendencies were apparent.

Product-moment coefficients of correlation were then calculated from the ungrouped data for every possible combination of the variables, excepting the Igoe vote.[21] These coefficients are presented in symmetrical form in Table 20, which is commonly known as a "correlation matrix."

We are now in a position to consider the relationship of the home-coverages of the different newspapers and the votes of the various candidates, keeping in mind some of the aspects of the total situation in which these relationships are found. In only 2 of the 44 possible combinations (variables a–d correlated with variables e–n with the addition of z) were there high zero-order coefficients (.50 or over) whose signs were just the opposite of what one might have expected in view of the recommendations and circulations of the newspapers concerned. (Cf. Tables 17 and 20.)

---

[21] The Igoe vote (letter symbol n) was not included because of lack of funds. The coefficients involving the newspapers and this vote were:

$$(News) \ r_{an} = -.80,$$
$$(American) \ r_{cn} = .00,$$
$$(Tribune) \ r_{bn} = -.76,$$
$$(Herald-Examiner) \ r_{dn} = -.24.$$

For a discussion of product-moment coefficients of correlation, see p. 106, above, and p. 210, below.

TABLE 20

INTERCORRELATIONS OF VARIABLES RELATED TO NEWSPAPER HOME-COVERAGE AND VOTING BEHAVIOR IN CHICAGO, 1930–36

(N = 47)

Letter Symbol	Variable	Newspapers				Percentages for Candidates										Political and Social Variables								
						Republican Primary 1930		Election 1930		Mayoralty Primary 1931			Election 1931	Election 1932	Election 1936									
		a	b	c	d	e	f	g	h	i	j	k	l	m	x	o	p	q	r	s	t	u	v	w
a	News		.87	.22	—.34	—.41	.49	—.66	.82	.18	.82	.06	—.79	—.05	—.87	—.31	—.84	—.57	—.67	—.91	—.85	—.69	—.82	—.90
b	Tribune	.87		.10	—.12	—.33	.58	—.65	—.75	.14	.76	.20	—.74	.10	—.79	—.35	—.84	—.87	—.54	—.86	—.75	—.63	—.86	—.77
c	American	.22	.10		.19	—.02	—.15	.25	.18	.10	.21	—.34	—.27	—.17	—.02	—.27	—.22	—.27	—.10	—.30	—.40	—.30	—.26	—.54
d	Herald and Examiner	—.34	—.12	.19		.27	—.20	.26	.39	.31	.31	.30	.23	.16	.32	.05	.24	.41	.41	.19	.06	.06	—.20	.13
e	McCormick	—.41	—.33	—.02	.27		.84	—.37	.68	—.03	.64	.07	.45	.14	.43	.17	.41	.46	.69	.40	.40	.35	.35	.45
f	Deneen	.49	.58	—.15	—.20	.84		.56	.54	.00	.61	.11	.55	.01	.52	.16	.54	.17	.60	.52	.43	.38	.52	.43
g	Lewis	—.66	—.65	.25	.26	—.37	.56		.61	—.01	—.67	—.10	.91	.35	.87	.26	.67	.29	.74	.68	.68	.47	.58	.54
h	Thompson	.82	—.75	.18	.39	.68	.54	.61		—.40	—.95	.39	.77	.01	.55	.30	.84	.74	.17	.11	.78	.68	.77	.81
i	Albert	.18	.14	.10	.31	—.03	.00	—.01	—.40		.10	.56	—.05	.41	—.06	—.30	—.22	—.92	—.82	—.81	—.07	.15	—.17	—.07
j	Lyle	.82	.76	.21	.31	.64	.61	—.67	—.95	.10		.18	—.81	.18	—.82	—.50	—.82	—.71	—.84	—.82	—.81	.67	.17	.84
k	Cermak	.06	.20	—.34	.30	.07	.11	—.10	.39	.56	.18		.15	.13	.59	—.12	—.04	.16	.13	.06	.19	.00	.10	.76
l	Roosevelt, 1932	—.79	—.74	—.27	.23	.45	.55	.91	.77	—.05	—.81	.15		.73	.96	.38	.85	.50	.78	.78	.84	.59	.72	.75
m	Horner	—.05	.10	—.17	.16	.14	.01	.35	.01	.41	.18	.13	.73		.44	—.38	—.04	.23	.36	.04	.30	.59	.10	.20
x	Roosevelt, 1936	—.87	—.79	—.02	.32	.43	.52	.87	.55	—.06	—.82	.59	.96	.44		.36	.81	.56	.80	.80	.82	.61	.73	.78
o	Voting interest	—.31	—.35	—.27	.05	.17	.16	.26	.30	—.30	—.50	—.12	.38	—.38	.36		.62	.71	.65	.71	.80	.33	.35	.42
p	Party voting	—.84	—.84	—.22	.24	.41	.54	.67	.84	—.22	—.82	—.04	.85	—.04	.81	.62		.52	.71	.65	.84	.52	.89	.83
q	Bond issue	—.57	—.87	—.27	.41	.46	.17	.29	.74	—.92	—.71	.16	.50	.23	.56	.71	.52		.48	.62	.61	.51	.61	.61
r	Wet vote	—.67	—.54	—.10	.41	.69	.60	.74	.17	—.82	—.84	.13	.78	.36	.80	.65	.71	.48		.62	.63	.49	.51	.48
s	Women	—.91	—.86	—.30	.19	.40	.52	.68	.11	—.81	—.82	.06	.78	.04	.80	.71	.65	.62	.62		.87	.75	.85	.90
t	Catholic origins	—.85	—.75	—.40	.06	.40	.43	.68	.78	—.07	—.81	.19	.84	.30	.82	.80	.84	.61	.63	.87		.72	.79	.85
u	Unemployment	—.69	—.63	—.30	.06	.35	.38	.47	.68	.15	.67	.00	.59	.59	.61	.33	.52	.51	.49	.75	.72		.72	.72
v	Median rental	—.82	—.86	—.26	—.20	.35	.52	.58	.77	—.17	.17	.10	.72	.10	.73	.35	.89	.61	.51	.85	.79	.72		.81
w	Taking no newspaper	—.90	—.77	—.54	.13	.45	.43	.54	.81	—.07	.84	.76	.75	.20	.78	.42	.83	.61	.48	.90	.81	.72	.81	

NATIONAL ELECTIONS

The home-coverage of the *Tribune* and the *News* tended to vary directly with the Republican vote in elections at which national issues were at stake. Both of these papers class themselves as independent Republican dailies, and in 1932, 1934, and 1936 they gave vigorous editorial support to the Republican candidates. The Republicanism of the readers of these papers was strongly marked at these elections, since the high negative coefficients of correlation indicate that, on the average, the home-coverages of the newspapers tended to vary inversely with the percentage of the total vote cast for Roosevelt. In those areas where the circulation of the *News* was high, the Democratic vote was low, and vice versa. From the zero-order coefficients it is not possible to say whether the readers were influenced by the newspapers or whether the editors were trying to follow the views of their public.

The close association of the home-coverages of the *News* and the *Tribune* with some of the other variables raises the question as to the net effect of their variations upon the Roosevelt vote when the influence of other variables is kept constant.[21a] The statistical device of partial correlation was used to throw some light upon this problem with reference to the 1932 election. Since the home-coverages of the *News* and *Tribune* are so closely related to each other, it was decided to use the *News* only as an independent variable in the equation of net regression which describes the 1932 Roosevelt vote as a dependent variable. The other independent variables selected were the wet vote, Catholic origins, and median rental. The equation shows clearly that the average change in the 1932 Roosevelt vote for a unit change in the home-coverage percentage for the *News* was practically zero when the other variables were kept constant. This would indicate that the voters in Chicago who supported Hoover in 1932 probably did so because they were drys, because they were Protestants living in good neighborhoods, rather than because they were convinced by the frantic pleadings of the *News*. At any rate, an increase in the circulation of the *News* seemed to

[21a] See Appendix C for equations.

make no difference in the Roosevelt vote where these other influences were taken into account.

While the 1932 election does not give much evidence to support the thesis presented at the beginning of the chapter, the 1936 election does. The last two years of the first Roosevelt administration were pounded terrifically by the Chicago newspapers, and yet Roosevelt's popular vote in Chicago was higher in 1936 than in 1932, when he had roughly half of the dailies with him. Was the press without influence during these years? A closer examination of the situation shows that the press was a factor to be reckoned with in many parts of the city. As a matter of fact, Roosevelt made practically no gains in those areas where the home-coverage of the *Chicago Tribune* and the *Daily News* was highest. For instance, in the Beverly Hills area, where there were undoubtedly many home-owners who profited from the H.O.L.C. and where there were countless others who benefited from the New Deal administration in other ways, there was no increase in the Roosevelt vote. In this area the cards were stacked two to one against Roosevelt in 1932, and he was up against the same situation in 1936. If the city of Chicago as a whole had been like Beverly Hills, where over 80 per cent of the families habitually read the papers of the morning and the afternoon colonels, Landon would have carried Chicago and he would have carried Illinois.

Roosevelt's great vote in Chicago in 1936 came in part from the areas where the daily newspapers printed in English were not habitually taken into the homes. Colonel McCormick and Colonel Knox could not influence persons who did not read their papers. The Democratic machine vote was concentrated in the lower rental areas, where there were large numbers of Catholics, a high proportion of unemployed and persons on relief, and a large ratio of persons without advanced education.

As in the case of the 1932 election, we are interested in the equation of net regression which will enable us to estimate how important the press was in relation to the 1936 result as compared with some of the other variables studied. Using the same variables as in the equation describing the 1932 vote as dependent variables, we discover a striking change. The new equation shows that the average change in the 1936 Roosevelt vote for a unit change in the home-coverage of the *News* was significant, and inverse when the wet vote, the ratio of persons of Catholic origins, and median rental were held constant.[22] In other words, the opposition papers cut into Roosevelt's popularity in 1936 in no mean fashion.

Since the newspapers cannot be expected to have any influence in areas where a large proportion of the families take no newspapers into the homes, it was decided to add the variable describing this situation (variable *w*) to the foregoing equation. This step in the analysis greatly increased the contribution of the *News* to the equation of prediction. In fact, in many areas in the city the home-coverage of the *News* was the most important factor in estimating the 1936 Roosevelt vote. In explaining the voting behavior of the inhabitants of Beverly Hills, we can say it was more important that the inhabitants read the *News* than that they paid high rents or owned their homes or that they were largely Protestant, well educated, and comparatively dry.

STATE AND PRIMARY ELECTIONS

An analysis of the interrelationships of the variables shown in Table 20 justifies the consideration of state and primary elections together.[23] The record of the newspapers in these elections has not been as clear-cut as in the case of presidential elections.

One of the occasions on which a newspaper seemed to be ineffective was the Republican primary of 1930, when the *Tribune* indorsed Mrs. McCormick and opposed Deneen. The variations in the home-coverage of the *Tribune* tended to follow those of the Deneen primary vote. This situation may be explained by the fact that Mrs. McCormick received some support in the primary from the Thompson faction of the Republican party. This faction drew its support from areas where the home-coverage of the *Tribune* was relatively low. In addition,

---

[22] See Appendix C for equation.

[23] H. F. Gosnell and M. J. Schmidt, "Factorial Analysis of the Relation of the Press to Voting in Chicago," *Journal of Social Psychology*, II (November, 1936), 375–85.

the *Tribune* was only lukewarm in the support of Mrs. McCormick because it did not want to appear to favor too strongly a person who was related by ties of marriage to the owner of the paper.[24] The *Tribune*'s indorsement of Mrs. McCormick probably helped her candidacy, but the situation was too complex to disentangle.

The other coefficient which had the opposite sign to that expected was the one measuring the relationship between the home-coverage of the *News* and the vote for Lewis in 1930. The *News* has been strongly Republican in national elections; but in 1930 it recommended, in its last-minute sample ballot, that its readers support Lewis in preference to Mrs. McCormick.[25] The indorsement of the *News* may have had some effect, but the election of Lewis was of such landslide proportions that the signs of this effect were drowned. The foundation of the Lewis vote was the normal Democratic vote, since the correlation between the Lewis and the Smith votes was high. The *News* was relatively scarce in the homes that were strongly Democratic.

Where a newspaper followed no consistent policy toward a candidate, it weakened its influence. This was the situation in the primary of 1931, when the *News* mildly backed Albert for the Republican nomination but did not always oppose Lyle, one of Albert's opponents. The figures indicate that the readers of the *News* supported Lyle, the candidate backed by the *Tribune*, more strongly than they supported Albert. This can be explained by the fact that Albert had comparatively little organization support. Lyle, on the other hand, had important factional support in the very areas where the readers of the *News* were relatively numerous. Table 20 also shows that there is a close relationship between the constituency of the *News* and the *Tribune*. It is probable that many of the readers of the *News* who also read the *Tribune* concluded that a vote for Lyle was the surest way to defeat Thompson. The votes that Albert received might be taken as a rough measure of what one newspaper can do almost single handed in a highly unfavorable situation.

The small size of the zero-order coefficients involving the two

[24] March 27, 1930.   [25] November 3, 1930.

Hearst papers indicates that the constituency of these papers
was different from that of the *Tribune* and of the *News*. The
American mildly indorsed Thompson in the mayoralty election
of 1931,[26] and its circulation showed a slight tendency to vary
inversely with the Cermak vote. A similar relationship held
also for the *Herald and Examiner* at this election.[27] While the
coefficients involving the *Herald and Examiner* were low in
every case, they were always positive for candidates indorsed
and negative for candidates opposed, except in the case of the
vote for Horner, where the relationship was very low. This
might mean that the morning Hearst paper anticipated the
political opinions of its readers or that it had some influence
upon them. In view of the intense editorial and cartoon campaign which this paper carried on for Roosevelt in 1932, its
relationship with the Roosevelt vote is low.

The *American* appeared to be working at cross-purposes with
the political attitudes of its readers on two occasions. Although
it favored Thompson in the mayoralty primary of 1931, the
percentage of the homes interviewed that received the *American*
tended slightly to vary inversely with the Thompson primary
vote. Likewise in 1932, when it indorsed Roosevelt for President, its home-coverage was apparently not closely associated
with the Roosevelt vote. An examination of the scatter diagrams for these two coefficients shows that, if the units where
there were many persons who read no newspaper at all were
eliminated, the coefficients would be positive.

ELIMINATING THOMPSON AND HIS COHORTS

Persons who are interested in proving the power of the press
in politics would have even less ground to stand on when first
glancing at the zero-order coefficients involving the 1932
Horner vote. However, it is highly significant that the vote for
Horner did not vary inversely with the home-coverage of the
News. Horner's name appeared in the Democratic party column under Roosevelt's. The *News* urged its readers to split
their votes, and presented marked ballots to show how they

[26] February 18, 1931.   [27] March 18, 1931.

could vote for Hoover and Horner. The equation of net regression for the Horner vote as a function of the *News*, the Cermak vote, and the Roosevelt vote shows that the stand taken by the *News* for Horner (plus a similar stand taken by the *Tribune*) was an important influence in the situation. The picture is even more striking when the coefficients of partial correlation are considered. The last one of these shows that, making allowances for the fact that Horner was on the Democratic ticket and that he was supported by the Cermak organization, variations in his vote are quite closely related to variations in the *News* home-coverage. This situation may also be studied in another fashion. If we subtract the Roosevelt vote from the Horner vote in each one of the areas, we find that the differences are positively related to the percentages for the *News* circulation.

While in parts of the city some conservative Jews might have voted for Hoover and Horner regardless of the recommendations of the papers, there were neighborhoods which had practically no Jews which showed just as wide a spread between the Roosevelt and the Horner percentages. In the areas under discussion, the aggregate vote for Horner was 39,719 greater than the aggregate vote for Roosevelt. By 1932 the overwhelming mass of the Jews in Chicago were Democratic. Furthermore, the sample studied did not include the heaviest concentration of Jewish population in the city. The author has collected sample ballots and attended political meetings during the entire period. We have interviewed hundreds of party workers. No evidence has come to our attention of any party faction which openly advocated tickets to be split for Hoover and Horner. In the Beverly Hills section, where there are few Jews, Roosevelt received 26.2 per cent of the total vote and Horner 61.2 per cent. The alderman of the Nineteenth Ward said that the newspapers and the churches were responsible for this independent voting. We can thus conclude that in this situation, the *News* (and the *Tribune*) probably had some influence. Additional proof of this is found in the zero-order coefficients which show the relationship between home-coverages and straight-party voting. The home-coverages were high where independent voting was high, and vice versa.

The success of the *News* and the *Tribune* in getting their readers to cut the Republican candidate for governor in 1932 was related to the bitter hostility which these papers had expressed toward the Thompson faction of the Republican party over a long period of time. Shortly after Thompson's first election as mayor in 1915, these papers began their campaign of adverse criticism. The animosities which the owners of these papers had harbored against former Senator William Lorimer were focused on a new object, Mayor Thompson, a henchman of the Lorimer faction. The readers of the *Tribune* and the *News* were conditioned by constant repetition of publicity which was bitterly unfavorable to Thompson and his cohorts. Len Small was the Thompson candidate who ran against Horner for governor in 1932. What relationship was there between the votes for Thompson, himself, and the home-coverages of these papers? This problem was studied on the basis of the mayoralty primary of 1931, at which the zero-order coefficients present a prima facie case showing considerable newspaper influence. The equation of net regression shows that for unit average change in the *News* home-coverage percentage there was a 27/100 average change in the Thompson primary vote in the opposite direction, while holding constant the relationship between the Thompson primary vote and the following variables, *Herald and Examiner* home-coverage, party voting, and median rental. The relationship is certainly a significant one.[28]

In order to counteract the influence of his journalistic opponents, Mayor Thompson denounced them at every platform appearance and sought an alliance with the two Hearst papers, the *Evening American* and the *Herald and Examiner*. He was most successful in recruiting supporters in the areas where there were many persons who read no newspapers and where the Hearst papers were relatively more popular. On the basis of the equation referred to in the previous paragraph, it can be said that for an average unit change in the home-coverage of

[28] See Appendix C for equation.

the *Herald and Examiner* there was, on the average, two-thirds of a unit change in the Thompson primary vote, while holding constant the *News*, party voting, and median rental. This relationship seems almost too high. We might reasonably expect a newspaper to influence about 10 or 20 per cent of its readers. The relationship appears more probable when the coefficients of partial correlation are considered and when it is remembered that the home-coverage figures for this paper greatly underestimate its circulation.

SUMMARY

While a number of candidates have carried the second largest city of the United States in the face of a bitter and overwhelming press opposition, this does not mean that the press is without influence or that its relative effectiveness is rapidly declining. An examination of newspaper home-coverage and voting responses in different areas of the city shows that there were many cases where the circulation and attitude of a newspaper were closely associated with the success of given candidates. By constant reiteration the newspapers had conditioned their readers to vote for candidates belonging to given parties or factions. One of the reasons why the press has apparently been overshadowed by other influences during the depression years is the fact that it has never reached some of the submerged groups. Many areas were found where a large proportion of the inhabitants took no daily newspaper.

There are certain typical situations in which the newspapers are important influences in those sections of the city where their circulations are largest. If they have followed a vigorous policy with reference to factional leaders in primary elections, they may be able to determine the fate of the candidates associated with these leaders. In general elections, if the papers have followed a consistent policy regarding a given party faction, they may be able to influence their readers to split their tickets in favor of, or in opposition to, that faction. Finally, if the press follows a tenacious policy during an economic crisis, it may be able to retard or prevent shifts from one major party to another.

HOW TO VOTE INTELLIGENTLY IN THE PRIMARY

From the "Chicago Tribune," April 5, 1932

CHAPTER IX

THE ROLE OF URBAN POLITICS

What is the balance sheet of machine politics in an urban center such as Chicago during a period of economic crisis? On the credit side of the ledger should be placed the success of the bosses in softening class conflicts. By granting petty favors to various nationalistic and local groups, by taking advantage of the subsidies offered by the national government, by keeping the attention of the voters distracted by factional quarrels and sham disputes, the party machines have kept minor party movements from gaining any headway. From the standpoint of the business leaders, this function of parties has been very useful. Some of the submerged groups may not be so appreciative; but the fact remains that during the years 1930-36 the city was comparatively free from violent labor disputes, hunger riots, and class warfare. The decentralized, chaotic, and inadequate character of the governmental organization of the city has discouraged far-reaching demands upon local authorities.

During the depression the machine has also acted as a kind of buffer for the various governmental agencies which have had to deal with the distressed. Eviction cases, emergency hunger cases, and emergency clothing shortages were sometimes cared for in first instance by the ward and precinct committeemen. The relief activities of the party workers were not systematic and, of course, were not disinterested, but they were devoid of red tape. Ward heelers asked no embarrassing questions, and they supplied at once any material aid they could. The demands of the period were such that the party organizations could not hope to meet more than a minute fraction of them, but they did leave the impression that they knew the ropes of the relief game.

The stability of the machine was reassuring to various groups that no upsetting innovations would be tried in local government. Ward leaders in particular showed an amazingly low

turnover, considering the stresses and strains that accompanied
the economic crisis. Business men, journalists, underworld
leaders, bankers, and labor chiefs knew that they could count
upon the local machine to do business in the old way in spite
of the changes that had taken place in the role of the national
government. Inefficiency in local government could be tolerated if it meant resistance to the extension of the local public
services. The largest industrialists, newspaper proprietors,
bankers, and gambling kings did not want a state income tax, a
modern tax-collection system, or an expansion of municipal
services and budgets. Party bosses were a bulwark against
such changes. Those citizens who might have benefited from
such modifications of the role of local government were indifferent, deficient in promotional skills, misled by the press, and
disillusioned by the failure of reform waves to leave many
permanent traces.

While the depression has not eliminated the influence of the
spoils tradition in the city hall, it has drastically purged one of
the major party organizations. The economic crisis greatly reduced national and local incomes and made the burden of taxation relatively much greater than it had been in the prosperous
twenties. A city can support more than one political machine
when real estate values are rising and incomes are going up.
During such times the taxpayers are not so tax conscious as in
lean times, and the general public is more indifferent to graft
exposures and wasteful expenditure of public funds. In a period
of economic depression there is graft enough for only one machine. The law of the pendulum in democratic countries operates against the party which is in power when the economic
deprivations are first being felt. Those major party factions
which were in power at the time of the stock market crash were
swept from the public offices. There has undoubtedly been a
decrease in the total amount of political grafting in the city
during the past eight years. Relative to the opportunities
available, there may not be any great decrease; but there are
fewer political mouths to feed out of the public crib, since local
political power has been concentrated in a single organization.

Under pressure from the financial interests the political bosses have been compelled, in the last few years, to make drastic economies. Tax collections have been insufficient to meet the local governmental expenses, and the unpaid public employee is not a great asset to the political machine. The banks have been unwilling to lend money unless total public expenditures were reduced. While many of the economies have not improved governmental efficiency, and there are still many strongholds of patronage and spoils, there have been some improvements, which have left the political bosses with less patronage. Greater publicity regarding tax assessments and collections has loosened the strangle hold which the corrupt politicians once had over a lucrative source of campaign funds. The demand for economy has aided the movement for the consolidation of overlapping authorities and the concentration of official responsibility for fiscal affairs.

In the field of public administration there have been a number of developments in recent years which have tended to lessen the influence of spoils. There has been a trend toward stricter supervision of the local tax authorities, and the newer forms of taxation are less open to political abuses. The Illinois sales tax, objectionable as it is from the theoretical point of view, is a tax which can be administered with comparatively little leakage. The advances which have been made in the field of public welfare administration have made the social service activities of the precinct committeemen more and more unnecessary. There have been fewer occasions when the party officials can step in and mitigate the harshness of the law. The growth of such services as parole, probation, community case work, rehabilitation, and public employment bureaus has reduced the importance of the precinct captain as a community agent. These gains have been achieved for the most part through the efforts of the state and national governments. The most that can be said for the local machine is that it has furnished no effective opposition to these innovations.

The depression has also brought greater recognition for the merit system in the municipal service. In Chicago the civil service rules were extended to certain park districts by the new Park District Law, to the Sanitary District by legislation in 1935, to the employees of the county assessor by the new taxation legislation, and to some of the other county employees by administrative action. While the Illinois civil service legislation has been reasonably sound, the practical application of the rules has left much to be desired. The spirit of the merit system has been violated by an excessive number of temporary employees, by a vicious system of waivers which nullifies the function of promotional examinations, by the old-fashioned practice of "framing" efficient employees, by the retention of inefficient political employees by means of legal chicanery, and from time to time by outright bribery and corruption. Leaders of both of the major parties have sinned against the civil service commandments. A pre-depression mayor of one party was frankly hostile to the merit system. Post-depression mayors of another party have given lip service to the system but have administered it as politicians.

One might expect that, when hard times brought a great relative increase in the size of the tax burden, the taxpayers would demand greater service and revolt against the perversion of government by spoilsmen. The defeat of established machines in New York and Philadelphia since 1929 might be interpreted in such terms. On the other hand, the depression has given to the citizens of Chicago no respite from boss rule. Economic deprivations have failed to break the political system in Chicago because of an unfavorable press situation, a lack of leadership, and the character of the party division at the beginning of the depression.

In New York and Philadelphia there were newspaper proprietors who were willing to crusade against political corruption and machine control in municipal government regardless of the personalities who happened to be in power. In times past, Chicago has had such newspaper proprietors, but in recent years local reform movements have been somewhat uncertain as to the possibility of strong press support. While daily newspapers of largest circulation have been unable to check the growing popularity of the New Deal administration except in a few areas where there are many persons of independent means, in local affairs they have had considerable influence in blocking change. Only in a state-wide primary battle, where some of the local newspapers were aided by the rivalry between the urban and rural sections of the state, did the press take part in a battle which involved some setbacks for the local machine.

The state of Illinois has furnished some national leaders during the economic crisis, but none of these has played a major role in city politics during recent times. Labor leaders in Chicago, until 1937, were very quiet as compared with their more active role in early post–World War period. Business and social leaders in the city have not cared to mingle in the rough and tumble of urban politics. Private philanthropy has furnished a much safer and more respectable avenue for their civic energies. Besides, Chicago has had no Frank Murphy, no Daniel Hoan, no Fiorello La Guardia.

At the beginning of the depression the balance between the two major parties in Chicago was fairly even, with the Republicans in possession of the city hall. It was inevitable, under the circumstances, that the Democratic party would be the chief beneficiary of any shifts in political attitudes. Political machines in general draw their chief support from the lower income groups, the persons in the lesser employments, the foreign born, and those who have had relatively few educational opportunities. These persons already belonged to the Democratic party in Chicago at the start of the economic crisis. The national policies of their party during the depression strengthened their party loyalty and made it very easy for the local leaders to build up an organization which was almost impregnable. On the other hand, in Philadelphia the party situation had been one-sided, with the Republicans normally in power; and when the depression came, many of the machine elements taken from the lower income groups were torn from Republican moorings. No such centrifugal forces were operating in the city of Chicago.

From the argument so far, the impression might be gained that the spoils system is inevitable in such a city as Chicago.

This is not necessarily so. The experience of such cities as Detroit, Milwaukee, and Cincinnati shows that patronage need not be the price of democracy. It may be that efficiency and expanding municipal services will sharpen class lines and the bitterness of city politics as in Milwaukee, where a socialist mayor has challenged the existing political and economic setup; but in some of the smaller cities the efficiency movement has frequently been an economy movement started by business men. New leaders, new movements, new attitudes, might arise in the future, just as the city itself rose from its ashes after the famous fire.

Assuming a new orientation in the civic organization of the community, there is no part of the political machine which is invulnerable. There are some people who take a defeatist view regarding the strangle hold which the spoilsmen appear to have upon the law-enforcing authorities. It is held that there will always be liberal elements in the great metropolitan communities and that these elements will furnish the basis for an alliance between the underworld leaders and the politicians. The wish to win money without effort, the desire for excitement, and the interest of mortals in the future are among the causes of gambling. When existence is precarious, the urge to take a chance is even greater, and it becomes almost impossible to keep gambling places from operating. Like bootlegging, protected gambling furnishes the basis for criminal gangs which ally themselves with the dominant party machine. However, it is likely that gambling is a practice which is less widely distributed than drinking was during the prohibition era. In addition, merchants generally frown upon the spending habits of persons connected with gambling houses. The experience of Cleveland shows that a determined and skilled public safety director can break up gambling rings and thereby cut away one of the foundation stones of a spoils machine. If such an administrator understands the arts of publicity, the party bosses will not be able to touch him. Any city administration would soon find out that an honest, courageous, intelligent, and well-trained director of public safety is a much better political asset than a bunch of thieving, double-crossing, cheating, gambling-house operators. It is true that gambling kings furnish party campaign funds, ballot crooks, a few jobs for the machine, and, in the case of the lesser games, a propaganda agency; but the power of these things melts away in the face of an aroused public which is beginning to take pride in having a safe city and an honest police force.

Those concerned with attacking the political machine should be interested in a number of changes in the election laws and their administration. The long ballot, the multiplicity of elections, the small size of the election precincts, and the lack of adequate safeguards against fraud are all factors which play directly into the hands of the political bosses. These trappings of an archaic rural democracy which assumed the existence of omnicompetent citizens function badly in the great metropolitan centers such as Chicago, New York, and Philadelphia. Illinois has a jungle ballot; and it is no wonder that the voters get lost trying to mark it, and are willing to be led by the suave representatives of the political bosses who take the time to show them sample ballots and to explain the mysteries of the slate. One of the best illustrations of cultural lag in the field of politics is the slow pace at which positive law is catching up with the unanimous recommendations of political scientists, over several generations, with reference to the short ballot. A shorter ballot in Chicago would make it much more difficult for the political machine to dodge its responsibilities, and the agitation to secure such a change would build up the anti-machine elements.

"Divide and rule" is an old saying in politics. It applies with particular emphasis to American municipal politics. The old-fashioned city council elected by wards is based on the principle that, if spoils are divided into small enough units, a great many individual citizens can be put under personal obligations to the machine. Thousands of citizens will not vote against the dominant machine because the local ward boss has done such favors for them as fixing their curbs, collecting their garbage, fixing the street lights, or aiding them in securing some

governmental service. That ward organization which delivers
the most votes is entitled to the biggest share of the spoils.
Fraudulent registration in the form of colonization, ballot-box
stuffing, alteration of ballots, and falsification of election returns
are practices which benefit ward politicians. In order to increase the controlled votes they can command, they put all
sorts of pressure upon their precinct workers, appoint criminals
as members of precinct boards of election, and organize gangs
of floaters and ballot tricksters.

Electoral corruption and petty graft weaken the faith of the
masses in democratic methods, and consequently it is necessary
to minimize their use if it is desired to strengthen democratic
ideology. If election precincts were made larger, the total number of election officials would be reduced and it would be harder
for the political bosses to manipulate each tiny unit of the
electorate. In Great Britain there are no precinct captains,
in part because the votes are not counted by small districts but
by large areas including around fifty thousand voters each.
In some parts of the United States fairly large precincts are
used, and in a number of cities ballots are centrally counted.

The control which the party machines have over the election
boards could be reduced by abolishing the requirements of
residence within the precinct and of representation of the two
dominant parties. For many years the city of Detroit has appointed precinct election officials on the basis of fitness and
integrity. Other jurisdictions have been able to keep persons
with criminal records off the precinct election boards. In Chicago it is very difficult in many areas to get properly qualified
persons living within their precincts to serve on the election
boards, and the requirement of party representation has not
prevented bipartisan conspiracies to perpetrate election frauds.
While the positive law remedy is well known, its adoption is
difficult because some of the legislators chosen under the present system have benefited from its defects and do not want to
weaken their own chances of re-election.

The substitution of a system of proportional representation
for the present ward plan would enable the anti-machine groups

to combine more effectively. Proportional representation would involve the selection of city councilors-at-large in accordance with a plan which would secure a city council reflecting with mathematical exactness the strength of the groups in the electorate. The underlying rationale of this system is the desire to prevent the exclusion of minorities from the benefits of the state—a rationale based on the democratic premise that, in the absence of some means of protection, minorities may be exploited by the majority. Proportional representation would do away with gerrymandering and chicanery in connection with the determination of ward boundaries; and it would automatically take care of any shifts in the population, thus eliminating such a rotten borough as the First Ward in the city of Chicago. Election at large would minimize organizational elements, since it would lessen the power of the primary relationships established by the ward heelers and magnify the importance of secondary contacts. Thus it would be possible for reform groups to elect candidates of their own by means of press and radio publicity. Such methods are not feasible in ward battles, inasmuch as neither a metropolitan newspaper nor a broadcasting station can give as much attention to fifty local contests as to a city-wide struggle. Cincinnati, Toledo, and Hamilton, Ohio, have shown that proportional representation can be used to defeat machine control.

If democracy is to survive in troublesome times like the present, it will have to have a firmer foundation than the cohesive power of public plunder. Too often the methods employed by party machines to finance their various activities have given rise to the charge that our democracy is a demagogic plutocracy. As long as the parties rely upon contributions from business men who are seeking special favors, criminal elements which are seeking protection against interference on the part of the law-enforcing authorities, and office-holders who regard their loyalty to the party above that to the state, cynicism regarding the electoral process will be widespread.

The power of money in American municipal politics could be regulated to a much greater extent than it is at present. The floodlight of publicity, before and after elections, regarding the sources of campaign funds and election expenditures, has weakened boss rule in a number of states and cities. In addition, the regulation of certain types of expenditures, such as the hiring of party workers and watchers on election day, has reduced the size of the machine vote where it has been tried. Many of the states have inadequate corrupt-practices acts, and Illinois is one of the states which has no law regulating the use of money in elections.

Legal regulations are necessary in the fight against the spoilsmen, but they are not sufficient. The American constitutional system is such that it has tended to inculcate a legalistic mode of thinking about social problems. We have had a naïve faith in the power of legislation—constitutional, statutory, and local —to change our habits and keep us good. The colossal failure of the "noble experiment" with the constitutional prohibition of the manufacture, sale, and transportation of alcoholic beverages has, to some extent, shattered this faith. Laws which run contrary to the mores of an important element of the population can only be enforced at a social cost which is prohibitive. On the other hand, a legal device designed to purify politics is workable only if someone is concerned with seeing that it does work. If machine candidates are elected to the important appointing offices, they will find methods for circumventing the civil service laws. Even the most perfectly drafted election law can be manipulated by unscrupulous politicians who are not carefully watched. The best that positive law can do is to create a legal framework which makes the perversion of public office for private profit risky and which facilitates the expression of civic points of view.

If the struggle against the party machine is to be successful, more democratic methods for financing political campaigns must be devised, local parties dedicated to the ideal of voluntary precinct work must be organized, and the citizens must be educated to demand services of the government rather than special favors from the politicians. That all of these things are possible to achieve in the present generation has been demonstrated by a number of cities, American and European. The will to achieve has been lacking in some places—high places as well as low places.

Looking at the problem of urban democracy in the United States from a long-run point of view, the picture does not appear as gloomy in all aspects as Thomas Jefferson painted it one hundred and fifty years ago. In the past seventy-five years or so, machine voters have been recruited for the most part from the ranks of the unadjusted foreign-born groups, the unassimilated migrants from rural areas, the transient workers, and other such elements. The sinews of campaign warfare came from the robber-barons of American industry, particularly the real estate and the utility magnates. With the cutting-off of immigration, the slowing-up of the migration from the farms to the cities, the declining of the birth-rate of the newer immigrant groups, the maturation of the industrial revolution in the country, the growing socialization of the policies of the government, particularly the national government, the machines will have fewer and fewer persons to draw upon as the years go by. That section of the electorate which reads no daily newspapers, which depends upon petty handouts from politicians, and which is deficient in formal civic training will grow less and less. It may be that at the end of the next seventy-five years the problem of building up civic morale in the great metropolitan centers will not seem so hopeless as Jefferson thought it was or as some who live in the twentieth century now think it is.

APPENDIX A

TABLE 21

VOTES FOR WARD COMMITTEEMEN

Year	Registered Voters	Republican			Democratic			Total Primary Vote Both Parties
		Wards with Contest for Ward Committeemen	Wards with No Contest for Ward Committeemen	Total	Wards with Contest for Ward Committeemen	Wards with No Contest for Ward Committeemen	Total	
				TOTAL VOTE CAST IN PRIMARY ELECTION				
1928	1,228,283	688,375	23,406	711,781	87,806	72,474	160,280	872,061
1930	1,297,055	545,152	20,208	565,360	145,040	61,826	206,866	772,226
1932	1,429,774	509,841	......	509,841	390,733	77,686	468,419	978,260
1934	1,396,151	285,663	33,434	319,097	281,316	216,417	497,733	816,830
1936	1,644,198	302,437	41,468	343,905	595,698	257,390	853,088	1,196,993

TOTAL VOTE CAST FOR WARD COMMITTEEMEN

Year	Republican				Democratic				Combined Vote for Committeemen Both Parties
	Wards with Contest	Wards with No Contest	Aggregate Vote for Successful Candidates	Total All Candidates	Wards with Contest	Wards with No Contest	Aggregate Vote for Successful Candidates	Total All Candidates	
1928	630,002	19,629	373,182	649,631	80,303	64,716	120,939	145,019	794,650
1930	495,283	16,581	297,838	511,864	133,235	55,557	148,644	188,792	700,656
1932	456,953	......	248,305	456,953	347,936	65,250	305,945	413,186	870,139
1934	259,935	28,516	184,008	288,451	250,927	193,541	379,743	444,468	732,919
1936	278,275	34,714	195,196	312,989	534,608	202,602	561,365	737,210	1,050,199

TABLE 22

DESCRIPTION OF 147 UNITS USED IN STUDY OF VOTING BEHAVIOR IN CHICAGO

Unit	Census Community	Census Tract	Ward Lines 1921	Ward Lines 1931	Total Number Registered October, 1930
1	1	1	50	50	1,774
2	1	2–8	49	49, 50	21,684
3	2	9–17	50	50	14,897
4	3	18	47	47	1,697
5*					
6	3	29–33	50	47, 50	7,285
7†					
8	4	40–42	47	47	3,503
9	4	43–50	50	47, 50	17,173
10	5	51–58, 65	47	45, 47	14,374
11	5	59,64	45	45	5,773
12	6	66–71	47	45, 47	8,508
13	6	72–77	45	45, 46	7,347
14	6	78–79	44	44	3,451
15‡					
16§					
17	7	100–104, part of 105	45	43, 44, 45	6,255
18	7	Part of 105, 106–13	44	43, 44	15,826
19	7	114–19	43	43	8,026
20	8	120–25	43	42, 43	9,892
21	8	126–37	42	42	16,822
22	9	138–40	41	41	2,598
23	10	141–46	41	41	5,258
24	11	147–52	41	41	7,021
25	12	153–54, 155	41	39, 41	1,739
26‖					4,141
27	13	157–59	40	40	4,141
28	14	160–61	41	39	4,036
29	14	162–67	40	39, 40	15,732
30	15	168–76	41	38, 39, 41	19,870
31	15	177–79	39	38	6,101
32	16	180–82	41	39	4,691
33	16	183–90	40	39, 40	18,071
34	16	191–92	39	39	2,764
35	17	193–94, 199–200	41	38, 41	2,821

* Divided into units 173, 174, and 175 below.
† Divided into units 176 and 177 below.
‡ Divided into units 178, 179, and 180 below.
§ Divided into units 181 and 182 below.
‖ Units dropped because of smallness.

TABLE 22—*Continued*

Unit	Census Community	Census Tract	Ward Lines 1921	Ward Lines 1931	Total Number Registered October, 1930
36.............	17	195–98, 201–2	39	38	3,011
37.............	18	203–5	39	36, 38	2,803
38.............	19	206–17	39	35, 36, 38	14,436
39.............	19	218–20	37	36	4,736
40.............	20	221–23	39	35, 36	3,614
41.............	20	224–26	36	34, 36	4,931
42.............	21	227	40	33	1,678
43.............	21	228–32	39	33, 35	10,854
44.............	21	233–35	38	33	4,285
45.............	22	236–38	39	33, 34, 35	7,390
46.............	22	239–48	38	33, 34	15,175
47.............	22	249–52	36	34	5,432
48.............	22	253–58	35	34	7,809
49.............	22	259–60	34	32	1,496
50.............	22	261–64	33	32, 33	3,072
51.............	23	265–67	36	34, 36	2,956
52.............	23	268–71	36	31	7,071
53.............	23	272–76	35	31, 34	6,575
54.............	23	277–79	30	30	5,729
55.............	23	280–82	28	28	5,951
56.............	24	283–86	35	31, 34	3,777
57.............	24	289–94	32	26, 28	12,238
58.............	24	295–304	34	26, 31, 32	13,997
59.............	24	305–12	33	32	10,370
60.............	24	313–20	31	26	11,344
61.............	25	321–39	37	30, 36, 37	41,473
62.............	25	340–44	30	30, 37	19,302
63.............	26	345–50	30	29, 30	12,905
64.............	26	351	28	28	836
65.............	26	352–54	29	29	7,210
66.............	27	355, 358–62	28	25, 27, 28	6,543
67.............	27	356–57, 363–73	29	25, 27, 29	18,414
68.............	27	374–75	25	25	701
69¶.............	.....	.....	.....	.....	.....
70¶.............	.....	.....	.....	.....	.....
71.............	28	388–409	25	20, 25, 27	12,039
72.............	28	410–24	27	20, 25, 27	18,974
73¶.............	.....	.....	.....	.....	.....
74¶.............	.....	.....	.....	.....	.....
75.............	29	444–45, 447–49	29	24	3,398

¶ Units with 20 per cent or more colored; dropped from calculation.

TABLE *22—Continued*

Unit	Census Community	Census Tract	Ward Lines 1921	Ward Lines 1931	Total Number Registered October, 1930
76............	29	446, 450–55	24	22, 24	17,551
77............	29	456–57	25	25	1,432
78............	29	458–59	21	25	575
79............	29	460–65	23	23, 24	11,737
80............	29	466–70	22	22	3,173
81............	30	471–75	21	25	3,306
82............	30	476–80	23	22, 23	11,948
83............	30	481–94	22	22	12,989
84............	31	495–98	26	21	5,233
85............	31	499–503	20	21	4,276
86............	31	504–10	21	21, 25	11,353
87**...........	....	....	....	....	....
88¶...........	....	....	....	....	....
89............	34	523–29	1	1	3,465
90............	34	530–33	11	11	632
91............	34	534	13	11	389.
92¶	....	....	....	....	....
93¶	....	....	....	....	....
94¶	....	....	....	....	....
95¶	....	....	....	....	....
96............	37	563–64	13	11	809
97............	37	565–70	14	14	4,159
98‖...........	....	....	....	....	....
99¶...........	....	....	....	....	....
100¶...........	....	....	....	....	....
101¶...........	....	....	....	....	....
102............	39	593–99	4	4	11,610
103¶...........	....	....	....	....	....
104¶...........	....	....	....	....	....
105¶...........	....	....	....	....	....
106¶...........	....	....	....	....	....
107††...........	....	....	....	....	....
108............	42	623–33	6	5, 6	29,038
109¶...........	....	....	....	....	....
110............	43	635–44	7	7, 8	28,621
111............	43	645–47	8	6, 8	5,400
112............	44	648–55	8	8, 17, 19	11,275
113............	44	656	19	17, 19	1,330
114............	44	657–58	10	8	1,447
115............	45	659	7	8	1,242

** Divided into units 183 and 184 below.
†† Divided into units 185 and 186 below.

TABLE 22—*Continued*

Unit	Census Community	Census Tract	Ward Lines 1921	Ward Lines 1931	Total Number Registered October, 1930
116............	45	660–61	8	8	2,510
117............	46	662–68	7	7, 10	12,298
118............	46	669–71	10	10	2,716
119‖	......	......	......	......	......
120............	47	673	10	8	460
121‖					
122‖					
123............	48	677–80	10	10	2,022
124¶	......				
125............	49	687–94	9	9	13,235
126............	49	695–96	10	8	556
127............	50	697–99	9	9	1,743
128............	51	700–704	10	10	1,732
129............	52	705–10	10	10	5,511
130‖					
131............	53	712–15	9	9	8,082
132............	54	716–17	9	9	601
133............	55	718–19	10	10	1,791
134‖	......				
135............	56	725–33	15	13	1,356
136............	57	734–37	12	13	798
137‖		......			
138............	58	739–51	12	12	12,149
139............	59	752–56, 758–59	12	11, 12	7,910
140‖					
141............	60	760–62, 764–78	11	11	13,941
142‖		......			
143............	60	779–81	13	11	3,055
144............	61	782–84, 787–88, 793–95, parts of 789, 790, 791, 792	13	11, 12, 14	6,671
145............	61	785–86, 796–805	14	14	12,024
146............	61	806–9, parts of 789, 790, 791, 792	15	14, 15	7,874
147‖					
148‖	......	......			
149............	63	815–17	12	12	791
150............	63	818–26	15	13, 15	10,935

TABLE 22—*Continued*

Unit	Census Community	Census Tract	Ward Lines 1921	Ward Lines 1931	Total Number Registered October, 1930
151.............	64	827–34	15	13	1,270
152.............	65	835–37	15	13	1,966
153‖...........					
154.............	66	839–45	15	13, 15	13,107
155.............	66	846–47	18	13	4,056
156.............	67	848–53	15	13, 15, 16	5,931
157.............	67	854–61	16	16	11,191
158.............	67	862–70	18	18, 13, 16	8,986
159.............	68	871–76	16	16	10,296
160.............	68	877–80	17	17	15,044
161.............	68	881–83	18	16, 18	9,607
162.............	68	884	19	17	2,725
163.............	69	885–94	8	6, 8, 17	17,687
164.............	69	895–98	17	6, 17	3,302
165.............	69	899–900	19	17	5,060
166‖...........					
167.............	71	903–7	18	18	8,897
168.............	71	908–14	19	17, 18, 19	15,761
169.............	72	915–21	19	19	7,045
170.............	73	922–27	19	19	8,286
171.............	74	928–29	19	19	959
172¶...........					
173.............	3	19–20, 22, 27	48	48	16,427
174.............	3	21	48	48	1,044
175.............	3	28	48	48	1,627
176.............	3	34–36, 38–39	49	48, 49	19,247
177.............	3	37	49	49	1,315
178.............	6	80–85, 88–95	46	44, 46	18,476
179.............	6	86	46	46	1,634
180.............	6	87	46	46	2,257
181.............	6	96–98	48	46	2,593
182.............	6	99	48	46	1,002
183.............	32	511–15	1	1	3,265
184.............	32	516	1	1	1,554
185.............	41	608–11, 613–22	5	4, 5	18,212
186.............	41	612	5	5	2,199
Totals for Chicago......					1,264,234

TABLE 23

UNITS USED IN THE STUDY OF THE RELATION OF THE PRESS
TO VOTING BEHAVIOR IN CHICAGO

Unit	Census Community	Census Tract	Ward Lines 1921	Ward Lines 1931	Total Number Registered October, 1930
1............	1	1	50	50	1,774
2............	1	2, 3, 5	49	49	10,960
3............	1	4	49	49, 50	3,079
4............	1	6-8	49	49	7,265
5............	2	12, 14, 16	50	50	4,477
6............	2	13, 15, 17	50	50	3,227
7............	3	34, 35	49	49	6,957
8............	3	36, 37	49	49	5,447
9............	3	38, 39	49	49	5,865
10............	4	44-46	50	47, 50	7,144
11............	9	139	41	41	1,663
12............	10	143-44	41	41	3,424
13............	14	162-63, 165-66	40	39, 40	10,237
14............	15	170, 172, 174	41	38, 41	7,208
15............	16	183-86, 188	40	39, 40	9,471
16............	22	238	39	33, 34, 35	3,893
17............	22	239-41, 244	38	33, 34	7,041
18............	22	253-56	35	34	6,339
19............	24	292-94	32	26	5,250
20............	24	309-12	33	32	8,049
21............	25	326-27, 330-31	37	36, 37	11,497
22............	25	334-35, 338-39	37	37	11,431
23............	26	346-47, 349-50	30	29, 30	9,285
24............	28	396-402, 404-9	25	20, 25, 27	6,930
25............	28	425-31	26	20, 27	4,722
26............	30	483-84, 490-91	22	22	6,980
27-28*........	38	576-78, 581-83	3	2, 3	14,157
29-30*........	38	585-88, 589, 592	4	3, 4	11,695
31............	42	623, 624	6	6	4,151
32............	42	626, 628, 630, 632	6	5	7,557
33............	43	635-39	7	7	12,506
34............	43	640-43	7	7	11,729
35............	49	648-49	8	8, 17, 19	5,147
36............	49	688-91	9	9	5,746
37............	52	707-8	10	10	2,591

* Units with 20 per cent or more colored population; dropped from calculation.

TABLE 23—*Continued*

Unit	Census Community	Census Tract	Ward Lines 1921	Ward Lines 1931	Total Number Registered October, 1930
38............	59	752–55	12	11, 12	5,290
39............	60	764, 770–78	11	11	5,863
40............	60	780, 781	13	11	2,391
41............	66	841, 843	15	15	5,344
42............	66	842	15	15	2,980
43............	67	855, 858, 861	16	16	4,091
44............	67	856, 859	16	16	2,487
45............	67	862–64, 868	18	16, 18	2,765
46............	68	881–83	18	16, 17	9,412
47............	68	884	19	17	3,210
48............	72	916–17	19	19	3,346
49............	72	918–19	19	19	2,213
50............	41	612, 621, 622	5	5	3,996
51............	41	613–14, 619–20	5	4, 5	6,624

FORM FOR INFORMATION REGARDING
WARD COMMITTEEMAN

Name.. Party............Date first elected............Ward.........
Address.................................   Last elected............Ward.........

ELECTIVE OFFICE-HOLDERS
(Ward Committeemen)

1. Elective positions held...

....

2. Dates holding office..
3. Occupation at time of first election..
4. Other early occupations..
5. Later occupations..
6. Present occupation..
7. Appointive positions held...
8. Military rank and experience..
9. Birthplace................................. 10. Date of birth..........................
11. Birthplace of father...
12. Age at first election............................. 13. Marital status......................
14. Date of arrival in Chicago........15. Years in Chicago before first election......
16. Places lived in before coming to Chicago...
17. Education; name and location of elementary school...........................
18. High school.............................College or university.........................
    Professional school.................Approximate years in school.............
19. Candidacies for other elective offices (Give dates)...........................

....

20. Religion (Give church)...
21. Membership in fraternal orders and clubs (Give names)....................

....

22. Activities in party organizations...
23. Factional alignments...
24. Connections with the underworld...
25. Outstanding accomplishments in office...

....

26. Reasons for entering politics...
27. Other comments..
                    Vote for his party in his ward...........................

REPORT ON PRECINCT COMMITTEEMAN

Name of prec. capt.....................

Address of prec. capt....................

...........Ward

...........Precinct

CHARACTER OF PRECINCT

...........Median rental

...........Education

...........Most numerous nationality

...........Percentage foreign born

...........Percentage unemployed

...........Most numerous occupational group

...........Last vote for ward committee-man.....................

...........Vote at last general election for congressman-at-large

Dem.....................

Rep.....................

CHARACTERISTICS OF PRECINCT CAPTAIN

...........Rep. (1); Dem. (2) faction.......

...........Sex: male (1); female (2)

...........Color: white (1); colored (2)

...........Height

...........Weight

...........Appearance: neat (1); untidy (2)

...........Speaking ability: pleasing (1); disagreeable (2); an orator (3)

...........Age

...........Present occupation:..............; govt. employee (1); lawyer (2); other professional (3); merchant (4); business exec. (5); domestic service (6); clerical (7); skilled laborer (8); unskilled (9); unemployed (X); no information (0)

Investigator.....................

Address.....................

Date.....................

...........Occupation before entering political work.....................

...........Birthplace:.....................; Chicago (1); other native Amer. (2); Brit. Empire (3); Ire. (4); Germany or Aus. (5); Scand. (6); Russia or Rumania (7); Poland (8); other. Slavic (9); Italian (X); other (r); no information (0).

...........Father's birthplace

...........Years in Chicago

...........Years in precinct

...........Ed.: no sch. (1); gr. non-grad. (2); gr. grad. (3); h.s. non-grad. (4); h.s. grad. (5); c. non-grad. (6); c. grad. (7); prof. non-grad. (8); prof. (9); no information (0)

...........Church:..................... Prot. (1); Cath. (2); Jewish (3); no religion (4); other religion (5); no church affiliation (6); no information (0)

...........Marital status: single (1); married (2); widowed (3); divorced (4); no information (0)

...........Fraternal affiliations.............

...........Early political mentors...........

...........Military experience...............

...........Start in politics...................

...........Reasons for moving into precinct.....................

REPORT ON PRECINCT COMMITTEEMAN—*Continued*

..........Years in political work

..........Public employee or office-holder..........
(Exact grade and office)..........

..........Salary

..........Other income from public sources

..........Former public-job-holder........

POLITICAL ACTIVITIES

..........Number of times precinct is canvassed

..........Arguments used to win votes

..........Ability to predict result..........

..........Ward headquarters: none (1); temporary for primary or election (2); permanent (3)

..........Political club..........

..........Social affairs in prec.: none (1); smoker (2); beer party (3); cards (4); dances (5); picnics (6)

..........Election-day activities: appoints judges and clerks (1); no control over judges and clerks (2)

..........Polling place: nothing to say about (1); selects (2)

..........Assistance to voters: given (1); not given (2)

..........Amount of money available for election-day expenses

..........Personal letters sent to voters: no (1); yes (2)

SOCIAL SERVICE AND FRIENDLY ACTIVITIES

..........Food: none given out (1); occasional gifts (2); Christmas baskets (3); Passover baskets (4)

..........Rent: none (1); month or so (2); longer period (3); eviction postponed (4); eviction prevented (5); helped to put in mun. shelter (6)

..........Coal: none (1); month or so (2); longer period (3)

..........Medical care: none (1); private doc. (2); county hospital (3); Oak Forest (4); Mun. T.B. San. (5)

..........Domestic difficulty adjusted: none (1); some (2); explain

----

..........Juvenile guidance..........
none (1); school transfer (2); advice to delinquent (3)

..........Scholarships:..........
none (1); yes (2)

..........Weddings:..........
none attended (1); attended (2)

..........Funerals:..........
none attended (1); attended (2)

..........Aid in naturalization:..........
none (1); advice on schooling (2); help with witnesses (3); coaching on examination (4)

..........Alleys and streets cleaned........
no attempt to see superintendent or alderman (1); situation handled (2)

..........Legal advice..........
none given (1); personal advice given (2); contact made with lawyer (3)

..........Advice *re* veteran's bonus........
none given (1); directions given (2)

REPORT ON PRECINCT COMMITTEEMAN—*Continued*

........Advice on Home Owner's Loan........

none given (1); directions given (2)

........Advice *re* relief agencies............

....

none given (1); directions given (2)

........Adjustment of taxes............

none adjusted (1); personal property tax adjusted (2); real estate (3); both (4)

........Adjustment of traffic violations............

none adjusted (1); yes (2)

........Aid in connection with trouble with law-enforcing authorities:

....

none given (1); bail raised or bond signed (2); friendly word to police, court clerk, coroner, state's attorney's assistant, or judge

........Permits secured............

none (1); yes: specify whether peddler's, milk, garage, build-

ing, other............

....(2)

........Adjustment of building or zoning regulation............

none (1); favor secured (2); use of law as threat (3)

........Public jobs secured for voters

....

....

none (1); city (2); county (3); park (4); Sanitary District (5); courts (6); state (7); federal W.P.A. (8); other federal (9)

........Public jobs formerly secured

....

....

........Employment for constituents in private concerns............

....

none (1); public utilities (2); numbers (3); other (4)

........Contacts with social agencies

....

....

none (1); friendly (2); hostile (3)

Use separate sheet for additional comments

APPENDIX B

FACTORIAL ANALYSIS

The correlation matrix (p. 109, Table 10) may be presented in a much simpler form by going through certain transformations devised by Professor L. L. Thurstone under the name of "multiple factor" analysis and described in his book *The Vectors of Mind, Multiple-Factor Analysis for the Isolation of Primary Traits* (University of Chicago Press, 1935). One purpose of multiple-factor analysis is to determine how many general and independent factors it is necessary to postulate in order to account for a correlation matrix. The word "factor," in the technical sense, means a reference variable in terms of which given variables can be expressed as linear functions.

The application of the centroid method to the data at hand brought out the fact that the 306 intercorrelations could be expressed in terms of three general factors. Further computations to see if there was a fourth factor indicated that three were sufficient. A three-factor solution means that it is possible to regard the three loadings for each variable as co-ordinates locating that variable as a point with reference to a given sphere. The points inside the sphere were projected to the surface (normalized), and the resulting pattern was studied so as to determine where the three planes of reference should pass. According to multiple-factor theory, the best solution out of an infinite number of solutions is the one which maximizes the number of zero loadings for each factor. Eleven of the points $(-d, e, j, m, -k, h, -u, -s, -l, -t, \text{and } f)$ tended to fall near a plane which was passed through the center of the sphere, the centroid of $-t$ and $-l$, and $-s$. A second plane was passed at right angles to the first and through v and j. Where the third plane of reference should have been passed, could not be determined without adopting an arbitrary rule, since the points did not fall in any definite triangular configuration. For purposes of convenience it was decided to make the third plane orthogonal to the other two. This enables an easy transformation from the co-ordinates to the original coefficients. Using the three planes described above, the factor loadings given in Table 24 were obtained for the eighteen variables. Since the factor loadings are derived from the correlation coefficients, it is possible to calculate the correlation between any two variables by employing only the factor loadings. The process of transformation is given by the equation

$$r = a_{11}a_{21} + a_{12}a_{22} + a_{13}a_{23},$$

where a_{11} is the loading of variable a in factor I, a_{12} is the loading of variable a in factor II, a_{13} is the loading of variable a in factor III, and a_{21}, a_{22}, and a_{23} represent, respectively, the loadings of variable b in factors I, II, and III.

Taking an actual example from Table 24, we find that the correlation of the 1932 Roosevelt vote with the 1936 Roosevelt vote calculated from the factor loadings is .95 and that the original coefficient is .96.

The next step is to name the factors. Mathematically, the solution may be quite satisfactory, but its meaning may not be clear. The method does not

TABLE 24

FACTORIAL MATRIX RELATED TO VOTING BEHAVIOR IN CHICAGO*
(FL=FACTOR LOADINGS)

	Letter Symbol	P Traditional Democratic Machine Vote†	E The Wet and Extravagant Tendencies of Renters‡	D Special Influences Favoring Democratic Candidates§	Communality
	(X)	$(r_{x \Lambda p})$	$(r_{x \Lambda e})$	$(r_{x \Lambda d})$	$(h^2 III)$
Smith.............	a	.811	.273	.416	.9053
Lewis.............	b	.675	.148	.527	.7552
Roosevelt, 1932....	c	.854	.208	.454	.9787
Igoe.............	n	.833	.192	.457	.9396
Roosevelt, 1936....	v	.832	.137	.460	.9226
Women...........	d	− .760	− .153	.007	.6010
Party voting.......	e	.934	.043	.009	.8743
Bond issue.........	f	.334	.620	− .051	.4986
Wet vote..........	g	.540	.637	.186	.7320
Voting interest.....	h	.459	− .229	− .112	.2757
Foreign birth......	i	.722	− .201	.322	.6654
Catholic origins....	j	.808	− .123	.262	.7366
Median rental.....	k	− .867	.227	.064	.8073
Home ownership...	l	.102	− .819	.066	.6855
Unemployment....	m	.890	− .138	.037	.8125
Mobility..........	s	− .598	.648	.003	.7775
Doubling-up.......	t	− .028	− .396	− .032	.1586
Education.........	u	− .884	.321	− .045	.8865
Actual........... {		5.657	1.395	3.030	13.0129
....		5.659	1.394	3.029	13.0130

* Calculated from centroid co-ordinates inside sphere.
† Distance of variable x from DE plane.
‡ Distance of variable x from PD plane.
§ Distance of variable x from PE plane.

insure that the factor loadings will be such that they can be readily labeled. The magnitude of the loadings, the signs, and the geometric solution must all be considered when arriving at names for the factors.

The most stable of the planes is the PE plane because it has the greatest number of points which are close to it. The distance of any given variable from this plane determines the loading which that variable has in factor D. The highest loadings for this factor, without reference to signs and arranged in order of magnitude, are: Lewis vote (.527), Roosevelt vote in 1936 (.460), Igoe vote (.457), Roosevelt vote in 1932 (.454), Smith vote (.416), foreign born (.322), and Catholic origins (.262). It is clear that this factor is a highly political one; it represents the extent to which the variables mentioned have peculiar qualities that distinguish them from the social and economic variables. However, since the loadings are low, it means that the political variables were separated from the social and economic variables only to a limited extent. The most independent of all is the Lewis vote, and this coincides with the logic of the situation, which has already been discussed. There were peculiar influences at work to accentuate the size of the Lewis vote and its relationship to the other variables. The other elections also had distinctive political characteristics which marked them off from the other variables. We may therefore name this factor "special influences favoring Democratic candidates."

Next to the PE plane, the PD plane is the most stable, since it has at least five points which are fairly close to it. Distances from this plane, or loadings in factor E as they are called, are given in the second column of Table 24. Disregarding signs, the highest loadings in the order of their magnitude are: home-ownership ($-.819$), mobility (.648), wet vote (.637), bond issue (.620), doubling-up ($-.396$), education (.321), Smith vote (.273), and voting interest ($-.229$). These loadings mean that variations in the proportion of home-owners had no definite linear relation to variations in party preferences. In Chicago, home-owners are highly tax conscious and dry whether their homes are palatial or extremely modest. On the other hand, the renters are wet and carefree about public spending. While it is hard to combine these descriptions, we may say that factor E represents "the wet and extravagant tendencies of renters."

Paradoxical as it may seem, the factor which has the highest loadings in the solution under discussion is the one which is the least stable. The plane DE has few points which are very close to it. Doubling-up is the nearest (a loading of only $-.028$), and home-ownership (.102) comes next; but it cannot be said that these are sufficient to determine the location of the plane, especially when the low communality of doubling-up is considered. There is no point which is close to the pole D, which marks the intersection of planes DE and PD. On the other hand, it is obvious that the loadings of the variables in factor P have considerable significance. They give a general view of the entire correlation matrix and show at a glance the high degree of relationship between the political variables and the social and economic variables. In the order of their magnitude, without regard to signs, the highest loadings are: party voting (.934), unemployment (.890), education ($-.884$), median rental ($-.867$), Roosevelt vote in 1932 (.854), Igoe vote (.833), Roosevelt vote in 1936 (.832), Smith vote (.811), Catholic origins (.808), women ($-.760$), foreign born (.722), Lewis vote (.675), mobility ($-.598$), wet vote (.540), voting interest (.459), and bond issue (.334). This factor is obviously related to the traditional Democratic machine vote, which is concentrated in the poor areas, where there are many Catholics of foreign extraction who have not gone very far in school and where women folks are relatively fewer on the registration rolls than in other sections. We may call this factor the "traditional democratic machine vote."

According to the multiple-factor solution, the 1936 Roosevelt vote very closely resembles the other Democratic votes in Chicago. The slight changes which took place between 1932 and 1936 in the various voting areas of Chicago tended to move the Democratic support ever so slightly away from the wet foundations which it had in 1928 (the Roosevelt vote has a lower loading in factor E than the Smith vote). As compared with the 1932 and 1934 votes, there were practically no special influences at work in 1936. Factorial methods corroborate correlational techniques in the conclusion that party tradition, as measured by previous voting behavior, was the most important influence in the 1936 election in Chicago.

APPENDIX C

FORMULAS AND EQUATIONS

I. EQUATIONS USED IN COMPUTATIONS

Mean, M:

$$M = \frac{\Sigma X}{N}.$$

Standard deviation, σ:

$$M = \frac{\Sigma X^2}{N},$$

$$\sigma = \sqrt{M_{X^2} - (M_X)^2}.$$

Product-moment formula for coefficient of correlation, r:

$$r_{XY} = \frac{p_{XY}}{\sigma_X \sigma_Y},$$

$$p_{XY} = \frac{\Sigma XY}{N} - M_X M_Y.$$

The Charlier check was used to test the accuracy of the cross-products of the variables.

General equation for straight line:

$$Y = a + bX.$$

Straight line of regression:

$$Y = M_Y - r\frac{\sigma_Y}{\sigma_X}M_X + r\frac{\sigma_Y}{\sigma_X}X.$$

Equation for coefficients of partial correlation:

$$r_{12 \cdot 34 \ldots\ldots n} = \frac{r_{12 \cdot 34 \ldots\ldots (n-1)} - r_{1n \cdot 34 \ldots\ldots (n-1)} \cdot r_{2n \cdot 34 \ldots\ldots (n-1)}}{(1 - r_{1n \cdot 34 \ldots\ldots (n-1)}^2)^{1/2}(1 - r_{2n \cdot 34 \ldots\ldots (n-1)}^2)^{1/2}}.$$

Methods outlined in Mordecai Ezekiel, *Methods of Correlation Analysis*, pp. 357–69, were adapted for computing the coefficients of multiple correlation and net regression, and the standard errors of partial regression coefficients.

II. EQUATIONS FOR CHAPTER V

a = Smith vote, 1928	k = Median rental, 1930
c = Roosevelt vote, 1932	m = Unemployment, 1931
e = Party vote, 1932	n = Igoe vote, 1934
g = Wet vote, 1930	v = Roosevelt vote, 1936
i = Foreign birth, 1930	w = Relief, 1933
j = Catholic origins, 1930	

Page 113:

The fourth-order coefficients of partial correlation are:

$r_{ca \cdot egjm} = .673$, $r_{cj \cdot aegm} = .069$, $r_{cm \cdot aegj} = .175$, $r_{cg \cdot aejm} = .206$,

$$r_{ce \cdot agjm} = .322.$$

$$X_c = 2.69 + .5428X_a + .2242X_e + .2002X_g + .0253X_j + .1063X_m.$$

$$S_{c \cdot aegjm} = 3.875.$$

Pages 118–20:

$$X_n = 10.59 + .8790X_c. \qquad\qquad S_{n \cdot c} = 3.667.$$

The second-order coefficients of partial correlation are:

$r_{ng \cdot ik} = .442$, $r_{ni \cdot gk} = .467$, $r_{nk \cdot gi} = -.297$.

$$X_n = 6.10 + .6799X_g + .4675X_i - .1610X_k. \qquad R_{n \cdot gik} = .8022.$$

$$S_{n \cdot gik} = 7.1825.$$

The third-order coefficients of partial correlation are:

$r_{nc \cdot gik} = .888$, $r_{ng \cdot cik} = -.141$, $r_{ni \cdot cgk} = .066$, $r_{nk \cdot gci} = .109$.

$$X_n = 14.35 + .9164X_c - .1076X_g + .0308X_i + .0285X_k.$$

The σ's of the b's are .040, .063, .039, .022.

$$R_{n \cdot cgik} = .962. \qquad\qquad S_{n \cdot cgik} = 3.304.$$

Pages 122–24:

$$X_v = 8.54 + .7079X_c + .0957X_g + .2918X_i - .0007X_k.$$

The σ's of the b's are .0327, .0498, .0293, .0164.

$$R_{v \cdot cgik} = .971. \qquad\qquad S_{v \cdot cgik} = 2.489.$$

$$X_v = 7.36 + .7126X_c + .0795X_g + .2960X_i + .0238X_k + .0825X_w.$$

The σ's of the b's are .0328, .0511, .0289, .0226, .0552.

$$R_{v \cdot cgikw} = .972. \qquad\qquad S_{v \cdot cgikw} = 2.453.$$

III. EQUATIONS FOR CHAPTER VIII

a = *News*, 1933	p = Party voting, 1932
d = *Herald and Examiner*, 1933	r = Wet vote, 1930
g = Lewis, 1930	t = Catholic origins, 1930
h = Thompson, 1931	v = Median rental, 1930
k = Cermak, 1931	w = Taking no newspaper, 1933
l = Roosevelt, 1932	z = Roosevelt vote, 1936
m = Horner, 1932	

Page 174:

The first- and third-order coefficients of partial correlation are:

$r_{la \cdot r} = -.568$, $r_{la \cdot t} = -.261$, $r_{la \cdot v} = -.496$, $r_{la \cdot rtv} = .065$, $r_{lr \cdot atv} = .556$, $r_{lt \cdot arv} = .539$, and $r_{lv \cdot art} = -.420$.

$X_l = -16.19 + .0402X_a + .9241X_r + .3098X_t - .1431X_v$.

The σ's of the b's are .116, .192, .093, .086.

$R_{l \cdot artv} = .8981$. $\qquad\qquad S_{l \cdot artv} = 6.263$.

$X_l = -27.999 + .0272X_a + .8055X_g + .3308X_r + .2070X_t - .0902X_v$.

The σ's of the b's are .074, .101, .143, .060, .055.

$R_{l \cdot agrtv} = .960$. $\qquad\qquad S_{l \cdot agrtv} = 3.990$.

Pages 175–76:

$X_z = 22.0 - .3123X_a + .7068X_r + .1491X_t - .0500X_v$.

The σ's of the b's are .157, .260, .126, .117.

$R_{z \cdot artv} = .9150$. $\qquad\qquad S_{z \cdot artv} = 2.691$.

$X_z = 38.11 - .4798X_a + .6360X_r + .3816X_t - .0599X_v - .5427X_w$.

The σ's of the b's are .1826, .2611, .1820, .1159, .3087.

$R_{z \cdot artvw} = .9166$. $\qquad\qquad S_{z \cdot artvw} = 2.667$.

Pages 178–80:

$X_m = -9.789 + .2418X_a + .6126X_k + .4743X_l$.

The σ's of the b's are .063, .087, and .084.

$R_{m \cdot akl} = .8467$. $\qquad\qquad S_{m \cdot akl} = 4.758$.

$X_m = 10.37 + .1386X_a + .7485X_l + .3200X_v$.

The σ's of the b's are .093, .101, and .076.

$R_{m \cdot alv} = .7547$. $\qquad\qquad S_{m \cdot alv} = 5.866$.

The second-order coefficients of partial correlation are:

$r_{ml \cdot ak} = .647$, $r_{mk \cdot al} = .728$, and $r_{ma \cdot kl} = .740$.

Pages 180–81:

$$X_h = 10.56 - .2738X_a + .6909X_d + .6014X_p - .0090X_v.$$

The σ's of the b's are .123, .369, .210, and .129.

$R_{h \cdot adpv} = .866.$ $\qquad\qquad\qquad$ $S_{h \cdot adpv} = 7.73.$

$$X_h = -53.92 - .1638X_a + .2558X_d + .4553X_p + .9484X_r.$$

The σ's of the b's are .096, .307, .135, and .194.

$R_{h \cdot adpr} = .916.$ $\qquad\qquad\qquad$ $S_{h \cdot adpr} = 6.20.$

The third-order coefficients of partial correlation are:

$r_{ha \cdot dpv} = -.321$, $r_{hd \cdot apv} = .280$, $r_{hp \cdot adv} = .446$, and $r_{hv \cdot adp} = .084$.

APPENDIX D

BIBLIOGRAPHY

DOCUMENTS

Board of Election Commissioners of the City of Chicago. *General Election Laws.*

Chicago. *Council Proceedings.*

Chicago Crime Commission. Records (unpublished).

Cook County Commissioners. *Official Record of Proceedings*, 1896–1900, 1904–10, 1929–36.

Illinois. *Illinois Blue Book*, 1877–1936.

United States Bureau of the Census. *Fifteenth Census.*

United States Congress. *Congressional Directory.*

United States Senate. *Hearings before a Special Committee Investigating Campaign Expenditures in Senatorial Primary and General Elections, 1926, 69th Congress, 1st Session*, Part II (Reed Committee).

———. *Positions Not under The Civil Service*, Document No. 173, 72d Congress, 2d Session.

———. *Select Committee on Senatorial Campaign Expenditures, 71st Congress, 2d Session*, Part II, Illinois (Nye Committee).

DAILY NEWSPAPERS

Illinois:

Chicago Daily News, 1928–36.

Chicago Evening American, 1928–36.

Chicago Herald and Examiner, 1928–36.

Chicago Tribune, 1928–36.

Daily Times, Chicago, 1928–36.

PUBLICATIONS OF CIVIC AND OTHER AGENCIES

Better Government Association of Chicago. Pamphlets, 1928–36.

Chicago Bar Association Record, 1928–36.

Chicago Bureau of Public Efficiency. *Bulletin*, 1928–36.

Chicago Daily News Almanac and Year Book, 1886–1937.

Citizens' Association of Chicago. *Bulletin*, 1928–36.

Civic Federation and Bureau of Public Efficiency. *Bulletin*, 1928–36.

Legislative Voters' League of Illinois. *Assembly Bulletin*, 1917–36.

Municipal Voters' League of Chicago. Reports, 1915–35.

Public Service Leader, 1930–36.

GOSNELL, H. F., and GILL, NORMAN N. "An Analysis of the 1932 Presidential Vote in Chicago," *American Political Science Review*, XXIX (December, 1935), 967–84.

GOSNELL, H. F., and SCHMIDT, M. J. "Factorial Analysis of the Relation of the Press to Voting in Chicago," *Journal of Social Psychology*, II (November, 1936), 375–85.

———. "Factorial and Correlational Analysis of the 1934 Vote in Chicago," *Journal of the American Statistical Association*, XXXI (September, 1936), 507–18.

———. "Relation of the Press to Voting in Chicago," *Journalism Quarterly*, XIII (June, 1936), 129–47.

HARRIS, JOSEPH PRATT. "The Practical Workings of Proportional Representation in the United States and Canada," *National Municipal Review*, XIX (1930), 337–83.

LOWRIE, S. G. "Organizing the Citizens for Good Government," *Public Management*, XII (November, 1930), 541–44.

MAYNARD, DAVID M. "Fraud and Error in Chicago Referendum Returns," *National Municipal Review*, Vol. XIX (March, 1930).

MOSHER, WILLIAM E. "Party and Government Control at the Grass Roots," *National Municipal Review*, XXIV (January, 1935) 15–18, 38.

OGBURN, WILLIAM F. "A Study of Rents in Various Cities," *Monthly Labor Review*, Vol. VIII (September, 1919).

OGBURN, W., and TALBOT, N. S. "A Measurement of the Factors in the Presidential Election of 1928," *Social Forces*, Vol. VIII (December, 1929).

RICHBERG, DONALD. "Gold-plated Anarchy, an Interpretation of the Fall of the Giants," *Nation*, Vol. CXXXVI (April 5, 1933).

SCHUMAKER, W. "People's Rule in Oregon," *Political Science Quarterly*, Vol. XLVII (June, 1932).

SEARS, KENNETH C. "Voting on Constitutional Conventions and Amendments," *University of Chicago Law Review*, II (June, 1935), 612–18.

STRATTON, IRA W. "American Citizenship and Australian Election Methods," *National Municipal Review*, XX (February, 1931), 90–94.

Survey Graphic, Vol. XXIII (October, 1934), special Chicago issue.

WOODDY, CARROLL H. "Jubilee in Chicago," *National Municipal Review*, XX (June, 1931), 321–25.

YARROS, V. S. "Presenting Big Bill Thompson of Chicago," *Independent*, November 5, 1927.

CASES

VALIDITY OF REFERENDUM AS A FORM OF GOVERNMENT:

People ex. rel. *Caldwell* v. *Reynolds*, 10 Ill. (1849) 1.

Erlinger v. *Boneau*, 51 Ill. (1869) 94.

People ex. rel. *Grinnell* v. *Hoffman*, 116 Ill. (1886) 587.

Rouse v. *Thompson*, 228 Ill. (1907) 522.

BOOKS AND PAMPHLETS

ADDAMS, JANE. *Democracy and Social Ethics*. New York: Macmillan Co., 1902.

ALTMAN, OSCAR LOUIS. "Chicago's Experiment in Personal Property Taxation, 1931–1936." Chicago: University of Chicago (Ph.D. thesis), 1936.

ANDERSON, NELS. *The Hobo: The Sociology of the Homeless Man*. Chicago: University of Chicago Press, 1923.

BENTLEY, HENRY. *Cincinnati Plan of Citizen Organization*. National Municipal League pamphlet, September, 1934.

BRIGHT, JOHN. *Hizzoner Big Bill Thompson*. New York: Jonathan Cape & Harrison Smith, 1930.

BURGESS, E. W., and NEWCOMB, C. (eds.). *Census Data of the City of Chicago, 1930*. Chicago: University of Chicago Press, 1933.

COUNTS, GEORGE SYLVESTER. *School and Society in Chicago*. New York: Harcourt, Brace & Co., 1928.

DOBYNS, FLETCHER *The Underworld of American Politics*. New York: Privately printed, 1932.

EZEKIEL, M. *Methods of Correlation Analysis*. New York: John Wiley & Sons, 1930.

GARDNER, C. O. *The Referendum in Chicago*. Philadelphia: University of Pennsylvania, 1920.

GOSNELL, HAROLD F. *Getting Out the Vote: An Experiment in the Stimulation of Voting*. Chicago: University of Chicago Press, 1927.

———. *Negro Politicians: The Rise of Negro Politics in Chicago*. Chicago: University of Chicago Press, 1935.

———. *Why Europe Votes*. Chicago: University of Chicago Press, 1930.

GREENE, SHIRLEY E. (ed.). *Re-thinking Chicago for 1936*. Chicago: Privately printed, 1936.

HARRIS, JOSEPH PRATT. *Election Administration in the United States*. Washington: Brookings Institution, 1934.

———. *Registration of Voters in the United States*. Washington: Brookings Institution, 1929.

HARTLEY, MARY. *James Breckinridge Waller: and Pioneering in the Wilderness of Politics*. Chicago: Privately printed, 1931.

HEMDAHL, REUEL G. "The Swedes in Illinois Politics." Evanston: Northwestern University (manuscript), 1932.

HOAN, D. *City Government: The Record of the Milwaukee Experiment*. New York: Harcourt, Brace & Co., 1936.

JACOBS, J. L. *Assessemnts of Real Estate and Personal Property in Cook County, Illinois*. Chicago: Office of the Assessor, 1934.

KENT, FRANK R. *The Great Game of Politics*. Garden City: Doubleday, Page & Co., 1923.

———. *Political Behavior*. New York: William Morrow & Co., 1928.

KEY, V. O. "Techniques of Political Graft in the United States." Chicago: University of Chicago (Ph.D. thesis). 1934.

KURTZMAN, DAVID HAROLD. *Methods of Controlling Votes in Philadelphia.* Philadelphia: Privately printed, 1935.

LANDESCO, JOHN. "Organized Crime in Chicago," *Illinois Crime Survey.* Chicago: Illinois Association for Criminal Justice, 1929.

LANG, R. O. "The Relation of Educational Status to Economic Status in the City of Chicago by Census Tracts, 1934," Chicago: University of Chicago (Ph.D. thesis), 1936.

LEPAWSKY, ALBERT. *The Judicial System of Metropolitan Chicago.* Chicago: University of Chicago Press, 1932.

LEWIS, LLOYD, and SMITH, HENRY JUSTIN. *Chicago: The History of Its Reputation.* New York: Harcourt, Brace & Co., 1929.

LOVETT, WILLIAM P. *Detroit Rules Itself.* Boston: Gorham Press, 1930.

LUNDBERG, F. *Imperial Hearst.* New York: Equinox Co-operative Press, 1936.

MARTIN, E. M. *The Role of the Bar in Electing the Bench in Chicago.* Chicago: University of Chicago Press, 1936.

MAYNARD, D. M. "The Operation of the Referendum in Chicago." Chicago: University of Chicago (Ph.D. thesis), 1930.

MERRIAM, CHARLES E. *Chicago: A More Intimate View of Urban Politics.* New York: Macmillan Co., 1929.

MERRIAM, CHARLES E., and GOSNELL, H. F. *Non-voting: Causes and Methods of Control.* Chicago: University of Chicago Press, 1924.

MERRIAM, C. E.; PARRATT, S. D., and LEPAWSKY, A. *The Government of the Metropolitan Region of Chicago.* Chicago: University of Chicago Press, 1933.

NEWCOMB, C., and LANG, R. O. (eds.). *Census Data of Chicago, 1934.* Chicago: University of Chicago Press, 1934.

OBERHOLTZER, E. P. *The Referendum in America.* New York: Charles Scribner's Sons, 1912.

ODEGARD, P. H. *The American Public Mind.* New York: Columbia University Press, 1930.

OVERACKER, L. *Money in Elections.* New York: Macmillan Co., 1932.

PEEL, ROY V. *The Political Clubs of New York City.* New York: G. P. Putnam's Sons, 1935.

POIS, J.; MARTIN, E. M.; and MOORE, L. S. *The Merit System in Illinois.* Chicago: Joint Committee on the Merit System, 1935.

RECKLESS, WALTER. *Vice in Chicago.* Chicago: University of Chicago Press, 1933.

RICE, STUART A. *Quantitative Methods of Politics.* New York: Alfred A. Knopf, 1928.

ROBERTSON, MRS. HARRIET M. (ed.). *Dishonest Elections and Why We Have Them.* Chicago: Women's Civic Council of the Chicago Area, 1934.

ROBINSON, C. E. *Straw Votes.* New York: Columbia University Press, 1932.

SALTER, J. T. *Boss Rule: Portraits in City Politics.* New York: Whittlesey House, 1935.

SCHIAVO, GIOVANNI E. *The Italians in Chicago.* Chicago: Italian American Publishing Co., 1928.

SIMPSON, HERBERT D. *Tax Racket and Tax Reform in Chicago.* Chicago: Institute for Economic Research, Northwestern University, 1930.

SMITH, T. V. *The Promise of American Politics.* Chicago: University of Chicago Press, 1936.

STEFFENS, LINCOLN. *The Autobiography of Lincoln Steffens.* New York: Harcourt, Brace & Co., 1931.

STUART, WILLIAM H. *The 20 Incredible Years.* Chicago: M. A. Donohue & Co., 1935.

TAFT, CHARLES P. *City Management: The Cincinnati Experiment.* New York: Farrar & Rinehart, 1933.

THRASHER, FREDERICK. *The Gang.* Chicago: University of Chicago Press, 1927.

UNION LEAGUE OF CHICAGO, PUBLIC AFFAIRS COMMITTEE. *Chicago Civic Agencies, 1927.* Chicago: University of Chicago Press, 1927.

WHITE, LEONARD D. *Prestige Value of Public Employment.* Chicago: University of Chicago Press, 1929.

WOODDY, CARROLL H. *The Case of Frank L. Smith.* Chicago: University of Chicago Press, 1931.

———. *The Chicago Primary of 1926.* Chicago: University of Chicago Press, 1926.

WOODS, ROBERT ARCHEY. *The City Wilderness.* Boston: Houghton, Mifflin & Co., 1898.

BRIEFER ARTICLES

FORTHAL, S. "Relief and Friendly Service by Political Precinct Leaders," *Social Service Review*, VII (December, 1933), 608–18.

Fortune. "The Chicago Tribune," IX (May, 1934), 14–25, 101–13.

———. "The Kelly-Nash Machine," Vol. XIV (August, 1936).

GOSNELL, HAROLD F. "Fighting Corruption in Chicago," *Polity*, July–August, 1935, p. 138.

———. "How Accurate Were the Polls?" *Public Opinion Quarterly*, Vol. I (January, 1937).

———. "A New Method for Counting Proportional Representation Ballots," *National Municipal Review*, XIV (July, 1925), 397–98.

———. "The Political Party versus the Political Machine," *Annals of the American Academy of Political and Social Science*, CLXIX (September, 1933), 21–28.

———. "Proportional Representation," *Encyclopaedia of the Social Sciences*, XII (New York, February, 1934), 541–45.

———. "The Swiss National Council Elections of 1931," *American Political Science Review*, XXVI (July, 1930), 351–54.

People v. *McBride*, 234 Ill. (1908) 146.

People ex. rel. *City of Springfield* v. *Edmands*, 252 Ill. (1911) 108.

People v. *Czarnecki*, 254 Ill. (1912) 72.

People v. *Hartquist*, 311 Ill. (1924) 127.

RECOUNT OF BALLOTS AND EVIDENCE IN CONTESTED ELECTIONS:

Welsh v. *Shumway*, 232 Ill. (1907) 54.

Shirar v. *Elbridge Township*, 249 Ill. (1911) 617.

Strubinger v. *Ownby*, 290 Ill. (1919) 380.

Hodge v. *Linn*, 100 Ill. (1882) 397.

MacGuidwin v. *South Park Commissioners*, 333 Ill. (1928) 58.

FORM OF BALLOT OR METHOD OF SUBMITTING QUESTIONS:

Clarke v. *Board of Supervisors of Hancock Co.*, 27 Ill. (1862) 304.

Union Co. v. *Ussery*, 147 Ill. (1893) 204.

People ex. rel. *Koch* v. *Rinaker*, 252 Ill. (1911) 266.

People ex. rel. *Brady* v. *Lu Salle Street Trust and Savings Bank*, 269 Ill. (1915) 518.

People ex. rel. *Vance* v. *Elledge*, 281 Ill. (1917) 592.

People ex. rel. *Mattingly* v. *Snedeker*, 282 Ill. (1918) 425.

Mitchell v. *Lowden*, 288 Ill. (1919) 327.

People ex. rel. *Forsythe* v. *The Cleveland, Cincinnati, Chicago, and St. Louis Ry. Co.*, 327 Ill. (1927) 611.

NUMBER OF VOTES REQUIRED FOR MAJORITY:

People ex. rel. *Husser* v. *Hedlund*, 309 Ill. (1923) 280.

Hagler v. *Small*, 307 Ill. (1923) 460.

Campe v. *Cermak*, 330 Ill. (1928) 463.

AMENDMENTS TO LEGISLATIVE ACTS AFTER SUBMISSION TO PEOPLE:

Waugh v. *Glos*, 246 Ill. (1910) 604.

Fields v. *Lueders*, 274 Ill. (1916) 562.

People ex. rel. *Egan* v. *City of Chicago*, 310 Ill. (1924) 534.

ELECTION EXPENSES:

Bolles v. *Prince*, 250 Ill. (1911) 36.

Johnson v. *County of Winnebago*, 256 Ill. (1912) 276.

Renneker Co. v. *South Park Commissioners*, 245 Ill. App. (1928) 513.

JURISDICTION AND CONSTITUTIONALITY OF ELECTIONS:

Sherman v. *People*, 210 Ill. (1904) 552.

POSTSCRIPT TO THE SECOND EDITION

CHICAGO POLITICS 1937–1967

Of all the great cities in the United States, the political power structure of the city of Chicago has probably changed the least during the three decades following 1937 when this book was first published. The Democratic party organization which held sway during the period continued to approximate the model of a political power elite led by the chief executive of the local government who was also the leader of the party organization. This party elite controlled Democratic nominations for city, county, and state offices; it participated in important political decisions made in the area; and it maintained party discipline. Of course it shared its powers with various economic and neighborhood groups depending upon the issues involved.[1] The social structure of the city was too complex and the problems too varied for anything but pluralistic leadership. The Democratic organization, however, furnished greater unity and, to use a local phrase, more "clout," or political power, than the party leadership in other cities. The Chicago political machine represented a survival of old-style party organization which served as a patron of minority groups and a broker for business.

In other large American cities, with some exceptions, a new style of party organization has been developing.[2] There has been a lack of unified leadership, and a number of voluntary organizations have been formed. In Los Angeles and Detroit, for instance, there have been no unified local party organizations which could control nominations and elections to city offices. Nonpartisanship has been strong in these cities, and

---

[1] Edward C. Banfield, *Political Influence* (New York: Free Press, 1961).

[2] Fred I. Greenstein, "The Changing Pattern of Urban Party Politics," in Lee S. Greene, "City Bosses and Political Machines," *Annals of the American Academy of Political and Social Science*, 353 (May, 1964), 1–13.

local elections have been won not by party machines but by combining various group interests and by exploiting the mass media, particularly television, in recent years.[3] In Detroit Eldersveld found that the political leaders were not arranged in a rigid hierarchy but held semiautonomous positions giving deference downward as well as upward. They held together subcoalitions of a highly divergent character. The top county leaders complained about the tenuousness of their control, the absence of patronage, and their own precarious position.[4]

A number of old-style party machines were smashed beyond repair during the period. The Democratic organization of New York City became a mere shadow of what it had been under Charles F. Murphy. Eleven years of Mayor LaGuardia, the passage of a new city charter, the strengthening of the merit system and the resultant drying up of patronage, the professionalization of the civil service, the splitting of the Democratic party into many factions, and the rise of minor parties with labor support and the development of independent citizens' groups meant the weakening of the organization and a loss of control over nominations and elections.[5] Even more dramatic was the collapse in 1939 of the Democratic machine led by Tom Pendergast in Kansas City. Pendergast's trial and imprisonment for income tax evasion for not reporting a large bribe received in connection with insurance rebates brought an end to his strong party leadership. Among the factors contributing to his downfall were diligence of the crusading press, the unflagging efforts of the Department of Justice and the Bureau of Internal Revenue, the determined opposition of the governor of Missouri, and aroused citizens' associations.[6]

Why has the political system of the city of Chicago changed

[3] Edward C. Banfield, *Big City Politics* (New York: Random House, 1965).

[4] Samuel J. Eldersveld, *Political Parties: A Behavioral Analysis* (Chicago: Rand McNally, 1964).

[5] Wallace S. Sayre and Herbert Kaufman, *Governing New York City* (New York: Russell Sage Foundation, 1960).

[6] A. Theodore Brown, *The Politics of Reform: Kansas City's Municipal Government —1925–1950* (Kansas City: Community Studies, 1958); Maurice M. Milligan, *Missouri Waltz* (New York: Scribner's, 1948).

less than that of other cities during the past three decades? A brief review of the main political events in the city since 1937 will furnish a background for the discussion of some of the factors related to the stability of the regime.

During the period there have been only three mayors, all Democrats, all of Irish extraction, and all of modest beginnings. They were: Edward J. Kelly, 1933 until 1947; Martin H. Kennelly, 1947 until 1955; and Richard J. Daley, mayor since 1955. All but Kennelly had started at the bottom of the party organization and served in a variety of political posts. None had been top leaders in the industrial or business activities of the city, but they all had demonstrated political managerial abilities. They should all be classified as political administrators.[7] Professor Wilson has characterized these three administrations as follows: "Where Kelly had appeared to be strong but corrupt, and Kennelly had been clean but weak, Daley would be strong *and* clean."[8]

The close relationship between the mayor of Chicago and the Cook County Central Democratic Committee was one of the keys to the stability of the Chicago political system. This committee controlled party nominations and the distribution of patronage, and it made possible by informal arrangements some form of unified action by the multitude of local governmental agencies in the metropolitan area. In the early part of the period, its chairman Patrick A. Nash, wealthy sewer contractor, worked hand in glove with Mayor Kelly. The Chicago Democratic organization was known as the Kelly-Nash machine. As pointed out above, Mayor Kelly's election in 1935 was a pushover. In 1939 and 1943, he met more serious opposition. In the first of these elections his Republican opponent was Dwight H. Green, former United States District Attorney, whose good showing in the election (43.5 per cent) was a factor in his selection as Republican candidate for governor the following year.

[7] Donald S. Bradley and Mayer N. Zald, "From Commercial Elite to Political Administrator: The Recruitment of Mayors of Chicago," *The American Journal of Sociology* (September, 1965), pp. 153–67.

[8] James Q. Wilson, *Negro Politics* (New York: Free Press, 1960), pp. 82–83.

His opponent in 1943 was George McKibbin, a Chicago lawyer who had served as state director of finance under Governor Green. McKibben made a slightly better showing (45.5 per cent). This was the closest anyone was to come to unseating the Chicago Democratic organization during the period.

Mayor Kelly inherited a political machine which he strengthened by skillful use of patronage, by careful cultivation of business interests, by his success in attracting federal grants-in-aid for various programs, and by his ability to reconcile the interests of labor, minority, and other groups. While he claimed that he believed that "good government was good politics,"[9] his regime was severely criticized for scandals in the administration of the schools, for manipulation of tax assessments, for padded payrolls, and for police corruption.

During the time that Kelly was mayor of Chicago, the Illinois Democratic organization played a significant role in national elections. While Secretary of the Interior Harold Ickes was critical of the Kelly regime because of his doubts about its honesty,[10] Postmaster General James Farley was impressed with the ability of the machine to deliver a large Democratic vote. In 1936 Mayor Kelly staged a mammoth rally for President Roosevelt. Both the 1940 and the 1944 Democratic national conventions were held in Chicago, in part because Mayor Kelly could pack the galleries and stage impressive demonstrations. In 1940 the Chicago delegation supported the nomination of Henry Wallace for vice president in accordance with Roosevelt's wishes, and in 1944 it participated in the scheme to drop Wallace and nominate Senator Harry S Truman in his place. Mayor Kelly put up Senator Scott Lucas as a favorite son in order to prevent Wallace from getting any votes from Illinois delegates on the first two ballots. He also participated in the preliminary conferences which led to the selection of Senator Truman. In 1936, President Roosevelt did not need a large

[9] Edward J. Kelly, with Walter Davenport, "Politics is People," *Collier's*, April 13, 1946.

[10] Harold L. Ickes, *The Secret Diary of Harold L. Ickes* (New York: Simon & Shuster, 1954), vol. 2, p. 561.

Chicago vote in order to carry the state of Illinois, but he did in 1940 and 1944.

When Colonel Jacob Arvey, a shrewd lawyer and a remarkable political manager, became Cook County Democratic Chairman in 1946, a new relationship between the party and the city government was established. Mayor Kelly was persuaded to retire in order to improve the image of the party, and the organization backed as the Democratic candidate for mayor in 1947 a businessman, Martin Kennelly, who had been active on the Crime Commission and was known as an antimachine civic leader. Although the tide was running in favor of the Republicans nationally, they put up a weak and unknown candidate. Kennelly promised to battle against party abuses and declared he did not subscribe to the principle "to the victor belong the spoils," but rather, "to the victor belongs greater responsibility." With the backing of the Democratic organization and a generally favorable press he was elected with a larger share of the votes than Kelly had received in his last two elections.

Mayor Kennelly, in relying chiefly upon his official powers, was not able to furnish as strong leadership as Mayor Kelly, with his control of the party machine. The new mayor could not control the City Council as well as his predecessor. In spite of this, he did much to create a better image of the city government by tightening police administration, by improving the administration of the schools, by enforcing the civil service laws, and by initiating plans for slum clearance and improved transportation facilities. With Colonel Arvey still serving as county chairman, and with strong press support, he was re-elected mayor in 1951.

One of the accomplishments of the Chicago political machine during this period was the bringing of Adlai Stevenson into the public eye as a candidate for elective office. In 1948 Colonel Arvey was looking for two strong candidates to bolster the fortunes of the Democratic party in Illinois. He needed one to run for United States senator against the isolationist Republican Senator C. Wayland Brooks and he needed another to run against incumbent Republican Governor Green. Three of Stevenson's lawyer friends urged him to run for senator and introduced him to Colonel Arvey. The Colonel decided to slate Professor Paul H. Douglas for senator and asked Stevenson if he would run for governor. After an agonizing weighing of the pros and cons, Stevenson consented to run. There has been much speculation about Arvey's motives in selecting two such high-class candidates. One view is that the Democratic party was in trouble and needed the best candidates it could find; another is that the war experience had elevated Colonel Arvey's political sights and that he was genuinely seeking to render public service. Both Stevenson and Douglas won by landslide majorities, and they helped President Truman obtain his narrow majority in Illinois.[11]

Early in 1952 Governor Stevenson was urged by President Truman and others to declare himself a candidate for the Democratic nomination for president but he refused to do so. He insisted that he only wanted a second term as governor of Illinois. This stand made it difficult for the Chicago Democratic organization to promote his candidacy for the Democratic nomination. Nevertheless, the Illinois delegation continued to exert pressure upon Governor Stevenson not to close the door to a draft. Just prior to the nominating speeches, Stevenson indicated his willingness to be a candidate. Colonel Arvey and his associates rounded up fifty-three of the sixty Illinois delegates for Stevenson, and they also participated in the strategy aimed at keeping the southern states from bolting the convention.[12]

In 1953 the Cook County Central Committee elected as its chairman Cook County Clerk Richard Daley, a lawyer and ward committeeman who had served in both houses of the Illinois Legislature and had been revenue director under Governor Stevenson. Chairman Daley decided in 1955 to seek the

[11] Kenneth S. Davis, *A Prophet in His Own County; The Triumphs and Defeats of Adlai S. Stevenson* (Garden City: Doubleday, 1957).

[12] Paul T. David, Malcolm Moos, and Ralph M. Goldman, *Presidential Nominating Politics in 1952: The Middle West* (Baltimore: Johns Hopkins Press, 1954), chap. 5, "Illinois."

Democratic nomination for mayor even though former Chairman Arvey opposed the move. Mayor Kennelly was invited to retire but refused to do so. In the primary Kennelly had strong press support but he went down to defeat. This showed that in Chicago a businessman who became mayor on a reform platform with the backing of the Democratic organization was vulnerable when the organization turned on him. The large vote Daley received in the wards inhabited largely by Negroes was crucial to his victory.

Candidate Daley's next test was to defeat the Republican nominee Robert E. Merriam, former alderman and son of the late Professor Charles E. Merriam of the University of Chicago, who had run for mayor in 1911 and 1919. Three of Chicago's four newspapers shifted to Merriam who, although young, was well known in the city for his activities on the crime committee. A private poll taken in 1954 indicated that he was almost as widely recognized as Mayor Kennelly.[13] Merriam campaigned against the machine and tried to attract dissatisfied Democrats and independent groups. He used radio and television extensively during his campaign, but this technique which worked well in Los Angeles and Detroit was apparently less effective in Chicago. Daley, who was not a polished television performer, won 55 per cent of the vote. His heaviest support came from the Black Belt and from the West Side wards where the Democratic machine was strongest.

When asked right after the election, "What do you regard as your biggest opportunity, your biggest task, that you can accomplish in four years?" Daley replied, "First, . . . restore, rebuild and revitalize the spirit of Chicago which did so much to build the city."[14]

Some critics thought that Mayor Daley would revert to the Kelly-Nash pattern, but he surprised everyone by adopting a number of reforms. He started out by making some excellent

[13] Robert E. Merriam and Rachel M. Goetz, *Going Into Politics* (New York: Harper, 1957).

[14] "Interview with Mayor of Chicago, Richard J. Daley," *U. S. News & World Report*, May 27, 1955.

appointments. He put the city finances in the hands of a distinguished comptroller. He appeared to demand and secure efficiency in street cleaning, street repair, garbage collection, water supply, sewage disposal, and public works. He helped push through projects for urban renewal, low cost housing, and the building of expressways. Some critics claimed that little was done on such basic problems as corruption, segregation, neighborhood decay, and general metropolitan confusion.[15] His opponents have included Republicans, some "liberal" Democrats, and many Negro and civil-rights spokesmen. At the same time he has maintained a strong party organization and won the support of many of the city's most influential business and professional men, labor chiefs, clergymen, and civic leaders.

Mayor Daley's leadership in state politics met with some reverses in 1956. Republican Governor William G. Stratton and his party were in deep trouble on account of the Hodge scandal. A newspaper investigation revealed the fact that the Republican auditor of public accounts Orville Hodge had been stealing from the state treasury. At the trial, the attorney general's office put the amount stolen at over one and a half million dollars.[16] The Democrats felt that Governor Stratton would be easy to defeat since the general public seemed to hold him responsible for not discovering the peculations and acting sooner. Mayor Daley persuaded the Democratic state organization to slate Herbert C. Paschen, then Cook County treasurer, as the Democratic candidate for governor. Paschen was not well known downstate but easily won the nomination since two-thirds of the Democratic state primary vote was located in Cook County.

The Paschen campaign started well enough, with the Democrats exploiting the Hodge scandal at every possible opportunity. In the middle of the campaign, however, it was revealed that in Paschen's office as Cook County treasurer there existed a $29,000 "flower fund" made up of contributions by banks

[15] Leon M. Despres, "A Big City Ripe for Reform: Corruption in Chicago," *Nation*, March 12, 1960.

[16] George Thiem, *The Hodge Scandal* (New York: St. Martin's, 1963), p. 117.

which had been favored with the deposit of county funds. While Paschen denied that this was a "slush fund" to be used for his political advancement, the Republicans were happy to turn the tables on the Democrats as far as scandal charges were concerned. Mayor Daley convinced Paschen that he should withdraw. He then persuaded the Democratic State Central Committee to nominate Chicago Superior Court Judge Richard B. Austin for governor. Judge Austin's reputation for honesty was beyond reproach, but the time was short and the judge was a very obscure person. Governor Stratton won reelection by a plurality of less than 1 per cent. Most observers believed that if Daley had presented a strong and well-known candidate for governor, the Democrats would have won the office.[17]

In the presidential race of 1956 the Chicago machine won no laurels, but it paved the way for very useful future connections. The Chicago delegation supported the renomination of Adlai Stevenson for president without great enthusiasm. When it came to the nomination of a vice president, however, the Daley organization supported the bid of Senator John F. Kennedy with great zest and vigor. Kennedy came close to winning and he laid the foundation for his presidential nomination four years later. In the 1956 election, the Chicago Democratic organization did very poorly against the popular President Eisenhower. For the first and only time during the period, the Chicago precincts failed to yield a Democratic majority in a presidential election. As compared with 1952, Stevenson's vote in Chicago was down some 19 per cent. Eisenhower gained only slightly in the city.

During his first term Mayor Daley succeeded in building up a favorable image of the city administration. He proclaimed himself a new leader type. As he put it, "The new objective of leadership is not what you can do for yourself, but what you can do for the people."[18] The Republican *Chicago Tribune* praised his record in these terms: "He is just about the most

[17] Austin Ranney, *Illinois Politics* (New York: New York University Press, 1960), p. 26.

[18] *Time*, March 15, 1963.

effective leader of a political party that this city has seen in living memory."[19] The City Hall publicity machine managed to detract attention from some of the shortcomings of the regime. The vote in the 1959 mayoralty election was light, but Mayor Daley won an overwhelming victory.

Within a year of his reelection Mayor Daley faced some serious setbacks. In January, 1960, the Republican states' attorney arrested a number of Chicago policemen on charges that they had conspired with a burglary ring. Some of the stolen goods were found in their homes. The scandal spread, and it was revealed that policemen had paid politicians for appointments and promotions and that policemen had protected such criminal activities as gambling, prostitution, narcotics, and liquor violations as well as burglaries.

The police situation called for drastic action, and the mayor appeared to rise to the occasion. He appointed Orlando W. Wilson, professor of police administration at the University of California, as the new police commissioner and promised to back him up in his efforts to purge the department of corruption and build a new and efficient police force. Daley obtained extra funds for the department so that it could hire 2,000 additional men and modernize its equipment. Commissioner Wilson thoroughly reorganized the police force and improved its morale. The city has been held up as a model of good police administration.

With city affairs calmed down somewhat Mayor Daley could turn his attention in 1960 to state and national politics. For the Democratic nomination for governor he turned down two prominent Democratic leaders, Joseph D. Lohman, the state treasurer, and Stephen A. Mitchell, former Democratic national chairman, and slated instead Cook County Judge Otto Kerner. Both Lohman and Mitchell challenged the machine choice in the Democratic primary. While Judge Kerner was not as well known as his two opponents, he swamped them by obtaining 70 per cent of the Cook County primary vote.

At the Democratic national convention the Daley forces were

[19] *Ibid.*

lined up solidly for John F. Kennedy. For four years Daley had
been a supporter and adviser to Kennedy in his drive for the
Democratic presidential nomination. At the convention Adlai
Stevenson toyed with the idea of a third nomination, as he was
impressed by the demonstrations on his behalf. He knew he
had to have some support from his home state as a base if such
a movement was to be launched, so he sought out Mayor
Daley. From the convention floor by telephone Daley informed
him that he had no support, and thus ended the boom for Stevenson.[20] In the November elections the Chicago machine performed mightily, delivering nearly two-thirds of the city's votes
to Kennedy. This gave Kennedy a city margin of 456,000,
which offset the Republican plurality downstate and gave him
a statewide edge of 8,858. Judge Kerner was also elected
governor.

Mayor Daley now had friendly state and national administrations with which to deal. He was able to obtain new state
laws which gave Police Commissioner Wilson top executive
authority. With state and federal grants a new Chicago campus
for the University of Illinois was established. Using every in-
strument of political power available to him and overriding
opposition from his own church and the Negro community,
Mayor Daley pushed ahead the South Side urban renewal project designed to improve the environment of the University of
Chicago. No serious challenge was presented to his reelection
as mayor for a third term in 1963. While the assassination of
President Kennedy was a great blow, the Chicago machine
soon established good working relationships with the Johnson
administration. In the Democratic sweep of 1964, Governor
Kerner was reelected.

During the sixties Mayor Daley had grave problems of race
relations to solve. The continuous migration of untrained and
poorly educated Negroes from the farms and small towns of the
South to Chicago created housing shortages, de facto segregation in neighborhoods and schools, unemployment, family dis-

[20] Theodore H. White, *The Making of the President 1960* (New York: Atheneum,
1961), p. 167.

integration, public welfare crises, and racial friction. While many whites left the city for the suburbs, the Negro proportion of the city's population increased from one-seventh in 1950 to an estimated one-third in 1967. The rising tide of Negro protest against poor housing and unsatisfactory school conditions included sit-ins, marches, and riots. Mayor Daley faced a difficult dilemma. To satisfy the Negroes he had to promise them more benefits, and at the same time he had to reassure whites that he would protect their interests. A climax was reached in 1966 when Dr. Martin Luther King, Jr. led civil rights open housing marches that led to serious disturbances. In order to stop the marches Mayor Daley reached an agreement with Dr. King. The reaction of some white elements was unfavorable to this agreement. In the fall elections, the Chicago machine failed to save the veteran Senator Paul H. Douglas from defeat by the Republican candidate Charles H. Percy, an attractive young industrialist, and the Republicans won eight out of twelve contests for county offices. These defeats were attributed in part to white backlash. In the spring elections of 1967, however, Mayor Daley was easily elected for a fourth term. The Negro revolt and the white backlash had not as yet affected the power of the machine to win city elections.

Analysis of the Parts of the Chicago Machine

We have now reviewed briefly some of the successes and failures of the Chicago machine during the past thirty years. What are some of the secrets of its durability? Why has the system changed less than that of other large American cities?

A central consideration has been the continuous availability of patronage in sufficient quantities to staff the old-style precinct organizations. The merit system has been extended during the period, but not as rapidly and thoroughly as in other jurisdictions. Patronage jobs with their political responsibilities have become less attractive than they used to be, but there are still many who will put up with the system. In 1961, following county, state, and national Democratic victories, the number of patronage jobs available to the Chicago organization was estimated by Alderman Leon M. Despres to be 35,000.[21] In addition to government jobs, the organization had working relations with business firms which would hire workers on the recommendation of local political leaders. Regarding how the machine operates, Alderman Despres wrote: "To participants, the machine offers income, careers, preferments, recognition, prestige, wealth, and protection. Does a man want to be a night watchman, federal judge, or park commissioner? Does he want to sell water coolers, build incinerators, or plan developments? The machine offers him an opportunity to realize his ambitions, and exacts only regularity, unwavering loyalty, work, devotion, contributions, and delivery of the vote."[22]

The form of the city government has been a factor which favors the continuation of the boss system. In contrast to Detroit where a council of nine is elected at large, the City Council of Chicago is a body of fifty aldermen elected by wards. The wards are relatively small in size and each has a Democratic committeeman elected by the primary voters every four years. The title of Chapter II of this book, "You Can't Lick a Ward Boss," still stands as a good description after thirty years. In the Democratic ward committeemen elections of 1948 there was only one upset, and in those of 1964 there were two contests and no upsets.[23] The advantage of the small wards from the standpoint of a machine is that a ward committeeman or ward boss can be close to ethnic, religious, nationality, color, religious, and business groups and can do things in his bailiwick which would not be tolerated in other parts of the city. In certain wards there has been a close linkage between crime and politics. Several mysterious murders of ward politicians occurred during the period. Various reform groups have advocated the abolition of the fifty wards and the election of a smaller council at large or by bigger districts. The Chicago machine has successfully blocked any such reform.

[21] Cited by Robert C. Nelson, "Chicago Machine Politics Described," *Christian Science Monitor*, July 10, 1961.
[22] *Ibid.*, July 8, 1961.
[23] *Chicago Tribune*, April 14, 1948, and April 15, 1964.

A characteristic of the Chicago organization has been the successful building of suborganizations or submachines among minority groups. Outstanding has been the construction of the Democratic organization among Negro voters, whose numerical importance has increased, as we have seen, from a seventh in 1950 to nearly a third in 1967. The leader of the Democratic organization in the so-called Black Belt for most of the period has been Congressman William L. Dawson, who was the first Negro to head an important House committee, the Committee on Government Operations. Originally a Republican and a militant battler for Negro rights, he became a Democratic leader who shunned publicity and kept to his legislative and party organization tasks.[24]

Congressman Dawson achieved success first as a Republican when he was elected alderman in 1933. Mayor Kelly spotted him as a coming leader and persuaded him to become a Democrat in 1939. In the following year Dawson was elected ward committeeman of the Second Ward and from this base he expanded his influence to six other wards inhabited largely by Negroes. He showed great shrewdness in distributing patronage and in selecting his lieutenants. In 1942 he was strong enough to win the Democratic nomination for Congress in the First Congressional District of Illinois, which had continuously returned a Negro since 1928. This was the beginning of his unbroken service in Congress of over a quarter of a century. Because of the nature of the Chicago political system, he was able to satisfy his constituents with material rewards furnished by the city organization and this left him relatively free to pursue policies in Congress that he thought were in accordance with the national interest. He went out of his way to divorce the activities of his Washington office from those of his Chicago office. In Washington he stressed the importance of being a member of the team, of being recognized as a successful legislator, and of being a party stalwart who did not raise divisive issues. In Chicago, on the other hand, he played the role of the

[24] Wilson, *op. cit.*; and Edward T. Clayton, *The Negro Politician* (Chicago: Johnson, 1964).

leader who could get more patronage and exercise more influence than possible rivals, who was very fair in his distribution of tangible favors, and who was willing to place the welfare of the organization above his own personal welfare. He did not appear to profit financially from his strategic position.

In spite of the growing militancy of Negro protest movements, Congressman Dawson has avoided public discussion of race goals. The leaders of some civil rights organizations have criticized him for not being more outspoken on racial issues. In answer to the criticisms, Dawson is quoted as saying: "How is it that after fighting all my life for the rights of my people, I suddenly awake in the September of life to find myself being vilified and abused, and those who know me well and what I have stood for are accusing me of being *against* civil rights? Not *for* civil rights? Why we made more progress toward civil rights under the Democratic Administrations under which I served and in which I had a hand in shaping the policy than ever in the history of the nation. . . . I have tried to fight for civil rights where it is the most effective, within the caucuses of my own party."[25] The criticisms of Dawson have not greatly affected his vote. He was challenged for renomination in 1966 by a much younger man, a social worker, who hoped to benefit from the civil rights marches led by Dr. Martin Luther King. The machine forces held, particularly in the poorer neighborhoods, and Dawson won by a comfortable margin.[26]

The Democratic organization led by Dawson has played a key role in city, county, and state politics. Dawson was elected vice chairman of the Cook County Democratic Committee. He played a leading part in the ouster of Kennelly in 1955 and his machine furnished a large portion of the votes Daley needed to win in the mayoralty primary. In the election a substantial part of the Daley plurality over Merriam was supplied by the South and West Side wards controlled by Dawson. In the presidential elections of 1948 and 1960 the state of Illinois could not

[25] *Afro-American*, January 26, 1957, cited by Clayton, *op. cit.*, pp. 83–84.
[26] Richard Cotton, "Negro Politics, Old Style and New: I. William Dawson Calls the Tune," *The Reporter*, August 11, 1966.

have been carried by the Democratic candidates without the crucial support of the Dawson organization.

Another factor which has contributed to the durability of the Chicago machine has been its strong position in national politics. In addition to producing crucial pluralities at the polls in presidential elections, the Chicago Democratic delegation to Congress has brought disciplined support to administration programs. While in New York City President Roosevelt helped defeat the Tammany organization by encouraging the formation of labor parties and fusion tickets, in Chicago the Roosevelt, Truman, Kennedy, and Johnson administrations generally followed a hands-off policy as far as internal city politics was concerned. Whereas Tom Pendergast in Kansas City was sent to jail for income tax evasion, Mayor Kelly was permitted to settle his income tax difficulties. Secretary Ickes contended that "he (Kelly) should have gone to jail and undoubtedly he would have gone had it not been for the improper leniency shown by the Administration for political reasons."[27] On the positive side, the Chicago machine took every advantage of the national trends which have produced more Democratic identifiers than Republican identifiers during the past thirty years. While conservative in local matters, it capitalized on the popularity of the New Deal, the Fair Deal, the New Frontier, and the Great Society policies, particularly among the less privileged. In the competition for federal funds the city of Chicago has done very well. It has obtained large sums of money from Washington to help pay for education, public welfare, public housing, health programs, urban renewal, federal public building projects, expressways, and airports. Federal aid has helped consolidate an entrenched organization. An example of the great power of the Chicago machine in national politics was the ability of the mayor to secure a reversal of an order by the Department of Health, Education and Welfare stopping federal funds to Chicago schools on alleged grounds of de facto segregation.

On balance, the leaders of the Chicago Democratic organi-

[27] Ickes, *op. cit.*

zation managed to maintain a favorable image of their city. The three mayors were always enthusiastic believers in a great future for their metropolis, and they cultivated the image that they placed the welfare of the city above that of their party. They were skillful in playing down unfavorable publicity and in emphasizing positive achievements. In particular, Mayor Daley obtained the solid backing of the business community, which gave him credit for improving transportation facilities, encouraging business expansion in the center city, improving city administration, keeping taxes down, and lowering the crime rate. In his twelfth year as mayor, he mobilized with business backing a massive campaign for a multipurpose $190 million bond issue which carried by more than two to one. While the Chicago Democratic machine has had its critics, in a showdown it has won the support of influential leaders and most of the general public. It has shown great powers of adaptation and considerable skill in building a general consensus without being subservient to any one group such as big business.

Chapter IX of this book suggested certain changes in laws, practices, and attitudes that might be made to improve Chicago politics. Only a few of these changes have taken place during the past thirty years. Improvements have been made in tax administration by the adoption of a city sales tax which lessens the burden on real estate and the chances for political abuses. The introduction of voting machines has reduced the possibility of certain types of fraudulent election practices. Employment of dinners to raise campaign funds has largely replaced reliance of the party on dubious sources of campaign revenue such as contributions from gambling interests. Many improvements have been made in police administration. In general, however, the progress of reform has been slow. The decentralized and chaotic structure of local government and the long and complicated ballot have not been changed. Chicago still needs many improvements in election administration, housing code enforcement, planning administration, and personnel administration. It also needs a more militant and crusading press, radio, and television and a larger number of citizens dedicated to performing political tasks on a voluntary basis. With all its faults, however, the Chicago machine, an old-style model, is still worth studying because of its durability.

INDEX

Adult citizens, number of, in Chicago, 53
Affirmative votes on propositions, 137
Albert, Arthur F., candidate for mayor: attitude of press toward, 163, 165–66; votes for, 170, 177
American Issue, cited, 147
Annexation propositions, 127, 132–34
Anti-saloon League: on the wet and dry polls, 145–47; attitude of, toward candidates, 164
Apprenticeship of party workers, 66
Assassination, role of, in Chicago politics, 14, 43, 88, 138
Assessment of job-holders, 75
Assessor, and party machine, 77
Audit of public funds, 19
Avalon Park, 122
Average votes, discussion of, 97

Balance sheet of Chicago politics, 183–93
Ballot frauds, 86, 190. *See also* Election frauds
Bank failures, relation of, to voting, 114, 116
Banker capitalism in New York, 25
Bankers, and Chicago politicians, 13, 17, 25, 185
Banking-law-proposition votes, 127, 132
Benevolent services of party, 61, 65, 183, 189
Beverly Hills: voting tendencies in, 106, 122, 148; newspaper home coverage in, 172, 175–76, 179
Bibliography, 214–19
Bipartisan deals, 19, 29, 44
Bipartisanship on election boards, 190
Black Belt, voting in, 120–22. *See also* Negroes
Blanket ballot, 133
Bohemians in politics, 60
Bond issues, referendum on, 99–100, 127–29, 136–42, 170
Bootlegging, and politics, 13, 17, 88
Bosses, role of, 183 ff.
Bradley, Edward R., race-track fan, 20
Brady, Peter J., 102

Brekke, Eden T., 102
Brennan, George: leader of Democratic party, 14, 89, 102, 126; and traction issue, 142; and wet vote, 146–47
Bribery of voters, 88–90
Brooks, C. Wayland: candidate for governor, 12, 168; candidate for congressman-at-large, 93
Building-inspector scandal, 76
Bundesen, Herman N., candidate for governor, 21
Busch, Francis X., 32
Business, political pressures on, 40
Business men, role of, in politics, 4–6, 8, 12–18, 25, 40–42, 46, 54–56, 77, 114, 125, 137–44, 149–55, 183–87, 193

Campaign finance, 5, 59, 75, 89–90, 94, 164, 191–93
Campaign techniques, of Mayor Thompson, 11, 165–67
Candidates and the press, 161–69
Canvassing techniques, 58–60, 81–83
Capone, Al, 45, 72
Cartoons of candidates, 162–63
Case studies of party workers, 58–68
Catholic origins, description of use of, 104, 171, 174
Catholics in Chicago, voting tendencies of, 17, 39, 63–64, 97, 102, 104, 107, 110, 113, 125, 149, 171–72, 174
Census of Religious Bodies, cited, 104
Census tract data: use of, 92; relation of, to newspaper home coverage, 157
Cermak, Anton J.: mayor of Chicago, 12–14, 21, 32, 39, 60, 93–94, 126; on wet issue, 146–48; attitude of press toward, 163, 165–67; votes for, 170
Charter amendments, 127
Chicago: retrenchment in, 4; taxation system of, 7; World's Fair, 11; general political complexion of, 25; ward lines in, 31; natives of, in politics, 45, 62–65; compared to other cities, 70, 78, 83, 88, 186–93; recognition of community interests of, 76; social composition of, 101 ff.; party system in, 106 ff.; geographical dispersion of votes in, 96, 121,

239

Democratic party in Chicago: and Insull,
6; in 1928, 8; and election reform, 22;
success of, 39, 94, 114; Christmas baskets distributed by, 73; patronage of,
74–75; straight votes for, 98–99; on
wet issue, 111; composition of, 112, 115,
117, 124–25, 187, 208

Democratic party workers, case histories
of, 56, 58, 64

Democratic vote, geographical distribution of, 96, 121, 175

Democratic ward committeemen and
legal profession, 47–48

Deneen, Charles S.: United States senator, 10; attitude of press toward, 163–
65; votes for, 170, 176

Dependent variable, Roosevelt vote as,
112–24

Depression, effects of, on politics, 3 ff.,
56–57, 68, 72–73, 86, 159–61, 184. See
also Bankers, Economic crisis, Home
owners, Unemployment

Detroit, politics of, 3, 188, 190

Dever, William E., mayor of Chicago,
traction plan of, 142

Doubling-up, relation of, to voting, 105–6,
108

Domestic difficulties, advice on, given by
party workers, 73

Downstate Illinois, and Chicago, 116, 120,
153

Dunne, Edward F., mayor of Chicago, 126

Dry organizations, on wet and dry polls,
144–48

Dry referendum, 18

Dry voters, characteristics of, 148–49

Drys, attitude of, toward polls, 144–48

Economic crisis, role of party during, 183–
84. See also Depression

Economic deprivations, effect of, on
voting, 114–16, 124–25

Economic status, relation of, to voting,
110, 112, 115–17

Economies in government, forcing of, 185

Edison Park, 122

Editorials on candidates, 162–63

Education: of ward committeemen, 46; of
precinct committeemen, 56–61; relation
of, to voting, 105–6, 108–10, 154–55

Eighteenth Amendment, agitation against,
100, 144–49

Election commissioners' office, 129

Election-day funds, 89–90. See also Campaign finance

Election frauds, 19, 22, 34, 42–43, 85–90,
129

Election laws, 189–91

Election machinery, control of, 33

Election precincts, 52–85, 189

Election prediction, 90, 120, 169

Elections, cost of, 15

Elective offices, number of, 33

Emergency-relief bond issues, 128

Emmerson, Louis, governor of Illinois,
133, 153

Endless chain fraud, 87

Englewood, a dry area, 148

Equation of net regression, use of: to explain voting, 115–24, 210; to study relation of press to voting, 174–81, 211–13

Eviction cases, provision for, by party
workers, 72–73

Factorial analysis, 206–9

Faherty, Michael, president of Board of
Local Improvements, 138

Farley, James A., chairman of Democratic National Committee, 14, 90

Fatigue curve of voting, 131–32

Federal government, party worker as
agent for, 56, 80–81

Federal judgeships, as political patronage,
21

Federal loans, substitution of, for bond
issues, 128

First Ward politics, 87–88, 98–100, 191

Food-dispensing activities of party, 71–72

Ford, Henry, 32

Foreign-born voters: voting behavior of,
98, 101–4; on wet issue, 149; on tax
amendments, 154

Forest preserves, 60

Formulas, 210–13

Forty-second Ward politics, 88

Fraud in referendum returns, 128–30

Fraudulent votes, 86. See also Election
frauds

Freedom, party workers' view of, 60

INDEX

Primary elections, relation of press to, 176–81

Primary laws of Illinois, 28 n.

Primary ticket, 66

Professional politicians, 47

Prohibition as a negative symbol for wets, 148

Prohibition-repeal issue, 100, 118, 144–49

Promotional skills in politics, 184. *See also* Canvassing, Press, Symbolism

Propaganda agencies, the press, 156 ff.

Proportional representation, 190–91

Proposition voting, 126 ff. *See also* Referendum

Protestants in Chicago politics, 104, 111, 125, 149, 174–76. *See also* Catholics

Public employment bureaus, 185

Public jobs and ward bosses, 39–41. *See also* Civil service, Patronage

Public Policy Act, 127, 132–34, 145

Public services, opposition of party machine to extension of, 184

Public welfare administration, 185

Publicity, art of, 161–69

Race-track handbook bill issue, 21

Racial groups, 14, 32, 44–46, 61, 64–66, 101–4, 154, 179, 193. *See also* Foreignborn voters, Jews, Negroes

Rational appeals, 59

Reapportionment, need of, 8, 30–33, 190

Reasons for entering politics, 48, 67

Recount of proposition ballots, 129

Referenda, special, 127

Referendum: increasing use of, 128; returns, 99–100

Reformers: scorned by party workers, 69–70; weakness of, 186–87

Refuse-removal, political control of, 76

Registered vote, 35, 53, 86–87, 100–101, 135

Registration frauds, 100, 190

Registration of voters, agitation for sound system of, 22, 86–87

Regression equation, use of, to explain voting relationships, 106–7, 122–24

Relief cases, and party workers, 7, 61, 65–66, 70, 74, 78, 183

Relief-rollers, voting of, analyzed, 124

Religion and politics in Chicago, 104. *See also* Catholics, Jews, Protestants

Religious affiliations of party workers, 64

Rent, payment of, by party workers, 72–73

Rentals, as a measure of economic status of voters, 104–5, 108–13; newspaper home-coverage and, 171–81

Rents, decline of, in Chicago, 3

Repeal of prohibition, 17, 128, 132

Republican party in Chicago: in 1928, 8; defeat of, 18; on election reform, 22; patronage retained by, 29; composition of, 38–39, 47, 59, 112, 117, 124–25; weakness of, 75–76; on wet issue, 111; relation of press to, 174–78

Republican ward committeemen, jobs held by, 43

R.F.C. and Chicago government, 7

Richberg, Donald: cited, 4; opponent of traction plan, 143

River wards, vote in, 97, 99, 154

Rogers Park, a dry area, 148

Roosevelt, Franklin D., president of the United States: and Cermak, 14; and Kelly, 19; vote for, 52–53, 93–98, 102, 106–16, 170–81; and the Igoe vote, 118–20; and the press in Chicago, 156, 163, 167–69

Rosenberg, Moe, Democratic politician, 6 n.

Russians in Chicago politics, 64, 101–3

Ryan, James W., 102

Saloon: importance of, in politics, 18, 82; as a negative symbol, 148. *See also* Liquor business

Sanitary District board, 16, 139, 186

Scandinavians in Chicago politics, 101–4

Scatter diagram, discussion of voting by means of, 106, 110, 122–23, 171

School board, and Chicago politics, 17

Separate proposition ballots, handling of, 129, 133

Serritella, Daniel, state senator, 12 n., 45

Service argument for votes, 82–83

Short ballot, 189. *See also* Long ballot

Short weight charges in 1931 campaign, 11–12, 72

Signature requirement for voting, 36–37, 87. *See also* Permanent registration

320.9773
G67
Date Due

85593

DEMCO NO. 295

OC 6 '69				
NO 3 '69				
DE 2 '69				
DE 5 '69				